CATHOLICISM   TODAY

Every scribe who is learned in the reign of God is like the head of a household who can bring from his storeroom both the new and the old.

— Matt. 13:52

Every truth without exception – whoever may utter it – is from the Holy Spirit.

St. Thomas Aquinas (1225-1274)

CATHOLICISM TODAY

A Theology of the Roman Catholic Church, a
Survey of Its Structure, and a Rationale
for Reform in the Twentieth Century

JEROME A. WELCH

JEWEL PUBLICATIONS
2417 HAZELWOOD AVENUE
FORT WAYNE, INDIANA 46805

Copyright © 1977 by Jerome A. Welch

ISBN: 0-917728-01-7   Clothbound Edition
ISBN: 0-917728-02-5   Paperbound Edition
Library of Congress Catalog Card Number: 76-29584

Cover Design by John N. Welch
Typesetting by Type, Inc., Fort Wayne, Ind.
Printed and bound in the United States of America by
Express Printing, Inc., Fort Wayne, Ind.

Published in the United States of America by
Jewel Publications
2417 Hazelwood Avenue
Fort Wayne, Indiana 46805

ACKNOWLEDGMENTS

The author expresses his gratitude to the following authors and publishers who kindly granted permission to reprint excerpts from copyrighted works:

Columbia Magazine, excerpt from "The Signs of the Times" by Fulton J. Sheen, copyright © 1970 by Knights of Columbus.

Encyclopaedia Britannica, Inc., excerpts from "Inquisition," "Papacy," and "Saint Peter," *Encyclopaedia Britannica*, 1965 edition, copyright © 1965 by Encyclopaedia Britannica, Inc.

Farrar, Straus & Giroux, Inc., excerpt from *Morality Is for Persons* by Bernard Haring, copyright © 1971 by Bernard Haring.

Fides Publishers, Inc., excerpts from *Contemporary Problems in Moral Theology* by Charles E. Curran, copyright © 1970 by Fides Publishers, Inc.; *A New Look at Christian Morality* by Charles E. Curran, copyright © 1968 by Charles E. Curran.

Harper & Row, Publishers, Inc., excerpts from *The Phenomenon of Man* by Pierre Teilhard de Chardin, copyright © 1959 by Harper & Row, Publishers, Inc.

Harvard University Press, Belknap Press, excerpts from *Contraception* by John T. Noonan, Jr., copyright © 1965 by the President and Fellows of Harvard College.

Hawthorn Books, Inc., excerpt from *Footprints in a Darkened Forest* by Fulton J. Sheen, copyright © 1967 by Fulton J. Sheen.

Holt, Rinehart & Winston, Inc., excerpt from *Are Parochial Schools the Answer?* by Mary Perkins Ryan, copyright © 1964 by Mary Perkins Ryan.

Macmillan Publishing Co., Inc., excerpts from *Man and Morals* by Celestine N. Bittle, O.F.M. Cap., copyright © 1950 by the Bruce Publishing Co.; *Church Triumphant* by J. P. Arendzen, copyright © 1948 by the Macmillan Co.; *Preface to Religion* by Fulton J. Sheen, copyright © 1946 by P. J. Kenedy & Sons.

McGraw-Hill Book Co., excerpts from *The World's First Love* and *The Priest Is Not His Own* by Fulton J. Sheen, copyright © 1952, 1963 by Fulton J. Sheen.

National Catholic Reporter, excerpts from "The State of the Priesthood" by Andrew M. Greeley; "Editorial" from the issue of March 31, 1972; "The Current Crisis in Theology as It Affects the Teaching of Catholic Doctrine" by Raymond E. Brown, S.S., copyright © 1972, 1973 by National Catholic Reporter Publishing Co., Inc.

John A. O'Brien, Macmillan Co., New York, 1958, copyright © 1958, University of Notre Dame, Notre Dame, Ind., present (1971) copyright holder, excerpt from *Truths Men Live By.*

Our Sunday Visitor, excerpts from the issues of Nov. 14, 1971 and June 9, 1972, copyright © 1971, 1972 by Our Sunday Visitor, Inc.

Paulist/Newman Press, excerpts from *Moral Theology* by Heribert Jone, O.F.M. Cap., copyright © 1951 by the Alien Property Custodian.

Seabury Press, excerpts from *Catching Up with the Church* by John A. O'Brien, copyright © 1967 by John A. O'Brien; *Contraception and Holiness* by Archbishop Thomas D. Roberts, S.J., and others, copyright © 1964 by Herder & Herder, Inc.; *The Future of Belief* by Leslie Dewart, copyright © 1966 by Herder & Herder, Inc.

Sheed & Ward, Inc., excerpts from *Theology and Sanity* and *God and the Human Condition*, Vol. I, by F. J. Sheed, copyright © 1946, 1966 by Sheed & Ward, Inc.; *Is It the Same Church?* by F. J. Sheed, copyright © 1968 by F. J. Sheed; *Authority in the Church* by John L. McKenzie, copyright © 1966 by Sheed & Ward, Inc.; *The Celibate Condition and Sex* by Marc Oraison, copyright © 1967 by Sheed & Ward, Inc.

Sherbourne Press, Inc., excerpt from *Sexual Self-Stimulation* by R. E. L. Masters (ed.), copyright © 1967 by R. E. L. Masters.

Simon & Schuster, Inc., excerpts from *A Modern Priest Looks at His Outdated Church* by James Kavanaugh, copyright © 1967 by Father James Kavanaugh; *Our Oriental Heritage, Caesar and Christ, The Age of Faith, The Pleasures of Philosophy*, and *The Reformation* by Will Durant, copyright © 1935, 1944, 1950, 1953, 1957 by Will Durant; *The Lessons of History* and *Interpretations of Life* by Will and Ariel Durant, copyright © 1968, 1970 by Will and Ariel Durant.

Tan Books & Publishers, Inc., excerpts from *An Introduction to Philosophy* by Msgr. Paul J. Glenn, copyright © 1944 by B. Herder Book Co.

Time, The Weekly Newsmagazine, excerpts from "Untangling Parochial Schools," July 12, 1971, and "Pilgrim of the Absolute," May 14, 1973, copyright © 1971, 1973 by Time, Inc.

U. S. Catholic Magazine, excerpt from "Let's Stop Knocking Bishops" by Peter J. Riga, copyright © 1972 by Claretian Publications.

My special thanks to Will Durant for his permission to quote from unpublished personal correspondence with the author.

Portions of Chapter IV appeared in the Fort Wayne, Ind., *Journal-Gazette*, May 16, 1971.

Picture of Cardinal Newman on p. xii courtesy of *Sign* magazine, Union City, N.J.

For
The Greater Glory of God

And
With Faithful Respect and Esteem for
His Holiness, Pope Paul VI

CONTENTS

PART IV

CATHOLICISM AND AUTHORITY

To live is to change; and to be perfect is to have changed often.

John Henry Cardinal Newman (1801-1890)

INTRODUCTION

Catholicism Today attempts to provide a summary of the essential doctrines of the Catholic Faith and a rationale for reform in this last quarter of the twentieth century. This is admittedly an ambitious undertaking for one volume, and the reader must judge for himself how successful the author has been. While I have written primarily with the general reader in mind, it is especially hoped that seminarians, priests, bishops, teachers, and all students of religion will find *Catholicism Today* useful, informative, and constructive. There is already enough polarization and confusion in Catholicism today. May this volume not add to, but rather decrease, this polarization and confusion. This study has been dedicated to "the greater glory of God." I have asked God's blessing upon these pages, that the efforts of one frail intellect may faithfully convey God's truth in the twentieth century.

Part I is devoted to Catholic doctrine from the viewpoint of traditional theology and its threefold division into apologetics, dogma, and moral. One ought to approach the problems besetting Catholicism today from the firm foundation of traditional theology before attempting to point out areas for development and reformation. One has no right to criticize what he does not adequately understand. For that reason this study begins with a statement of the traditional orthodoxy of Catholicism.

It is hoped that Part I will serve as a refresher course for Catholics who have been long separated from formal instruction in Catholicism. Part I will aid the non-Catholic reader to learn what the Catholic Church really teaches, as distinguished from hearsay and caricatures of Catholic doctrine. I have tried to keep the presentation as nontechnical as clarity, accuracy, and the subject matter itself would permit, and to manifest a fluency and consistency in Catholic doctrine. Numerous references are given in the text in hope that the reader will pursue in greater detail those topics of special interest. Theology is especially characteristic of the Christian religion; Christians are the greatest sceptics in the world, always demanding reasons and explanations.

Part II deals with the controversial topic of abortion, which in recent years has become a burning social issue. The problem has become identified with the women's liberation movement and with the increasingly popular view that the state has no right to interfere with private morality.[1] But that is the crux: is abortion a purely private concern between a woman and her doctor or does abortion involve the lives of two distinct (though not separate) human beings — one being completely helpless to defend itself? The answer to this question has profound social significance. Either life is sacred or it isn't. The state may not be recreant in the preservation of life and providing for the common good, including the good of the yet unborn. I have concluded from philosophical, theological, biological, and sociological premises that deliberate abortion, at any stage of pregnancy, is morally unacceptable. The only possible exception would obtain where the life of the mother is put in serious jeopardy by the continued pregnancy. It certainly seems to be the lesser of two evils to allow the death of a nonviable fetus than to permit the death of both mother and fetus.

Part III takes on the subject of reform in Catholicism in this last third of the twentieth century. Ten areas for reform are cited, along with background information and my personal recommendations for reform. Statements in this part will disturb the comfortable and comfort the disturbed. Peter's barque may be rocked somewhat — not an unusual occurrence for the Church over a period of two thousand years; but there is no danger that Peter's barque will capsize as it moves forward in the mainstream of human life and civilization. On the contrary, the Catholic Church thrives on dialectic and a hammering out of truth on the anvil of history.

Part III considers the most significant areas for reform in Catholicism today. An enlarged democratic base for the election of the pope and bishops is proposed. Optional celibacy for the secular clergy is recommended. The permission of any medically safe form of contraception is justified. The ordination of women is advocated. New vistas for Catholic education within the framework of the public school and the liturgy are pointed out. A critique, mostly favorable, is given of Teilhardism. Polygenism is regarded as a tenable option regarding the origin of man. And the removal of the penalty of mortal sin for nonattendance at Mass on Sundays and Holy Days is recommended. Each proposal is prefaced with a historical review, placing the issue in proper perspective. I have made a genuine effort to come to grips with the pressing issues besetting Catholicism today. "To hold a pen," said Voltaire, "is to be at war."

Part III asks more questions than it answers. I make no claim to have solved all of the problems of contemporary Catholicism. The task is simply too great and too complex for one person and even one generation to solve. But I do modestly hope that I have at least pointed out directions in which the Church must move in the future. In the words of Robert F. Kennedy, the future is not a gift; it is an achievement. My proposals for reform seek to achieve the future for Catholicism. They are offered only in a spirit of love and respect for the Faith in which I was born and raised. Never do I threaten the Church with extinction if my proposals are not adopted; to do so, as some have done, would not only be an act of supreme arrogance and folly on my part, but would also do violence to the historical nature of the Church and the guarantee of Christ to be with His Mystical Body all days unto the consummation of the world. The Church is above any one mind, other than the mind of Christ. Nor do I ever recommend or suggest disobedience to current ecclesiastical legislation. Obedience remains a virtue; and one must remain a "child of obedience" — as Teilhard phrased it — in all matters which do not violate one's own conscience. However much one may disagree with current legislation, the virtue of obedience should prevail until such time as change comes from within the Church itself. The life of Christ is the supreme example of a life of obedience.

Rome moves slowly. Change usually starts with the theologians, and sometimes is initiated by the laity. It was the Emperor Constantine, a layman, who convened the Council of Nicea. It was not till 1854 that the dogma of Mary's Immaculate Conception was defined and not till 1950 that the dogma of Mary's Assumption was defined — though both doctrines were commonly held in the Church's tradition. Papal infallibility, for that matter, was not formally defined until the reign of Pius IX. I recall that twenty years ago my proposal for an English Mass was held to scorn by some fellow seminarians. Latin had been used for so long, more than a thousand years, and it would be close to heresy to suggest a change. Today, the English Mass is a reality, and Catholics are the better for it. The Church has always been able to sift the chaff from the wheat, the worthwhile and the valuable from the frivolous and the ephemeral.

The reforms proposed in the Church's teaching on human sexuality are admittedly both controversial and far-reaching. Here again the Church moves slowly. It was not till 1951 that a pope explicitly acknowledged that conception may be deliberately and conscientiously avoided by the use of the sterile period. I ask of the reader that all prejudgmental attitudes be laid aside and that my conclusions be judged solely on the basis of their agreement with reason. A philosopher can ask no more and expect no less. I ask this in the absence of any specific Biblical precept. The disciplinary laws of the Church are only as good as the rationale behind them; hence, they are always subject to review and reform.

Part IV describes the structure of the Catholic Church and defines the meaning of authority and its function in the Church. The problem of authority in the Church has always been extant, but has become more acute in the last few decades. I chose to complete this study of Catholicism today with the topic of Church authority because all that has been said before finds its ultimate significance in the teaching and governing authority of the Church. The times call for a reaffirmation of faith in that teaching and governing authority. This is not to downgrade efforts for reform and renewal, but to see these efforts as a part of the total life of the Church, working not against authority but with it and for it.

The Epilogue offers some final thoughts concerning the future of Catholicism.

The year given in the bibliographical entries is the year of copyright. Citations from Sacred Scripture and from the documents of Vatican II are given in the text immediately following the quoted material. Doctrinal heads of dogmatic theology as well as all nouns and pronouns referring to the Deity have been capitalized. I have not quoted exclusively from a single version of the Bible; but most of the Biblical quotations are from the Confraternity edition cited in the Bibliography.

Each chapter is prefaced with a number of significant quotations which place in bold relief the central themes of the chapter. The work abounds with references for further reading, both historical and contemporary. The documents of Vatican II provide a frame of reference throughout the study. I have sought to generate light, not heat, upon the topic at hand, blending traditional orthodoxy with an openness to modern insights. I have appealed to no other ultimate criteria than the demands of truth and the mind of Christ, Who claimed to be the Way, the Truth, and the Life.

Without compromising essential Catholic principles, the work offers wide areas with which non-Catholics can identify, thus contributing to the ecumenical movement. It is hoped that these pages will offer to thinking persons of all persuasions a stimulating philosophy of religion and a positive guide to a happy and meaningful life.

Catholicism Today is not a "catechism." Catechesis is primarily concerned with the faithful and accurate teaching of the official doctrines of the Church as promulgated by its magisterium. Polemics, apologetics, theological opinion and speculation, and proposals for reform are not proper matter for a catechism. Catechisms, of course, are absolutely necessary and indispensable. *The Catholic Catechism* (1975) by Father John A. Hardon, S.J., and *The Teaching of Christ* (1976) published by Our Sunday Visitor, Inc., are superb in performing the catechetical function. But, I submit, there is also a necessary and valid place for the present work — best described as "theological" — which, in addition to accurately communicating the official doctrines of the Church, employs a methodology of self-examination, constructive criticism, and the possibility of reform. The role of the prophet, seldom with honor in his own country, is never easy. Prophets are generally hung, notes Father John L. McKenzie; or, what's worse, they're ignored. Catechisms will not "rock the boat"; they can hardly be expected to perform a prophetic function of convicting an institution of its sins.

One of the finest tributes ever paid to mankind was written by William Shakespeare, who made Hamlet say:

What a piece of work is a man! How noble in reason! how infinite in faculty! in form and moving how express and admirable! in action how like an angel! in apprehension how like a god! The beauty of the world! The paragon of animals!

The atheist philosopher Nietzsche wrote: "The finest clay, the most precious marble — man — is here kneaded and hewn."

St. Catherine of Siena received a special revelation from Christ, Who showed her the ravishing beauty and splendor of a human soul. She said that the human soul appeared almost as a god.

Freud gave considerable attention to the human subconscious, especially in its libidinous tendencies. I say with Archbishop Sheen that the *treasures* of the human subconscious remain to be explored — this new frontier of the inner man and the human psyche. Man's potential for good is vastly superior to his capacity for evil. Man, of course, is capable of the most heinous crimes; but the thrust of mankind in general is toward the good. With the Greeks, President John F. Kennedy liked to define happiness as the full use of one's powers along lines of excellence.

I espouse a true Christian humanism, which has been well described by Jacques Maritain.[2] False humanism has man lifting himself by his own bootstraps, breathing in the air he exhales. True humanism acknowledges the brotherhood of all men under the fatherhood of God. A true humanism sees the human soul as the image and likeness of God Himself. All war is seen, in the words of Adlai Stevenson, as civil war. All killing in warfare is internecine destruction. It is, as Wendell Willkie pointed out, one world — this space ship, planet Earth.

Christianity is an integral and supremely important element in the world community. Christian truth will continue to operate in the world, sometimes in subtle ways, othertimes in more obvious ways. My hope is that the papacy will become a more influential force in human affairs, that the pope will be able to function more effectively as a peacemaker and a moral leader to the world, to be truly "the Holy Father" for all mankind.

The tragedy of Vietnam has caused all of us to re-examine our consciences and to reassess what is done in the name of justice and freedom. More than ever it has become obvious that the defense of freedom throughout the world must be in the hands of an international organization which is strong enough to administer international justice. It is less obvious that any one nation has the right, or the duty, to unilaterally engage in war — other than the defense of its own borders — apart from an international sanction to do so. An unconscionable squandering of human life in defense of a corrupt regime engaged essentially in a civil war and in a war without international approbation, is a sin crying to Heaven for vengeance. No wonder our young people are rebelling.

No one can claim to be an instant expert. I have been studying Catholicism for more than twenty years, giving attention to the full spectrum of commentaries on Christianity and Catholicism — from the thought of atheists to agnostics to liberals to conservatives. Nothing I have ever heard or read has diminished my faith in the truth of Christianity and the truth of Catholicism. The value of my opinions must be judged by the reader for himself on the basis of their rationality and harmony with revealed truth. The words of Montaigne are apropos: "Although we may be learned with the learning of others, at least we can only be wise with our own wisdom." The thrust of my proposals for reform is admittedly liberal. I have tried to avoid the terms *liberal* and *conservative* as much as possible because they have no absolute, only a relative, meaning in themselves. Every liberal must be willing to conserve what is true and good and right in the past; every conservative must be willing to allow change to what is true and good and right for the future.

There is an open-ended side to all truth. "Sixty years ago," writes Will Durant, "I knew everything. Now I know nothing. Education is a progressive discovery of our own ignorance." I am not implying that true and certain knowledge is impossible for man; I am saying that there is a tentative and even a precarious aspect to all truth. As I shall develop in Chapter V, all truth is subject to development, qualification, and refinement. One ought to be humble before the arcana of divine truth. Christ told us that we shall know the truth; but He also reminded us that we are to come to divine truth with the innocence and pristine faith of a little child. There is no place for smugness in theology.

Four acknowledgments are in order. First, I am indebted to my good parents, brothers, teachers, and fellow tertiaries in the Third Order of St. Francis, St. Charles Fraternity, Fort Wayne, Ind., from whom I learned the Christian Faith by both word and example.

Secondly, I am grateful to the following who read the manuscript: Rev. James Ballemans, O.S.C., of the Fort Wayne, Ind., Crosier House of Studies; Rev. Lawrence A. Gollner, *Censor Librorum* of the Diocese of Fort Wayne-South Bend; Msgr. J. William Lester, my pastor at St. Jude Church, Fort Wayne; Mr. Scott Meredith; Rev. Richard P. Hire, Director of Religious Education, Diocese of Fort Wayne-South Bend; my uncle and aunt, Mr. and Mrs. Edgar B. Welch; and Mr. Lambert Wilson.

Thirdly, I wish to acknowledge the help of the competent staff at the Public Library of Fort Wayne and Allen County, Ind., which on more than one occasion came to the author's rescue in locating some valuable reference material. Our excellent libraries are living witnesses to what the wise Aristotle said long ago: "In prosperity education is an ornament; in adversity, a refuge."

Lastly, I am most indebted and grateful to the employees of Type, Inc., which did the typesetting; to Robert Stoppenhagen of Express Printing, Inc., which did the printing and binding; and to my brother, John N. Welch, president of Screen-Art Advertising Co., Fort Wayne, Ind., for his outstanding cover design for this volume. Their patience and expertise have brought the manuscript through its various stages of gestation to full term.

Catholicism Today has been more than five years in the writing. After many solitary hours at desk and typewriter, I send this work on its way, with the prayerful hope that these pages will provide light and be an instrument of faith, where there is now darkness, obfuscation, and scepticism; hope and confidence, where there is now despair and distrust; brotherly love, unity, and understanding, where there is now animosity and dissension. If even one reader is brought to a deeper love of God and a better appreciation of Catholicism today, then the author's efforts will not have been in vain.

Jerome A. Welch

Fort Wayne, Indiana
May 27, 1976
Ascension Thursday

PART I

CATHOLICISM AND THEOLOGY

*You shall know the truth, and
the truth shall make you free.*

—John 8:32

CHAPTER I

CATHOLICISM AND APOLOGETICS

The Rationale of the Catholic Faith

Lead, kindly Light, amid the encircling gloom,
Lead Thou me on!
The night is dark and I am far from home;
Lead Thou me on!
> — Cardinal Newman, "The Pillar of the Cloud"

I fled Him, down the nights and down the days;
I fled Him, down the arches of the years;
I fled Him, down the labyrinthine ways
Of my own mind . . .
> — Francis Thompson, "The Hound of Heaven"

I, Lord, went wandering like a strayed sheep seeking Thee with an-
xious reasoning without, whilst Thou wast within me.
> — St. Augustine, *Confessions*

If anyone assert that the one true God, our Creator and Lord, can-
not be known with certainty from created things by the natural light of
human reason, let him be anathema.
> — First Vatican Council

The works themselves which I do give testimony of Me, that the
Father has sent Me.
> —John 5:36

The Catholic Church is the only good church to die in.
> — Oscar Wilde

Alexander, Caesar, Charlemagne and I myself have founded em-
pires; but upon what do these creations of our genius depend? Upon
force. Jesus alone founded His empire upon love; and to this very day
millions would die for Him.
> — Napoleon

"**MAN** was made to know," states the opening line of Aristotle's *Metaphysics*, bravely, affirmatively, optimistically. We begin our study of Catholicism today on that theme: man was made to know; man is able to know; man wants

3

to know; and man needs to know. Who am I? Where did I come from? Where am I going? How do I get there?

I. INTRODUCTION: THE SCIENCE OF THEOLOGY

Theology (Greek, *theos,* God; *logos,* word or study) means literally the study of God. *Theodicy* is the philosophical science that proves the existence of God from reason alone. *Theology*, as distinct from theodicy, may be defined as the science that establishes the existence and content of God's special Revelation to man. St. Anselm (1033-1109) defined theology as "faith seeking understanding."

First, theology is a science, inasmuch as it is a systematized body of knowledge that is governed by certain laws and arrives at definite conclusions with certitude.

Secondly, theology establishes the existence of God's special Revelation to man. *Revelation* literally means the removing of a veil. God may reveal Himself to man either through the ordinary channels of nature or in a supernatural manner. We can know of God naturally by a study of His creation and by the use of our own reason; however, God may wish to impart knowledge to us that would be impossible to know by the use of our native powers of reasoning alone. This knowledge might be either natural or supernatural in substance which God would reveal to us in a supernatural manner. Whether or not God has so revealed Himself is part of the job of theology to determine.

Finally, theology studies the content of God's special Revelation. Once having determined that God has spoken to man, theology proceeds to formulate the truths of that Revelation.

Theology is called a divine, rather than a human, science, inasmuch as its ultimate criterion of truth and motive of certitude rest on God's own word. First of all human reason established the fact that God has spoken. Once in possession of the fact of Divine Revelation, we *believe* not because reason *sees* the truths of Revelation, but because God has spoken.

Theology and philosophy should be, and are, mutually beneficial. Philosophy helps theology by providing the motives of credibility, by showing that God has spoken in a particular case. Philosophy also helps us to understand divine truth in a human way by expressing these truths in language familiar to us. Philosophy also establishes by reason some of the truths that God has seen fit to reveal to us. Thus, God's own existence, the immortality of the human soul, an eternal reward for a virtuous life — these truths are known by reason alone, even though God has revealed them to us in a special way.

Philosophy is "the handmaid of theology" in the above sense: it establishes the foundations and helps to express the truths of theology. Critics of Scholasticism frequently charge that it is only a disguised theology and that philosophic truths are twisted to fit theological dogmas.[1]

We can only say that the philosophic truths of Scholastic philosophy speak for themselves and stand on their own intrinsic worth. Truth is its own defense. Furthermore, the Aristotelian elements in Scholasticism, which are many, were first enunciated long before medieval philosophers began developing them and relating them to theology.

Theology is the completion and fulfillment of philosophy. The history of philosophy is a record of man's search for fundamental truth. Throughout the welter of confused thought, so characteristic of man's philosophic endeavors, runs a thread of helplessness, an inadequacy, a need for direction and supernatural aid. Even St. Thomas Aquinas admitted that the great truths of philosophy can be known by "only a few, after much effort, and then with an admixture of error." The great thought of Aristotle was sprinkled with error (mainly of a scientific nature). Philosophy needs theology as a guiding light, providing divine certitude on the essential questions of life.

There can be no real conflict between philosophy and theology. Both are from God, the Author of all truth in Whom there is no contradiction. Each has its own particular way of arriving at truth; but the God of philosophy and the God of theology are one and the same. True, theology asks us to accept mysteries, i.e., truths that are beyond the power of reason to either establish or comprehend. As we have mentioned, we are not unreasonable in believing these mysteries, for our reason tells us we must believe them once we have established the fact that God has revealed them. Furthermore, theology does not have a monopoly on mystery, for a little reflection will show that our modern world of science is replete with mysteries that we accept on the word of scientists.

St. Thomas Aquinas expressed it well:

Although the doctrines of faith surpass the truths of human understanding, there can be no opposition between them. Both proceed from God in their respective orders of Grace and nature. And the doctrines of faith become as indubitable through the evidence of the divine authority revealing them, as the primary truths of reason do through their self-evident testimony.

What about the alleged conflict between theology and science? Hasn't modern science shown theology to be rife with superstitious belief in a supernatural world? Once again, we can only say, *a priori*, there can be no real conflict in genuine truth, be it philosophic, theological, or scientific. God does not contradict Himself in the various ways He has revealed Himself to man. Science deciphers nature's hieroglyphics and reads the handwriting of the Almighty written in natural law. Science and theology operate in essentially different spheres, science dealing with the proximate, experimental aspects of natural phenomena and theology dealing with fundamental, spiritual truth. True, modern science has discovered proximate cause-effect relationships that have supplanted what was once thought to be immediate divine action. But the basic premises and conclusions of theology remain intact. In fact, science has given us a more exalted and grandiose concept of God by pointing up more vividly the omniscience and omnipotence required to bring this tremendous, complex universe into being.

More often than not, the apparent conflict has arisen as a result of theologians playing the part of scientists, and vice versa. The case of Galileo is a capital example. Galileo Galilei (1564-1642), professor of mathematics at the University of Padua, defended the Copernican theory of astronomy, which stated that the sun is the center of our system and the planets revolve around the sun. Most theologians of the day, including the learned Cardinal Bellarmine, condemned the theory as being contrary to Sacred Scripture, especially Josue 10:12, which seems to clearly indicate the mobility of the sun. Likewise did many notable scientists of the day hold for the traditional Ptolemaic theory of geocentrism. For the theologians, here was a classic example of the error of making a textbook of physical science out of the Bible, something it was never intended to be.

Likewise, many scientists, untrained in the sciences of metaphysics and theology, are guilty of making rash pronouncements on philosophical and theological questions. Being an eminent physicist does not in itself make one an authority on philosophical and theological matters. Alfred North Whitehead, for example, said that a new cosmology suggests a new religion. The *reductio ad absurdum* of a scientist speaking as philosopher was the pronouncement of an astronomer of note, who said he had scanned the universe and nowhere had he seen a being called God.

Is there one, true theology? Reason immediately suggests that there is. Surely if God has revealed Himself supernaturally to man, He would do so in connection with certain signs and marks whereby His Revelation could be clearly recognized by all.

First, His Revelation would be essentially one, a harmonious whole without contradictions. That there could be even two true theologies, holding divergent views on God and the world, is absolutely repugnant to reason and opposed to the veracity of God. Secondly, God's Revelation would be in harmony with man's highest aspirations and not repugnant to right reason. Thirdly, His Revelation would be complete, i.e., contain all the truths He wishes to reveal. The foregoing would be the internal marks of God's Revelation. Externally, God's Revelation would be marked by a historical setting and tradition and be accompanied by unusual signs, or miracles, putting the divine stamp of approval on that Revelation.

Finally, we come to the question of the subject matter of theology. Objectively speaking, the content of theology would be all the truths, be they of the natural or supernatural order, that God has seen fit to make known to man in a supernatural manner. These truths are the *dogmas* of theology. The science of theology also includes those "secondary" truths that are required to amplify and explain the basic dogmas of theology.

Theology is divided into apologetics, dogma, and moral. (1) *Apologetics* studies the reasons for belief, the evidences from reason that a Divine Revelation has taken place. Apologetics determines which of the many existing theologies is the one, true theology. (2) *Dogma* is the study of the doctrinal content of Revelation, i.e., those truths that God has made known to man supernaturally. And, (3) *moral* is the special study of the laws of ethical conduct that God has revealed to us, ultimately leading man to his supernatural end. Moral theology also makes a study of ecclesiastical law, or the disciplinary laws of the Church in regard to the Commandments and the Sacraments, as expressed in the Code of Canon Law.

It is important to note the distinction between "theology" and the "Christian Faith." The *Christian Faith* refers to the content of Divine Revelation, whereas *theology* refers to the human expression of and reflection upon Divine Revelation. Upon analysis one can see that the distinction between the two is a logical, not a real, distinction. Divine Revelation is intended for human beings and must necessarily be expressed in human language. Ready-made statements of the Christian Faith coming from Heaven simply do not exist. Even the utterances of Christ are clothed in the habiliments of the Aramaic idiom spoken by the Jews of His day.

Every statement of the Christian Faith will necessarily be a theological formula. From time to time in the history of the Church, the magisterium has declared certain theological formulas to be valid and adequate reflections of divine truth, while declaring other theological formulas to be invalid or inadequate. Some theological formulas the Church has neither denied nor affirmed; they remain open questions.

Pope St. Pius X, in his encyclical *Lamentabili*, condemned the proposition that "Revelation, constituting the object of the Catholic Faith, was not completed with the apostles." Vatican Council II stated: "We now await no further new public Revelation before the glorious manifestation of Our Lord Jesus Christ." Pope Paul VI, on Jan. 19, 1972, stated: "Revelation . . . must be regarded as closed and completed with the apostles."

There is an archconservative element in Catholicism today that would interpret the foregoing statements as a condemnation of all theological change and would regard all theological investigation as suspect and a threat to the Faith. This mentality fails to sufficiently recognize the dynamic and historical aspects of all truth, including Divine Revelation. Divine Revelation is one and complete, ending with the apostles; but Divine Revelation and its theological expression did not *die* with the apostles. Divine truth is alive today and, like any living thing, is subject to development, change, and growth. There are no new doctrines of the Faith, but only a better understanding and application of the one Christian Revelation.

To assert that divine truth is subject to development and modification is not to say that all theology becomes "process theology," that there is no finality or certitude regarding Revelation, that theological doctrines are "up for grabs." On the contrary, the magisterium of the Church has fully committed itself to certain basic theological doctrines, as defined by the Ecumenical Councils and the infallible teaching of the papacy, and reflected in the Jan., 1973, publication by the American bishops of the *Basic Teachings for Catholic Religious Education;* in the *General Catechetical Directory* (1971); and in Pope Paul's "The Credo of the People of God" (*Professio Fidei*). From these basic dogmas a faithful Catholic will not waver. But the fact that all statements of the Faith are necessarily limited by human language and understanding and are, to some extent, historically conditioned makes it possible and even inevitable that theology will manifest a dynamic, developing, and changing character. Ultimately, the magisterium of the Church decides upon the validity of a theological statement. No theologian, as such, has the power to formulate and define doctrine; his function is to investigate, to propose, and to contribute to the whole Church's understanding of divine truth. The role of the theologian in the Church is vital and necessary.

Christian theology is not handcuffed to an *a priori*, static worldview and methodology. Theology is and must be always open to new findings in science and more refined theological insights based on Christian experience and reflection.

The topic of religious truth and change is taken up in more detail in Chapter V. Here we note that writers such as Hans Kung, Charles E. Curran, and Raymond E. Brown are giving eloquent expression to the rationale for a more historically conscious, *a posteriori* theology. An *a priori* theology, for example, finds it extremely difficult to accept a change in the Church's position on contraception. Such a change is readily accepted and justified by an *a posteriori*, historically conscious theological methodology. One might also cite the rationales for evolution, the ordination of women, optional clerical celibacy, the choosing of a pope and bishops, and the declaration of Vatican II on religious liberty as examples of a more historical theology.

Loyalty to Christian truth is not measured by one's ability to ignore problems and sweep them under the sanctuary rug. True Christian theology endeavors to come to grips with the pressing issues of the day. "Despite the annoyance caused by these archconservatives," writes Father Raymond E. Brown, "our great assurance for the future is that the real organs of Catholic theological education are solidly in the hands of those who accept modern insights."[2]After a dearth of theological brilliance for the last two centuries, Catholic theology is once more coming alive.

II. DIVINE REVELATION

The Creator speaks to man, His creature, in various ways: through the sanctuary of the human heart; through the interior Sinai known as conscience; through the senses and the beauties of nature; through the intellect and the light of reason; through the physical laws of the universe. All nature reflects the wisdom, the power, and the goodness of the Almighty; all nature is a natural revelation of and a sacramental bridge to the First Cause and Final End of the created world.

Yet, there is "that Love we fall just short of in all love"; we live in a universe that promises more than it can give. Anticipation is always greater than realization concerning the things of this world. The testimony of history cries out that this earth is not man's lasting city.

Philosophy has always been plagued by the problems of evil, death, and suffering. Why must life be mixed with death, health with sickness, truth with error? Likewise, philosophy alone has never been able to adequately deal with the remoteness of God. Aristotle's Prime Mover is cold, impersonal, and seemingly couldn't care less about human affairs. Was man created for only a natural end? Why is the world characterized by war, confusion, travail, wrangling, and disease? Was all of this intended by the Creator?

The pre-Christian world longed for redemption. Aeschylus wrote in *Prometheus Bound:* "Neither look for any respite from this agony, unless some god appear as a voluntary successor to thy toils, and of his own free will goeth down to sunless Hades and the dark depths of Tartarus."[3] Socrates said, "Wait for a wise man who is to come, who will tell us how we are to conduct ourselves before God and man."[4] Confucius, in his *Morals,* wrote: "The Holy One must come from Heaven Who will know all things and have power over Heaven and earth."[5] Buddha said, "The Buddha Who will come after me will be known as *Maitreya,* which means, 'He Whose name is Love.' "[6]

Mythology was man's naive attempt to account for natural phenomena with a supernatural explanation. The myths expressed man's elementary desire to know the causes of the effects that he sees. Chesterton put it well: "We all feel what is meant by Prometheus stealing fire from Heaven, until some prig of a pessimist or progressive person explains what it means."[7]

Aristotle's God was deistic, far removed from the affairs of men; He set the world in motion and let it run according to its own inherent laws. Deism has never answered and fulfilled the deepest yearnings of man. Indeed, it is the position of Teilhard de Chardin, who sees everything in an evolutionary context, that the universe naturally tends toward "Christogenesis": in the historical person of Jesus, Point Omega appears tangibly for the first time.[8]

Even a superficial study of history indicates that the un-aided natural reason of man has been unable to achieve a pure form of natural religion. The great minds of Plato, Aristotle, Socrates, Seneca, and Marcus Aurelius made flagrant errors in developing a moral code. Slavery was generally condoned; cruelty and sexual promiscuity were often permitted. Man needed, and still needs, a special communication from his Maker, to guide his faltering footsteps and to guarantee the truth concerning the supreme issues of life.

How can man recognize a Divine Revelation? Theologians distinguish between the manner and the substance of revelation. Revelation may be transmitted in a *natural* manner, by the use of the senses and reason alone; or Revelation may be transmitted in a *supernatural* manner, by a direct intuition or infusion of divine truth, or by the testimony of a divine messenger. Thus, man knows *naturally* of the existence of God, the freedom of the will, the immortality of the human soul, and many precepts of natural ethics. Revelation may be natural or supernatural in substance: i.e., the truths revealed in a supernatural manner might be known by reason alone (e.g., life after death) or they may be beyond human reason to establish (e.g., the Trinity, the Real Presence).

From the foregoing it follows that Revelation that is supernatural in substance must be revealed in a supernatural manner. Revelation that is natural in substance may be revealed in either a natural or supernatural manner.

It stands to reason that if God chose to reveal Himself in a supernatural manner to mankind, such a Revelation would be accompanied by distinguishing marks to be recognized by all. First, the substance of the Revelation would be consonant with man's deepest convictions and fulfill his highest aspirations. A Divine Revelation cannot contradict a natural truth; nor can a true Revelation contradict itself. The foregoing constitutes the *internal* evidence of a Revelation. The external evidences of a special Divine Revelation are miracles and prophecies. A *miracle* is defined as "an unusual event or occurrence perceptible to the senses and beyond the power of nature."[9] God is the Author of the physical laws of this universe; He alone, therefore, has the power to suspend a law of nature in a particular instance. When a miracle occurs, we may be sure that the event gives testimony of God's approval and sanction. Likewise with prophecies: "A prophecy is the clear foretelling of a future event which depends in some way upon the exercise of free will."[10] A prophecy is a kind of miracle of the intellectual order. Since God alone knows the future acts of a free creature, a prophecy must be traced to God as its primary Author.

We conclude that pantheists, materialists, and deists are in error when they deny the possibility or existence of miracles. Miracles and prophecies put the divine stamp of approval upon a Revelation, so that all men may know and recognize the divine authorship. Vatican Council I issued the following definition: "If any one assert that miracles are imposible . . . and that the divine origin of the Christian religion cannot be properly demonstrated by them; let him be anathema."[11]

III. THE TRUTH OF CHRISTIANITY

Postulates. In establishing the truth of the Christian religion, we must rely upon certain postulates, or presuppositions. First, we must accept the trustworthiness of human reason in acquiring true and certain knowledge. The philosophical science of epistemology establishes this postulate.[12] Secondly, we assume the principle of sufficient reason, which states that everything (including God) has a sufficient reason to explain its existence. This principle is a self-evident postulate established by the philosophical sciences of logic and ontology. Thirdly, we assume the existence of God, which is established by the philosophical science of theodicy.[13]

(1) Sceptics deny that man is able to acquire true and certain knowledge. But they use their *intellect* in denying the possibility of trustworthy human knowledge. One can immediately see the futility of scepticism, which is intellectual suicide. Of course, one cannot prove the innate capability of the human mind to acquire truth. Such a "proof" would itself involve a begging of the question. The trustworthiness of human reason is an *a priori*, self-evident postulate of all human sciences; without

this postulate life would indeed become a snare and a delusion, a "tale told by an idiot, full of sound and fury, signifying nothing." The truth of Christianity assumes that man was made to know and that man is able to know. Truth may be apprehended only partially and incompletely; truth may be subject to development, intensification, and clarification; but the truth of Christianity assumes that valid, certain knowledge is possible for man.

(2) Philosophy has its first principles, all of which are assumed to be true in establishing the truth of Christianity. A thing is what it is (the principle of identity); a thing cannot be and yet not be at the same time under the same respect (the principle of contradiction); a thing either is or is not (the principle of excluded middle); everything (including God) has a sufficient reason to explain its existence (the principle of sufficient reason); every effect has an adequate cause (the principle of causality). David Hume (1711-1776) — who first interrupted Kant's "dogmatic slumber" — questioned the ontological reality of the principle of causality, which he reduced to a mere *a posteriori* sequence of emperical events. It is useless to speak of the truth of Christianity unless one is willing to accept the above-mentioned first principles as being self-evident and necessary postulates of all human thought and objective reality.

(3) The truth of Christianity assumes the existence of God. Even God has a sufficient reason, namely, Himself. God is His own sufficient reason, the self-subsistent being, the *ens a se* (being from itself). Unlike God, all creatures have a cause which is extrinsic to themselves; they are, therefore, *ens ab alio* (being from another). In the thirteenth century Thomas Aquinas wrote that best arguments ever written for God's existence. Kant denied the validity of these arguments; but we subscribe to the Scholastic position that these arguments are as valid today as they were when Aquinas wrote them.

The five arguments of Aquinas, briefly paraphrased, are:

First, there is motion (*motus*, change, evolution) in the universe; but such motion must ultimately lead to a prime mover which is itself unmoved, unchangeable, and pure act. Such a being men have called God.

Second, efficient causality is manifested in the universe; but no being is the efficient cause of itself. There must be a first cause, itself uncaused, which men have called God.

Third, the universe is composed of finite, contingent beings which might or might not exist; but such beings presuppose the existence of a necessary being which is not in potency and not dependent upon, nor limited by, another being. This necessary, infinite being men call God.

Fourth, there is a gradation, or hierarchy, of perfection in the universe: from chemicals, to plants, to animals, to man; these perfections must find their source in a supramundane being possessing all perfections in their plenitude and without limit. This being is called God.

And, fifth, there is order, design, and purpose (teleology) in the universe, which bespeaks of a supreme intelligence and a master architect, whom men have called God.[14]

Fideism denies that the existence of God can be known with certitude by reason alone; God's existence is known only by an act of faith. Kierkegaard spoke of "the leap of faith." Aquinas maintained that the existence of God is not self-evident, but can be readily demonstrated by a simple application of the principle of causality. Vatican Council I defined as part of the Catholic Faith that unaided reason is capable of knowing God. It is upon this firm foundation of reason that the truth of Christianity is built.

A final postulate to the truth of Christianity should be mentioned: the necessity of good will and an upright conscience. Conduct colors belief. We tend to trim our beliefs to suit our conduct, rather than making conduct conform to belief. When one says he cannot believe in the Trinity, Confession, or the Real Presence, he may mean he is unwilling to live the Christian life. The difficulty is not so much with the Creed as it is with the Commandments. One never falls away from Christianity to become a better person. A sincere heart and a clear conscience are necessary prerequisites to knowing God's truth; this may be what Our Lord had in mind when He said: "Blessed are the clean of heart, for they shall see God" (Matt. 5:8). It may also be what Cardinal Newman inferred when he said, "Syllogisms make but sorry rhetoric with the masses." Necessary and important though they are, logic and argumentation are not enough in coming to God's truth. Newman warned about winning an argument and losing a soul. St. Thomas Aquinas said he learned more through prayer at the foot of the Crucifix than from all the books he had read. God is not simply a philosophical abstraction to be defined but a living presence to be shared.

The foregoing postulates having been established, our purpose is to show that a Divine Revelation is a historical fact; that the Christian religion is of divine origin; that Jesus Christ proved Himself to be the bearer of Revelation; and that Jesus Christ is the divine Son of God.

The New Testament as a Historical Document. The claims of Christianity to be a divine religion are subject to historical scrutiny and verification. Any work of history is *authentic*, or geniune, inasmuch as it is truly the work of the author whose name it bears; a work is historically *reliable* inasmuch as its author was trustworthy, truthful, and informed; and a historical work possesses *integrity* inasmuch as the text is complete and substantially as it left the author's hand.

How does the New Testament stand up under the scrutiny of historical criticism? From many sources that we could cite, we have decided to quote the testimony of Will Durant, who knows his history and is frequently critical of Christian theology:

The contradictions are of minutiae, not substance; in essentials the synoptic Gospels agree remarkably well, and form a consistent portrait of Christ. In the enthusiasm of its discoveries the Higher Criticism has applied to the New Testament tests of authenticity so severe that by them a hundred ancient worthies — e.g., Hammurabi, David, Socrates — would fade into legend . . . That a few simple men should in one generation have invented so powerful and appealing personality, so lofty an ethic and so inspiring a vision of human brotherhood, would be a miracle far more incredible than any recorded in the Gospels. After two centuries of Higher Criticism the outlines of the life, character, and teaching of Christ, remain reasonably clear, and constitute the most fascinating feature in the history of Western man.[15]

"Viewed simply as historical documents," writes John A. O'Brien, "the Gospels present in a trustworthy and reliable manner the Revelation of Jesus Christ to mankind."[16]

Christ, the Bearer of Revelation. The Gospels record that Christ both made and fulfilled prophecies. "Search the Scriptures; . . . the same are they that give testimony of Me" (John 5:39). He foretold His own death by crucifixion and His Resurrection on the third day (cf. Matt. 20:18-19). He foretold Judas' betrayal and the threefold denial of Peter.

Likewise, Christ performed miracles. He restored Lazarus to life; He multiplied loaves and fishes; He changed water into wine; He walked on water; with a single word He cured a paralytic. He rose from the dead, both fulfilling a prophecy and giving the mightiest evidence of His own divine character and mission. He appealed to His works as giving testimony of His divine mission (cf. John 5:36).

Moreover, Christ taught a sublime doctrine of love for God and neighbor; His appeal was to the noblest elements in man; and He answered the deepest aspirations of the human heart. His doctrine is one of mercy, love, forgiveness, kindness, justice, and fidelity. He promised life everlasting to those who believe and love.

We conclude that Christ was indeed the bearer of Revelation and deserves to be acknowledged as such by all mankind.

Christ, the Son of God. Christ asked His disciples, "But who do you say that I am?" He asks the same question of all of us. Each must answer the question for himself. Some reject Christ altogether as a charlatan and an imposter Who suffered from a monomania; some consider Him to have been a noble teacher with a winsome personality, and list Him with Socrates, Aristotle, Confucius, and even Albert Schweitzer, of our own time; still others answer with Peter, "You are the Christ, the Son of the Living God" (Matt. 16:16).

Did Jesus of Nazareth claim to be divine? It is difficult to see how one can read the Gospels, openly and sincerely, and not conclude that Jesus indeed claimed to be divine, one in nature with God. He claimed true sonship with the Father (cf. John 5:17-36); He claimed to have the same nature as God the Father (cf. John 10:25-39).

The apparent contradictions (cf. John 17:3; John 14:28, "The Father is greater than I"; Matt. 20:23; and Luke 18:19, "Why do you call Me good?") are readily explained by the context in which the words were spoken.

We conclude that Jesus Christ, besides being the bearer of a Divine Revelation, claimed to be God incarnate and, in fact, went to His death on the cross rather than retract this claim. Christ was not just "a good man" or "a noble teacher," for good men and noble teachers do not lie. We must say with Chesterton that if Jesus of Nazareth was not the Christ, then He was Antichrist. We further conclude that Christianity is the one, true, divine religion authored and sanctioned by God Himself and that it is incumbent upon all to come to know, love, and serve Our Lord and Savior, Jesus Christ.

Nearly two thousand years after the Eternal Galilean redeemed the world and gave to mankind His religion of love, peace, hope, and joy, we find only about one-third of the earth's people regarding themselves as Christians. More than two billion people know not Christ, or at least have not made some kind of visible commitment to Him. Christianity itself continues to find itself divided into differing sects. Why have not the person and life-giving doctrines of Jesus had a more universal effect upon mankind? Christ is still asking His Church and the world, "Who do you say that I am?"

The impact and influence of Christianity upon the world cannot be evaluated solely in terms of numbers. Christ once referred to His "little flock." Karl Rahner wonders if the description may be literally accurate in terms of the future of Christianity. Christ never promised the total conversion of the world to Christianity; but Christians have the divine mandate to work to bring about such a total conversion.

Christ is the Light of the world. Such notables of history as Napoleon, Goethe, Voltaire, and Rousseau were willing to acknowledge the singularity and profound appeal of the man from Galilee. Rousseau wrote in *Emile*: "If the life and death of Socrates were those of a sage, the life and death of Jesus were those of a God." Voltaire, never a friend to Christian theology, wrote: "I have two hundred volumes on this subject, and, what is worse, I have read them. It is like going the rounds of a lunatic asylum." Though he continued to end many of his letters with *"ecrasez l'infâme* (crush the infamy [Christianity])," toward the end of his life Voltaire seemed to respond more warmly to the singular appeal of Christ, sometimes referring to Him as "my brother" and "my master." Nietzsche thought the world had seen only one Christian, and He died on a cross on Good Friday. The scandal of so-called Christians living un-Christian lives continues to frustrate God's purposes in this world. Much of Voltaire's objections to Christianity was based on caricatures of Christian doctrine, on anticlericalism, and on immoderate and irrational practices, such as the Inquisition. Yet the Pilgrim Church, ever conscious of its frailty and sinfulness, continues to proclaim Christ crucified and rejoices with hope and confidence in the great Paschal Mystery of the death and Resurrection of Christ. Even those who do not formally regard themselves as Christians may indeed be seeking first the Kingdom of God and His justice, and are therefore Christians at heart.

The essential thrust of Christ's distinctive message can be summarized by five key Greek words which appear in the New Testament: (1) *kerygma*, whereby the good news of salvation and the love of Christ are to be proclaimed to the world; (2) *metanoia*, calling for an ongoing coversion and change of heart in response to the love of Christ and the promptings of the Holy Spirit; (3) *koinonia*, calling for fellowship and communion among all Christians; (4) *diakonia*, calling for service and charity to all mankind; and (5) *parousia*, the final coming of Christ to establish the new Heaven and the new earth, which give all Christian labors and perseverance their eschatological significance and fulfillment.

"Why has not Christianity succeeded?" asks the sceptic. "What has Christianity done for the Third World of underdeveloped nations?" "Why are there still poverty, war, disease, ignorance, and injustice in the world?" Apologetics cannot give complete and final answers to these questions. Vatican II eloquently proclaimed the mystery of the Church which is a Pilgrim Church with a mission to perform: to be the salvation of the world. Christ did not totally succeed in His own day when He trod the dusty roads of ancient Palestine. He was rejected by His own people and executed by the civil authority of the day. The saddest words of Scripture are those of Our Lord when He said: "Thou wouldst not." The rejection of Love has to be the most tragic event in the universe. Christianity exists in a finite, imperfect world tainted with Original Sin and its consequences.

The Eternal Galilean continues to proclaim Himself to mankind through His Pilgrim Church making its way through the vicissitudes of this world. The Great High Priest continues to offer Himself to the world as the Way, the Truth, and the Life. As *The Imitation of Christ* tells us, without the Way there is no going; without the Truth there is no knowing; without the Life there is no living. Yes, we say with Peter: "Thou art the Christ, the Son of the living God!"

Christianity has not failed; only we Christians have failed — with our scepticism, fears, materialism, triumphalism, sensuality, egotism, and indifference. Christlike Christians will continue to work to bring about the new Heaven and the new earth. There will be setbacks, pitfalls, and times of discouragement; there will be times when Christ will seem to have been defeated, as on Good Friday; but the Paschal Mystery shall prevail, as Christ prevailed on Easter Sunday. Evil has its hour;

but it is God Who wins the day. The beautiful words of Jean Paul Richter are prophetically true: "The purest among the strong and the strongest among the pure, Christ lifted with His wounded hands empires from their hinges and changed the stream of ages."

Joseph Stalin, the Soviet dictator, once asked how many armed divisions the pope had. Christianity possesses no tanks, machine guns, or nuclear warheads. Christians, in their battle against diabolical forces, are armed only with

the armor of God, . . . having girded your loins with truth, and having put on the breastplate of justice, and having your feet shod with the readiness of the Gospel of peace, in all things taking up the shield of Faith, . . . the helmet of salvation, and the sword of the spirit, that is, the word of God (Eph. 6:11 ff.).

An army composed of men and women like Francis of Assisi, Thomas Aquinas, Dominic, Ignatius Loyola, Thomas More ("a man for all seasons"), the Curé of Ars, Vincent de Paul, Catherine of Siena, Elizabeth of Hungary, Joan of Arc, Teresa of Avila, Bernadette Soubirous, and America's own Mother Cabrini and Elizabeth Seton — along with the legions of "uncanonized saints" performing their prosaic duties in a Christlike manner in a workaday world — such an army would be invincible! The battle rages on; but every Christian is deeply aware that victory is assured. "I have overcome the world," said the Captain of the Cross. The words of Julian the Apostate were true when he spoke them, are true now, and will be true forever: "O Galilean, Thou hast conquered!"

IV. THE TRUTH OF CATHOLICISM

Christ's Church. How did Christ intend to teach, to govern, and to sanctify subsequent generations? The question is moot, and twentieth-century Christianity is divided over the answer. Catholics, numbering about 52 percent of all Christians, believe Christ founded a visible Church headed by the pope, the successor of St. Peter. Protestants, numbering about 27 percent of the world's Christians, de-emphasize the institutional Church and lay stress on private interpretation of Sacred Scripture and justification by faith alone. Eastern Orthodoxy, accounting for about 21 percent of all Christians,[17] agrees with Catholicism on many points but does not accept the primacy and jurisdiction of the pope of Rome.

The Bible records that Jesus identified Himself with three others: (1) with His heavenly Father, when He said He was one with the Father; (2) with the poor, when He said that whatever was done for them was the same as doing it for Him; (3) with His Mystical Body, the Church, when He called it "My Church" and said that He was the vine as we are the branches. Catholics believe that Matt. 16:18-19, where Peter is named the foundation of the Church, is given the keys of the Kingdom, and is given the power to bind and loose, is cogent testimony of Christ's intention.

Tradition supports the view that, *de facto*, the papal office has been exercised from the time of Peter. The *Encyclopaedia Britannica* states candidly that the evidence points to Peter having lived in Rome and having been martyred there.[18]

Besides the arguments from Scripture and tradition, Catholics believe that *reason* supports their concept of Christ's Church. Man is social by nature, and God deals with man according to his nature. The history of the Old Testament gives a venerable place to "the people of God," to the *qahal* (religious body) presided over by a visible head.[19] The Hebrew word *qahal* became the Greek word *ecclesia*, when Christ spoke of "My Chruch." Man's nature demands order, government, unity, and coherence; the institutional Church, presided over by the pope and bishops, provides the structure intended by Christ to best fulfill the needs of the individual Christian.

The Catholic believes that Christ's Chruch is identifiable by certain marks, or qualities. (1) Christ's Church would necessarily be *one*; that there could be even two Churches of Christ, holding contradictory beliefs, is absolutely repugnant. Christ prayed for unity, "that all may be one." (2) Christ's Church would be *holy*, in the sense that it possesses the means to holiness given to it by its divine Founder, Who is holiness itself. (3) Christ's Church would be *universal*, inasmuch as it teaches all that Christ taught and would embrace all nations. And, (4) Christ's Church would be *apostolic*, tracing its origin in a continuous and direct line to its Founder, Jesus Christ.

Catholics believe that such a Church does exist on earth today, that Christ's Church is the Roman Catholic Church. To say this is not to say that all other Christians are totally in error, that the Holy Spirit does not work through them, or that all non-Catholics are doomed to Hell. When Catholicism teaches that the Catholic Church alone is the true Church of Christ, it

makes a claim based, first on its own inner consciousness of its
divine origin and mission and, secondly, on a claim grounded in
Scripture, history, and reason.[20]

A Critique of Protestantism. The religious revolution of the
sixteenth century produced what is now generally known as
Protestantism; most historians agree that this revolution could
not have succeeded without the aid of the nationalist movement
and the help of the secular princes of the day.[21] The principle of
private interpretation of the Scriptures along with the rejection
of papal authority introduced a divisive element within Christianity. In the United States there are over four hundred distinct Protestant sects. The Protestant would justify this division as a necessary price to pay for religious freedom; the
Catholic, on the other hand, views this division as something
tantamount to religious chaos and anarchy. A principle in religion that produces such disunity, doctrinal chaos, and a prolifer-
ation of sects surely cannot be a sound principle nor representative of the mind of Christ.

The doctrine of the Bible as the sole rule of faith ignores the
fact that the Church was antecedent to, and mother of, the
Bible in its completed form; we find the Church in the Bible and
the Bible in the Church. The Bible needs an authoritative interpreter; the Holy Spirit absolutely does not guarantee that
each one's interpretation will be infallible. Witness the many
contradictory interpretations existing within Protestantism;
God certainly does not bear witness to contradictions. On the
natural level, what would happen to our country if each citizen
were free to interpret the Constitution as he saw fit?

Justification by faith *alone* is a one-sided exaggeration of a
theological truth: that faith is necessary for salvation. St.
James said explicitly that faith without works is dead (James
2:26); Luther, rejecting what he wished from Sacred Scripture,
called the Letter "an epistle of straw." Christ said, "Not
everyone who says to Me, 'Lord, Lord,' shall enter the Kingdom
of Heaven; but he who does the will of My Father in Heaven
shall enter the Kingdom of Heaven" (Matt. 7:21).

The fundamental premise of Protestantism that religion is
essentially a private affair sins against reason by its ultrasub-
jectivity. Many like to regard Martin Luther as the first existentialist of modern times. But as Fulton J. Sheen has pointed
out so well,[22] each one does not have his own sun, his own

planet, his own atmosphere, his own government, his own
school, or his own multiplication table. How justify having one's
own religion? How justify going to Heaven "my way" when only
God's way will suffice?

We conclude that Protestantism, which did not see the light
of day until the sixteenth century, minimizes the importance of
religious unity, social solidarity, objectivity, historical tradition,
and authority. To say this is not to deny that Protestants are
sincere, intelligent, devoted followers of Christ. All Christian
denominations are partly to blame for the scandal of
twentieth-century disunity; all must work assiduously to
further the ecumenical movement, "that all may be one."[23]

A Critique of Eastern Orthodoxy. The origin of the Eastern
Orthodox Church, also called the Greek Orthodox Church, can
be traced to the ninth century when Photius, the Patriarch of
Constantinople, was excommunicated by Pope Nicholas I.
Reunion with Rome took place after Photius' death, but the
schism took a more permanent form in 1054 A. D. with Michael
Cerularius, who was excommunicated by Pope St. Leo IX. The
split from Rome, except for brief periods in the thirteenth and
fifteenth centuries, has persisted to this day. Strictly speaking,
there is not *one* Eastern Orthodox Church, since there exists a
federation of thirteen autocephalous Orthodox Churches, accounting for about one-fifth of the world's Christian population.
The ecumenical patriarch of Constantinople is the head of the
federation but only as *primus inter pares.*[24]

Eastern Orthodoxy retains a valid priesthood and valid
Sacraments. In the course of time, in addition to not accepting
the primacy of jurisdiction of the Bishop of Rome, Eastern
Orthodoxy has developed more than twenty doctrinal differences with Roman Catholicism.

Prior to 857 A. D. there was no separate Eastern Orthodox
Church; thus, the quality of apostolicity cannot *licitly* be
claimed by the Eastern Orthodox Church, even though the validity of its priesthood has remained intact. The marks of unity
(as we have noted), catholicity (by not accepting Christ's commitment to Peter), and a licit apostolicity are missing from
Eastern Orthodoxy.

We must conclude that Eastern Orthodoxy, like Protestantism, errs in not accepting the authority of St. Peter's successor,
the Bishop of Rome. There are, of course, a number of signifi-

cant social, political, and cultural factors involved in this separation from Rome; the blame for the schism does not necessarily fall entirely on one side. Yet we must conclude, *a priori*, that the fundamental reason for the separation of both Protestants and Orthodox from Roman Catholicism is an unwillingness to submit — in the spirit of faith, humility, and obedience — to the pope in matters of faith and morals. Such submission isn't easy, even for the Catholic in certain cases; but the Catholic is convinced that Christ intended such submission, that both the Bible and tradition make it imperative to do so. How and when this Christian dilemma of disunity is to be resolved is known only to the Holy Spirit.[25]

V. COMPARATIVE RELIGION[26]

Principles to Be Observed. One can distinguish three aspects of the science of comparative religion: (1) *hierography*, which is concerned with the observation of religious phenomena for the purpose of knowing and describing them; (2) *hierology*, which formulates and coordinates general principles and laws; and (3) *hierosophy*, which adds a metaphysical approach to determine the intimate nature, fundamental laws, and value of religious phenomena. The first observes; the second coordinates; the third interprets.

The principle of demarcation makes a distinction between method and doctrine; simply to observe and describe a particular religion is not to have fully explained or evaluated that religion. The principle of the primacy of the spiritual states that in every human work primacy belongs to the invisible element and the idea, or intention, which is the soul of the human act. The principle of organic unity states that the details of a religion must be studied in relation to the whole, and not merely in comparison to another religion.

A true science of comparative religion should not rest on the following false assumptions: (1) The crudest forms of religion practiced today necessarily represent the religion of primitive man. (2) The supernatural is impossible, or at least unknowable. (3) If there is one, true, divine religion, it must be different in every respect from all other religions. (4) All religions have a sociological explanation. (5) All religions have a psychological explanation.

The Non-Christian Religions of the World. Hinduism, Buddhism, Confucianism, Taoism, Judaism, and Islam constitute, in the main, the world's non-Christian religions. About 15 percent of the world's population are either animists (pagans) or atheists.

(1) About 12 percent of the world's population are classified as *Hindu*. This religion of India and the Orient is probably the oldest living religion. Its contradictions have never been resolved, and no iron orthodoxy is imposed upon its followers. The *Upanishads* sets forth the whole philosophy of ancient India, which is called Brahmanism. The world is illusion (*maya*); Brahma is the basic reality, indwelling in all things (pantheism); life is evil; existence involves an infinite series of births and deaths; the goal of existence is release from this endless cycle of rebirth by ascetic discipline. Thus, individuality is lost by a sinking into the universal self, which is Brahma.

(2) *Buddhism* was an outgrowth of Hinduism. Buddhists constitute about 11 percent of the earth's people. Prince Siddhartha, a member of the Gautama clan, was probably born about 563 B.C. After profound meditation while sitting under the *Bodhi*-tree, he was "enlightened"; he saw birth as the origin of all evil. The only answer to pain and sorrow is to sink into the cool quietude of *Nirvana*, by the practice of asceticism and following "the Eightfold Path."

Buddha, which means "Enlightened," never claimed that God was speaking through him. He stayed clear of metaphysics altogether. "There is nothing stranger in the history of religion," writes Will Durant, "than the sight of Buddha founding a worldwide religion, and yet refusing to be drawn into any discussion about eternity, immortality, or God."[27] Again, "At times this most famous of Hindu saints passes from agnosticism to outright atheism."[28] Buddha claimed no ability to work miracles.

Buddhism is not a miracle religion. Nor does its founder claim to be anything but a man. Buddha simply claims to have had the best insight of any man on the best way to live.

(3) *Taoism* is attributed by tradition to Lao-tze (640-531 B.C.), which, like Buddha and Christ, is a title given to a historical figure. *Lao-tze* means "The Old Master"; his real name was Li.[29] Taoism is a pacifist faith which preaches submission and humility and a philosophy of inaction: "doing everything without apparently doing anything." Taoism as a religion turned toward sorcery and magic.

(4) *Confucius* (the Latinized form of K'ung-fu-tze, a title given to K'ung Ch'iu by his pupils, meaning K'ung the Master) was born in 551 B.C. Like Buddha and Lao-tze, Confucius eschewed metaphysical speculation; one can rightly ascribe to him a kind of agnosticism as to a transcendent God and a personal immortality. His master passion was for morality. Anticipating Christ, Confucius gave us the Golden Rule, stated negatively: "Not to do unto others as you would not wish done unto yourself." He taught courtesy, propriety, reverence, and respect for authority. He preached *Tao*, a very ancient Chinese principle which stands for the unchanging unity and harmony of the universe.

Taoists and Confucianists constitute about 14 percent of the world's population.

(5) *Judaism* has a venerable history. From the start the Jewish people were "the people of God," Who had made a special covenant with Israel. God is Yahweh, transcendent, personal, the Lord of history. God transmitted a primitive Revelation to the progenitors of the human race; by the call of Abraham God entrusted the true religion with the Jewish people and prepared for the coming of the Savior of the world; Moses proved his divine mission by miracles and prophecies. Judaism is pre-eminently a miracle religion, monotheistic and providential in character. Modern Judaism, of course, still looks for the coming of the Messiah. Jews make up about 0.45 percent of the earth's people.

(6) *Islam* is the name given to the religion founded by Mohammed, whose name means "The Praised One." The Prophet was born in Mecca, Arabia, probably in April, 569 A.D. At his birth he is reputed to have exclaimed, "God is great! There is no god but Allah; and I am his prophet." Mohammed had nine wives at the time of his death. Spasmodic convulsions always accompanied his visions — attributed by many to his epilepsy. The Prophet was a strange contradiction: at times he was cowardly and deceitful; other times, loyal, generous, kind, and forceful. In later years he gave way to gross sensuality.

Mohammed claimed to be the sixth Great Prophet, following Adam, Noah, Abraham, Moses, and Jesus. Hilaire Belloc thought Islam to be a Christian heresy. The miracles of Christ are frankly acknowledged by Mohammed, and he claimed no power to work miracles himself.[30] Mohammed never claimed to be more than an envoy.

The six cardinal points of Islamic belief (*Imân*) are: (1) God and His unity; (2) angels, good and bad spirits; (3) belief in the Koran and revelation; (4) belief in the Prophet; (5) belief in the resurrection and judgment day; and (6) God's absolute rule of the world. Significantly, the Nineteenth Chapter of the Koran contains forty-one verses on Jesus and Mary; Mary is the true *Sayyida*, or Lady. Mohammed foretold the coming of a Messiah, *Al-Mahdi*, who will restore the glory and power of Islam.

Hell everlasting is only for the followers of other religions; Paradise is a sensuous place embellished with beautiful gardens, trees, rivers, maidens, and appetites that increase as the delights are enjoyed. The blessed will always see the face of God and praise Him. Allah intended religion to be easy, "lest we all be hypocrites."

Moslems constitute about 13 percent of the world's population.

A Critique of the World's Religions. (1) Christiantiy alone of the world's religions claims complete and necessary adherence. Hinduism, Buddhism, Taoism, Judaism, and Islamism do not claim to be the final, complete Divine Revelation of God to man; both Judaism and Islam look for a Messiah yet to come. Buddha referred to a successor, *Maitreya*. Confucius said a Holy One was yet to come. Christianity claims to be final and complete, "unto the consummation of the world."

(2) Christianity is not identified with only one ethnic group or people. Originating in the Near East, which is midway between the great civilizations of the world, Christianity alone is able to unite both East and West. The Founder of Christianity commanded that the Gospel be taught to all nations; and He expressed the desire that there be but one fold and one shepherd. The sense of mission to convert and teach the world is missing from the other world religions. Buddhism is concentrated mainly in India; in China and Japan Buddhism takes the form of Shinto. Islam is essentially the religion of Arabia and northern Africa; the spread of the religion followed a pattern of military conquest. Christianity alone has an essentially universal character and commission.

(3) None but Christianity has a Founder Who is identified with history itself, so that all time has been reckoned as either before His birth or after His birth (B.C. and A.D.). The birth of Christ, unlike the birth of Buddha, Lao-tze, Confucius, or Mohammed, hit history with such an impact as to split time in two. Even one who would deny that Christ ever existed would have to date his denial as A.D.

(4) None but Christianity has a prehistory and lays claim to miracles as evidence of the divine character of the religion. The birth of Christ was foretold in Genesis 3:15; Isaiah 9:7 said He would be born of the family of David; Moses declared that He will be a great Prophet (cf. Deut. 18:18); Psalms 2:7 gives the eternal prehistory of Christ: "Thou art My Son, this day have I begotten Thee." Quoting Isaiah 61:1, Christ declared, "This day is fulfilled the Scriptures in your ears" (Luke 4:21). None of the other founders of world religions can lay claim to such a remarkable record of prophecy concerning their birth, character, and mission.

Christ alone, among the founders of world religions, claimed to work miracles and appealed to them as evidnece of His divine mission. As we have noted, Buddha, Lao-tze, Confucius, and Mohammed made no such claim. Judaism, of course, also appeals to miraculous events to support the validity of its religious claims; the Christian readily acknowledges the truth of Judaism. It was a pope who said, "Spiritually we are all Semites." But the Christian believes that Judaism errs in not accepting Christ as the Messiah, Who came "not to destroy, but to fulfill the law" (Matt. 5:17). The absence of geniune evidence of miraculous support for the other world religions gives one a sufficient reason to question their divine authorship.

(5) Only Christianity fulfills the highest aspirations of mankind; only Christianity gives an acceptable and coherent explanation of pain, death, sin, and error; and only Christianity successfully heals the breach between this world and the next.

Buddhism explains suffering and pain as intrinsic to existence itself; relief from "the pains of existence" can be achieved only by a complete self-abnegation in a kind of nonexistence called *Nirvana*. On the contrary, Christianity teaches that life is good; that pain, suffering, and death are the result of a misuse of freedom at the beginning of human history; and that the fullness of life will be achieved in Heaven through the merits of Christ, the Savior. Christianity affirms life; the Oriental religions tend to deny it. Christ said He came to give life "more abundantly."

Only Christianity gives philosophy its due. Buddha, Lao-tze, and Confucius refused to engage in metaphysics. But since the true God is the Author of reason as well as the Author of faith and Revelation, one would feel that philosophy would flourish as a companion to the true religion. History shows that philosophy has flourished, in the Scholasticism of the Middle Ages, as a companion and a support to Christian theology. Christianity rests on a firm philosophical basis that is characteristic of no other world religion.

Finally, and most important of all, (6) only Christianity has a Founder Who claimed to be divine; Buddha, Lao-tze, Confucius, and Mohammed never claimed to be anything but human, in spite of the efforts of some of their followers to deify them. Christ claimed to be the Way, the Truth, and the Life; He asked that all would believe in Him. Buddha pointed to Four Noble Truths and the Eightfold Path; Confucius promulgated the Golden Rule; Christ said He *was the Way*. Christians are not asked to follow an abstract formula; they are asked to know, love, and serve a *person*, Jesus Christ, the Son of the living God.

Conclusion: the Transcendence of Christianity. We conclude that Christianity alone, of the world's religions, is unique in its divine authorship and divine sanction. Christianity is not just better than the other religions; Christianity *transcends* comparison and possesses historical superiority. To say this is not to say that all other religions are in total darkness. Every religion possesses a segment of the circle of truth: Buddhism is right in stressing self-denial and the control of one's passions; Confucianism is right in teaching moderation, meekness, courtesy, and obedience; Judaism is right in teaching the Ten Commandments and man's need for redemption; Islamism is right in teaching the unity of God and personal immortality. The Holy Spirit works through these religions in His own mysterious way. "How unsearchable are His ways," St. Paul reminded us.

Nor does the transcendence of Christianity imply that the Christian religion is unique in every way. Thus, Frazer pointed out in *The Golden Bough* that human sacrifices were offered to appease the Deity by a number of primitive cults; H. L. Mencken compared the "god-eating" of primitives with the Holy Communion of Christianity. These facts do not vitiate the Christian doctrines of Redemption and the Holy Eucharist. The truths of natural religion belong to mankind in general, and it is certainly reasonable to assume that the true religion would build upon the best in human nature: *Gratia perficit naturam* (Grace perfects nature); *Gratia praesupponit naturam* (Grace presupposes nature). Furthermore, the principle of the primacy of the spiritual demands that one look to the inner, invisible meaning of any human act to determine its true significance. The truths of Christianity, while containing many human elements common to all mankind, are sparked and animated by divine authority itself. Man's nature inclines toward sacrifice as a religious act; man aspires to communion with the Supreme Being. Christianity took hold of these natural inclinations and aspirations and gave them a supernatural significance.

Apologetics leads to God. All His servitors, in "their traitorous trueness and their loyal deceit," point to the Almighty.

The Son of Man shed tears over the death of His friend Lazarus and over the city of Jerusalem, which had rejected the divine visitation. Let it never be said that it is unmanly to weep! Sam Levenson has observed that the world today needs a good cry, which can serve as a kind of catharsis for the soul. God is never closer to one than in moments of trial, frustration, and suffering. The peace of Christ — that deep, inner peace which He alone can give — is always available to one who is willing to remove the obstacles to that peace. The Christian apologist sees all moments of gloom as "the shade of His hand, outstretched caressingly." The "Hound of Heaven," described so poignantly by Francis Thompson, beckons to ignoble man: "Rise, clasp My hand, and come!"

CHAPTER II

CATHOLICISM AND DOGMATIC THEOLOGY

The Truths of the Catholic Faith

Jesus said to him [Thomas]; 'I am the Way, and the Truth, and the Life. No man comes to the Father, but by Me.'

— John 14:6

And Simon Peter answered Him: 'Lord, to whom shall we go? You have the words of eternal life.'

— John 6:69

An ounce of Revelation is worth a ton of philosophy.[1]

— F. J. Sheed

A child of God on his knees sees more than a philosopher on his tiptoes.

— Anon.

I feel the difficulties of unbelief as well as those of belief. But I trust that the good Lord will accept intellectual conscience as well as the humility of faith.[2]

— Will Durant

I. CHRISTIAN DOGMA

THEOLOGY is a precise science, like any other science worthy of the name. Diction, semantics, and even syntax can be crucial; a slip of the pen and one finds himself in heresy. Furthermore, theology does not admit of scientific verification by techniques of the laboratory. Orthodoxy (which does not necessarily exclude originality, freshness, and creativity) ought to be uppermost in the mind of one who writes on theology. And the ultimate criterion of what is orthodox must be the judgment of the infallible magisterium of the Church.

The Meaning of Dogma. *Dogma* comes from a Greek word, *dokein*, to think. Webster defines dogma as a doctrine or body of doctrines of theology formally stated and authoritatively pro-

31

claimed by a church or sect. Vatican Council I defined dogma as a truth contained "in the word of God, written or handed down, and which the Church, either by a solemn judgment or by her ordinary and universal teaching, proposes for belief as having divinely been revealed."[3]

Dogma has taken on an odious connotation in modern times. For many the term smacks of narrow-mindedness, intolerance, and fanaticism. Some advocate a "religion without dogmas" (which is itself a "dogma"). One cannot have education without truth, government without law, chemistry without formulas. How achieve religion without dogma? Every science has its dogmas.

One frequently hears, "It doesn't matter what you believe so long as you do what is right." The statement ignores the fact that we tend to act on our beliefs. Hitler acted on Nazism and produced a world war. Truth does count and ought to be taken seriously. After all, it was the truth of Christ's divinity, which He refused to deny, that was the deciding factor in His Crucifixion.

A paramount distinction must be made concerning dogmas, theological conclusions, theological opinions, and private revelations. *Dogmas* are formally contained in Scripture and/or tradition; these truths are believed on "divine faith." *Theological conclusions* are "secondary truths" intimately connected with, and derived directly from, dogmatic truth. They are not dogmas in the strict sense. The Church, as the guardian of Christian dogma, teaches them infallibly, and they are accepted by "ecclesiastical faith." *Theological opinions* are more remote conclusions, philosophical justifications, and other statements intended for amplification and discussion; they do not bear the mark of infallibility. Since the deposit of Christian Revelation ended with St. John's writing of the Apocalypse, about 96 A.D., subsequent *private revelations* (e.g., Lourdes, Fatima) are not binding upon the Christian community at large; nor do they carry the guarantee of infallibility.[4]

The chief dogmas of Christianity are contained in the various creeds of the Church. The *Apostles' Creed* certainly dates from the first century. The *Nicene Creed* emphasized the divinity of Christ. The *Creed of Constantinople* declared the divinity of the Holy Spirit. The *Creed of St. Athanasius* was held in high regard by both Greeks and Latins as an expression of Christian doctrine. The *Lateran* profession of faith defended the doctrine of the Blessed Trinity. The profession of faith of the *Council of*

Trent is a comprehensive statement of Catholic doctrine, directed against the errors of the sixteenth-century Reformers. Vatican Council I declared the infallibility of the pope. Vatican II made many significant pastoral pronouncements.

The following branches of dogmatic theology can be distinguished: *pneumatology* studies spirits (angels); *anthropology* studies man, his original state and his Fall; *ponerology* and *hamartiology* study evil and sin, respectively; *soteriology* studies redemption and salvation; *Christology* is the study of Christ, especially His person and nature; *Mariology* is the study of Mary, especially her role in the Redemption; *ecclesiology* is the study of the Chruch; and, finally, *eschatology* studies the last things: death, Judgment, Heaven, and Hell.

The Sources of Dogma. The sources of dogma are twofold: Sacred Scripture and sacred tradition. Strictly speaking, there is one source of Revelation, viz., God's word revealing through tradition; Sacred Scripture is a part of sacred tradition, as protected and transmitted by the Church. The Church existed before one word of the New Testament was written; the Church decided which books of the Bible are canonical and which are apocryphal; and the Church preserved and transmitted the inspired writings. "I should not believe the Gospel," said St. Augustine, "unless I were impelled thereto by the authority of the Catholic Church."[5] The Scriptures hold a unique place as a source of dogma: they are truly the word of God, written by inspired authors *(de fide divina).*

Sacred tradition contains divine truth as expressed in the solemn definitions of the Councils and the *ex cathedra* declarations of the pope *(de fide definita);* Christian dogma is also contained in the ordinary and universal teaching of the pope, bishops, and theologians dispersed in time and space *(de fide Catholica).* The tradition of which we speak is called *sacred,* in contrast to human tradition, inasmuch as sacred tradition is preserved from error by a divine guarantee.

II. THE BLESSED TRINITY[6]

The Trinity in Scripture and Tradition. The dogma of the Trinity is not taught explicitly in the Old Testament. Yet a number of oblique references to the Trinity can be cited. "Let *us* make man to *our* image and likeness," states Genesis 1:26. The triple *Sanctus* of Isaiah 6:3, "Holy, holy, holy, the Lord God of hosts," seems to point to the Trinity. Genesis 18:2 tells of three men appearing to Abraham, who "adored down to the ground." The liturgy of the Church says that Abraham saw three and adored one. Psalms 2:7 speaks of the divine sonship: "Thou art My Son, this day have I begotten Thee."

Most of the references to God in the New Testament refer to one or more Persons of the Trinity. Karl Rahner counts forty-four such references. Matthew 28:19, where Christ commands that all nations be taught and baptized "in the name of the Father, and of the Son, and of the Holy Spirit," is the only occasion in the New Testament where the three Persons are so named together. In other cases the terminology varies. St. John refers to the Father, the Word, and the Holy Spirit as being one (cf. 1 John 5:7). The Trinity is clearly evidenced at the baptism of Christ, recorded in Matthew 3:16-17. One should note that every such reference to a Person of the Trinity considers the Person as identical with God Himself.

Many profound minds have dwelt on the doctrine of the Trinity. Even Plato wondered what God did in the loneliness of eternity. Aristotle, in a flash of philosophic insight, called God "Thought of Thought." St. Augustine (354-430) spent seventeen years composing the fifteen books of his most systematic work, *De Trinitate.*[7] St. Thomas Aquinas (1225-1274) devoted Questions 27-43 of the First Part of his great *Summa Theologica* to the study of the Blessed Trinity. Mohammed considered any suggestion of a divine trinity as blasphemous. Arius created a major split in Christianity by his denial of the divinity of Christ.

The *Apostles' Creed* professes belief in the Trinity. The *Creeds of Constantinople, Athanasius,* and the *Fourth Lateran Council* defended the Catholic doctrine of the Blessed Trinity. The Protestant sect known as Unitarian denies the doctrine of the Trinity.

Theologians speak of "the divine processions." God the Father begets God the Son, which is called *generation;* God the Son is begotten of God the Father, which is called *filiation;* both God the Father and God the Son spirate God the Holy Spirit, which is called *spiration.* The Son proceeds from the Father; the Holy Spirit proceeds from the Father and the Son. The Father knows Himself perfectly and infinitely, so as to generate a distinct Person, the *Logos* or Word, the Son of God. The Father and the Son have an infinite love for each other, so as to "spirate" or "breathe" a distinct **Person, the Holy Spirit. Each** Person is in full possession of the Godhead; each Person is distinct, though not separate, from each other. Theologians have made many other refinements concerning the doctrine, which space forbids us to consider.

The Trinity and Reason. Philosophy could not, and did not, establish the truth that there are three Persons in the one God. The dogma is known only by the Christian Revelation. But once in possession of this truth, philosophy can shed some light on the doctrine by telling us what is meant by nature and what is meant by person.

Nature, according to Aristotle, is the essence of a being, considered as the principle of its activity. *Person,* as defined by Boethius in the fifth century, is "an individual substance of a rational nature." Nature tells *what* a thing is; person tells *who* a thing is. God, angels, and man are persons because they possess intellect and free will.

In God there is but one nature, which is divine. In God there are three really distinct Persons, each in full possession of the divine nature, each distinct from the others; yet there is no separation in the divine substance or nature. Reason falters here; after fifteen volumes Augustine concluded that the Trinity is not *against* reason, but *above* it.

The analogy of the shamrock gets us nowhere. That 1 times 1 times 1 still equals 1 helps but little. That matter can take the form of a solid, liquid, or gas (three states of the same element or compound) does not solve the mystery of the Trinity. Philosophers speculate as to whether a created spirit could be simultaneously possessed by more than one person, reflecting the inner life of the Godhead. We are in deep water here; the question will probably not be solved this side of eternity.

Only the Second Person, God the Son, became incarnate. All other "appropriations" are logical distinctions based on the real relations of the Persons. We think of the Father as the almighty Creator, the Son as the Redeemer and source of wisdom, the Holy Spirit as the Sanctifier and source of love and goodness. The attributes and external works of God are actually common to all three Persons.

The doctrine of the Trinity answers Plato's question. God is eternally fecund and eternally in love. The doctrine has "vital equivalents" (to use Frank Sheed's phrase) for mankind. God is affirmative and fruitful, a far cry from "the God of total indifference," or Whitehead's "harmony of epochal occasions," or Dewart's "open background of consciousness and being." The doctrine of the Trinity has not been sufficiently appreciated by Christians. We need to make the doctrine our own.

III. CREATION AND THE FALL OF MAN

Creation: Angels, Atoms, Organisms, Man. *Creation* is defined as the total production of a thing from nothing. Creation thus defined never occurs in this universe. Every finite being owes its existence in some way to a pre-existing finite being. God alone can create. "Nothing is new except arrangement" is the way Will Durant has put it.

The opening line of Genesis tells us the world was created and had a beginning: "In the beginning God created the heavens and the earth" (Gen. 1:1). The Greek philosophers generally held for the eternity of matter. Thomas Aquinas agreed with Aristotle that an infinite series of *secondary, accidental* causes is ontologically possible, so that time could extend endlessly into the past. But both Aristotle and Aquinas maintained that an infinite series of *primary, substantial* causes is not metaphysically possible; one must ultimately come to the prime mover, the uncaused cause, which men generally call God. Aquinas held that only by Divine Revelation do we know that the world had a first moment, a beginning.

Most Scholastic philosophers today reject the idea of "an infinite series" or "an eternal creation." The difficulty is not with God, but with the very nature of finite reality. Every act of God is "from eternity," but the effects of God's acts take place in time. An infinite series of anything — time, space, or matter — involves an inherent contradiction: any series can always be added to or subtracted from; anything that is really infinite is incapable of increase or decrease. By this definition God alone is infinite. Time cannot extend *endlessly* into the past; nor can the universe extend *endlessly* in space.

Do angels exist? Is there a Devil? These questions have been revived by some modern writers who suggest that Christian theology would be better off to get rid of all good and evil spirits. In the time of Christ, the Sadducees denied the existence of angels. Angelology has currently become moot in view of the increased interest in exorcism and demonic possession.

Science can neither affirm nor deny the existence of angels, since purely spiritual reality lies beyond the purview of the laboratory scale and test tube. Reason alone would suggest the possibility of a spirit world, of spiritual creatures above human nature but less than divine. The pagan philosopher Aristotle believed that spirits moved the heavenly bodies. Primitive religions and the ancient pagan world abounded with spirits and deities. An essential tenet of Islam is belief in angels.

The existence of angels can be known with certitude only by Divine Revelation. In the Bible their presence is affirmed consistently from Genesis to the Apocalypse. Sacred Scripture never attempts a systematic apologetic for the existence of angels. They are simply taken for granted, a kind of "given." The account of creation in Genesis makes no mention of angels. But the Evil One soon makes his appearance in the Garden of Eden, tempting man and woman from their pristine state of innocence. An angel, known by an ancient tradition as Uriel, guarded the gate of the lost Eden with a fiery sword. Angelophanies in Sacred Scripture mention only three angels by name, each an archangel: Gabriel, who announced to the Virgin Mary that she was to be the mother of the Messiah; Michael, who cast Satan (the dragon) from Heaven (cf. Apoc. 12:7-9); and Raphael, who, according to the apocryphal Book of Enoch (chap. 20), heals the earth which the fallen angels had defiled. The Church Fathers, interpreting the words of Jesus in Luke 10:18, assigned the name of Lucifer ("lightbearer") to the angel, supposedly the most intelligent, who became Satan. Moslems believe that Gabriel dictated the Koran to their Prophet.

From Scriptural texts it is possible to name nine choirs of angels (from the lowest order to the highest): Angels, Archangels, Principalities, Powers, Virtues, Dominations, Thrones, Cherubim, and Seraphim. Daniel 7:10 indicates the existence of a vast multitude of angelic spirits. Thomas Aquinas, consistent with his belief in the possibility of an infinite series of contingent beings, believed in an infinite ascending hierarchy of spirits who reflect, but do not exhaust, God's infinite perfection. The Angelic Doctor further tells us that each angel was directly created by God, and each is a distinct species.[8] No two angels have the same nature or are equal in intelligence and Grace.

Theologians commonly hold that angels are immortal; they cannot perish. They are not subject to time as we know it, and are

independent of the laws of space. The duration of angels is called
aeviternity, which is a succession of spiritual states independent
of material movement. Angels are pure (i.e., bodiless) spirits,
having only intellect and free will. Augustine seemed to favor the
view that angels possessed some kind of ethereal body. Angels
can exert power on the material world by a will-act, but they
cannot perform miracles except with God's power and permission. Angels cannot err within their own sphere of nature and
cannot reverse a decision once taken. Angels cannot coerce the
free will of another intelligent being, either human or angelic.
Angelic knowledge is intuitive and has been infused by God,
whereas human knowledge is discursive (i.e., is derived from the
senses and reason). Angels do not know the future unless it has
been revealed to them by God. Being pure spirits, angels experience no sensuous appetite, no passion, feeling, or emotion.

Theologians further teach that the angels were created in
Grace. They were raised to a level of life above their natural life
whereby they would share in the very life of God Himself.
Aquinas taught that the angels were placed in the Empyrean
Heaven (*Caelum Empyreum*), with their destiny being to ascend
to the Heaven of the Holy Trinity (*Caelum Sanctae Trinitatis*). In
the latter they would enjoy the Beatific Vision. Some of the
angels freely rejected their supernatural destiny as planned by
God. Aquinas suggests that they preferred their own natural
glory to that of supernatural glory freely offered by God, or chose
to act *as if* they were God by attaining supernatural beatitude
through their own power. Francisco Suarez (1548-1617), the pre-
eminent Jesuit theologian, held as "probable" that God revealed
to the angels that God the Son would become hypostatically
united with a subangelic human nature. With this knowledge
some of the angels refused to worship God the Son and submit to
the supernatural order of Grace — an order which would permit
human nature to exceed angelic natures in degrees of Grace. St.
Paul believed that God gave to man the power to judge even
angels. Lucifer's *"non serviam"* changed him into Satan; he and
his fellow angels were cast into Hell after a great heavenly war
was waged between the rebellious angels and the faithful angels.

The repercussions of this primordial *non serviam* were felt
on earth. Scripture refers to Satan variously as a dragon, the
prince of darkness, the prince of this world, Beelzebub, a murderer, the father of lies, a deceiver, and a roaring lion seeking
whom he can devour. Satan would not submit to God's super-

natural design, and he continues to do his best to subvert that plan in relation to mankind.

Some present-day theologians point out that the existence of angels is not a formally defined article of faith. We may concede this fact. But it would be temerarious (a favorite word of conservative theology) to dismiss gratuitously a doctrine firmly ingrained in the tradition and liturgy of the Church, and upheld throughout Scripture.

Christ Himself spoke realistically of the angels and of Satan. The evangelists have angels present at all the major events in the life of Christ: His Annunciation, Birth, Baptism, Temptations, Agony, Resurrection, and Ascension. Christ spoke of the little children's angels who always behold the face of God. The Son of Man was tempted by Satan in the desert; and He cast out devils. A theme that is so ubiquitous and consistent throughout Sacred Scripture should not be easily dismissed as a mere literary figure or rhetorical device representing the good and bad influences upon mankind.

The constant tradition of the Church has regarded Mary as Queen of Angels, higher in Grace than any other creature, human or angelic — a doctrine repeated by Vatican Council II (cf. *Lumen Gentium*, n. 69). The Canon of the Mass for centuries implored Almighty God "to command that these things be borne by the hands of Thy holy angel to Thine altar on high . . . ." Thomas Aquinas himself claimed to have been girded by an angel with the mysterious *cingulum* of perfect chastity. And the diabolical harassment of the Curé of Ars is well known.

There will always be sceptics, of course. Will Durant, for example, observes in *The Age of Faith:* "Thomas writes ninety-three pages on the hierarchy, movements, love, knowledge, will, speech, and habits of the angels — the most farfetched part of his far-flung *Summa*, and the most irrefutable." The order of Grace is a thing of majesty, symmetry, proportion, and continuity. And from Divine Revelation we know that the angels are an integral part of that grand design. They act as God's messengers and guardians of the human race, and, along with the faithful of the human race, they will sing forever God's praises in the new Heaven and the new earth.

How did atoms, organisms, and man come into existence? For many centuries the Judeo-Christian tradition assumed the direct, immediate creative act of God in producing the genera and species of living things, as well as the stars, planets, and other heavenly bodies. Augustine warned about taking the six days of creation, recorded in Genesis, too literally. His doctrine of *rationes seminales* (germinal causes) was a dim reflection of modern evolutionary theory. Evolution, as first proposed by Lamarck in 1809, is now a highly probable theory. If proven to be true, evolution would simply be God's method of creation; in no way does the theory diminish the necessity of God or undermine the authority of the Bible — which was never intended to be a text of natural science. Regardless of the *method* God used in producing His creatures, each can truly claim God for its Creator.[9]

Is man the product of evolution? *Humani Generis*, promulgated by Pope Pius XII on Aug. 12, 1950, said that one may accept the evolution of man's body from pre-existing forms of life as a possible explanation of the natural origin of man's body. As to the origin of man's soul, the encyclical warns against theories that question the direct creation of the human soul by God; the encyclical also warns against theories of polygenism (a plurality of human progenitors), saying it is not "clear" that such theories can be reconciled with the doctrine of Original Sin. Pierre Teilhard de Chardin, for example, believed that the human soul came into existence by gradual stages, with the "noosphere" emerging from the "biosphere." Even according to Teilhard, however, God is still the first cause of every development in the cosmos.[10]

Our personal opinion is that theology should "keep its options open" — to use a currently popular phrase. We have come a long way since Dr. John Lightfoot, in the seventeenth century, calculated from Biblical chronology that "Heaven and earth, centre and circumference were all created together, in the same instant"; and "this work took place and man was created by the Trinity on October 23, 4004 B.C. at nine o'clock in the morning."[11] Paleontology indicates that real human beings walked the earth one million years ago. The origin of man's soul is a philosophical as well as a theological question. Theology should welcome any help it can receive from the other sciences. The doctrine of Original Sin does not stand or fall on monogenism or the direct creation of the human soul.[12]

Unlike the angels, man is a hylomorphic creature, composed of matter and form, a material body and a spiritual soul. The Greeks called man a "microcosm," a little world in himself. In some way he contains all of the perfections of the cosmos.

According to Aristotelian-Thomistic psychology, every living organism possesses a *soul*, which is defined as the *principium vitae*, the principle of life. The vegetant soul enables plants to perform functions of nutrition, growth, and reproduction; the sentient soul enables animals, in addition to their powers of vegetation, to experience sensation and sensuous appetency; the rational soul of man, in addition to possessing the faculties of vegetation and sensation, gives human creatures the powers of intellection and volition.

The human soul is spiritual, i.e., immaterial, states Thomistic psychology. Since man is capable of spiritual ideogeny, of thinking universal ideas which prescind entirely from the material and the particular, there must be a sufficient spiritual principle in man to account for such activity. Man can conceive of God, essence, truth, unity, justice, beauty, goodness, relation, etc., and particular things in their general or universal aspects; man can reason, inferring conclusions from premises; man can idealize, conceiving of things not as they are but as they might be; man can think of himself as a self-conscious *ego*; man alone of all living creatures knows of the inevitability of his own death; man is aware of conscience, of a sense of morality and "oughtness" — all of which point to a spiritual, immaterial principle in man, which has traditionally been called the human soul.

The human soul is endowed with free will. First, human consciousness intuitively recognizes that some choices are made freely, without a necessary intrinsic or extrinsic compulsion. The will can freely choose what is to be the final practical judgment of the intellect. Secondly, the entire moral order is predicated on the assumption that man is essentially free in at least some of his fundamental options. Eternal reward for the good and eternal punishment for the wicked become a hollow mockery apart from personal responsibility, which presupposes personal freedom. Thirdly, practical, everyday experience presupposes freedom of choice. A meaningful human society would be impossible if it were composed of mere automatons blindly and mechanically following their predetermined instincts. All commercial advertising assumes that human beings are capable of changing their minds and making free and independent choices. Behaviorists such as J. B. Watson, phenomenologists, materialists, fatalists, and determinists deny the freedom of the human will.

The spiritual nature of the human soul demands its essential freedom in moral acts involving fundamental options.

Human freedom, of course, is a natural mystery and defies human explanation. Many profound thinkers of the past have tried to reconcile human freedom with divine providence, governance, concurrence, and the efficacy of divine Grace. St. Augustine seemed to opt for a form of predestination. *Molinism* contends that God *simultaneously concurs* in man's free acts. *Bannesianism*, following the Thomist school of thought, teaches that God supplies a *physical premotion* in man's free acts. The controversy has never been settled conclusively. How God can be both totally free yet totally necessary is no less a profound mystery. The solution to the problem does not lie in abandoning the concept of freedom, but in recognizing that there are some secrets of human existence and the divine nature that God has kept for Himself.

The human soul is immortal. This truth follows from the spiritual nature of the soul, which is intrinsically and substantially independent of matter in its spiritual operations. The soul is simple, i.e., not composed of parts which are subject to disintegration and decay. Plant and animal souls are intrinsically dependent upon matter in all of their operations; hence, these infrahuman souls return to the potency of matter with the disintegration of the organism, when the material body is no longer an apt receptacle for the soul. The simple, spiritual soul of man survives bodily death. Such is the Scholastic rationale concerning the human soul.

The Scholastic concept of soul is based on Aristotle's cosmological theory of hylomorphism. According to the hylomorphic theory, all corporeal creatures are composed ultimately of two incomplete substances, or co-principles: prime matter and substantial form. Prime matter is the determinable, potential, indeterminate principle of a bodily being; substantial form is the determining, actuating, determinate principle of a bodily being, making it *this* being with *these* properties. The substantial form of living creatures is called the *soul*.

Physical science has made giant strides in recent times; in the light of nuclear physics and chemistry, the hylomorphic theory as an explanation of the ultimate composition of bodies does not seem to hold up well. Celestine N. Bittle believes that "hylosystemism," which explains the essential constitution of bodies in terms of subatomic particles, ought to replace traditional hylomorphism. Regarding *living* bodies, however, Father

Bittle retains a modified hylomorphism as a reasonable explanation for vital activities; the soul is not strictly the "form" of the living body, but is its life principle, making the body a functioning, integral organism.

How do the foregoing doctrines on the human soul relate to the Christian Revelation? W. Wilmers believed that the Council of Vienne defined the rational soul of man as the *form* of the body; the existence of the rational soul, said Wilmers, is therefore not merely a philosophical question, but is intimately connected with the dogma of the Incarnation. The Church was justified in defining the existence of the human soul as a necessary "theological conclusion," or "secondary truth." Not all theologians today would agree with Wilmers. The true humanity of Christ and human survival beyond the grave are assuredly essential doctrines of the Christian Faith; but these doctrines do not stand or fall necessarily with the hylomorphic theory of Aristotle. The philosophy of soul gives the best rationale so far devised by man in explaining the phenomenon of life and human nature; but the dynamic and historical character of truth forbids one to close the door forever on the possibility of an even better and more accurate explanation.

The term *soul* is used a number of times in the Bible. The Old Testament equates "spirit" with "the breath of life"; Genesis 2:7 says that God "breathed" into man the "breath of life," and "man became a living being." No purely spiritual concept of soul, and certainly not a hylomorphic concept of soul, is to be found in the Old Testament. Christ referred to His own soul when He said, "Now My soul is troubled" (John 12:27). Our Lord balanced a human soul with all the riches of the world: "For what does it profit a man, if he gain the whole world, but suffer the loss of his own soul?" (Matt. 16:26). Mary stated in her Magnificat that her soul magnified the Lord (cf. Luke 1:46). The concept of spirit as immateriality is clearly evidenced in the New Testament. The concept of soul, in a theological sense, is valid insofar as the term represents that part of man which constitutes him the natural image of his Maker in virtue of his spirituality, freedom, and immortality.

Finally, regarding the origin of the human soul, we have already cited the position of Pius XII, and the view of Teilhard that the human soul has been in production since the first moment of creation. A number of possible theories can be mentioned:

(1) Concerning life in general, *abiogenesis* (spontaneous generation, absolute emergence) states that life is generated spontaneously from nonliving matter. Aristotle, Aquinas, and many of the medieval Schoolmen held this view. Modern science, with the experiments of Francesco Redi in 1668 and Louis Pasteur, begun in 1860, has shown conclusively that spontaneous generation never occurs; *omne vivum ex vivo* (all life comes from life) was the conclusion of Redi in 1698.

(2) *Direct creation* states that the first living creatures, including man, were created immediately and totally by a special act of God; the human soul, being spiritual, was and continues to be created directly by God.

(3) *Mediate creation* (restricted emergence) states that God used pre-existing material from which were educed plant and animal souls by His special creative act; the human soul was infused by God into pre-existing matter, or into a pre-existing organism.

(4) *Traducianism* states that in the process of human reproduction, the souls of the parents are capable of generating another human soul to animate the fetus, like one torch lighting another without being thereby diminished. St. Augustine seemed inclined toward this view.

Most Scholastics have been steadfast in maintaining that each human soul, being spiritual, is created immediately and individually by God, just as angelic spirits have been individually created. Based on the principle *nemo dat quod non habet* (one cannot give what one does not have), the Scholastic doctrine holds that matter, *in and of itself*, is incapable of producing the spiritual soul of man. No effect can transcend its cause. Abiogenesis is never observed by science; and it is gratuitous to assume that matter alone was ever capable of producing life, no matter how many eons of time may have elapsed. Teilhard took a much less restricted view of matter, regarding it as "prelife" rather than "nonlife."

We fail to see that the question of how and when plant, animal, and human life came into being has any great theological significance *provided* that one is willing to acknowledge that God is the first and adequate cause of all life. A theory of abiogenesis which denies the necessity of a supramundane cause is certainly unacceptable to Christian Faith as well as doing violence to the principle of causality, which demands that every effect have an adequate cause. Life exists; and matter alone is an insufficient cause of life. Life must have a living cause, which is but another argument for the existence of God. However, a theory of abiogenesis which states that *God put into matter* the potency to evolve into plant, animal, and even human life we do not find to be repugnant to the Christian Faith. Such a theory is substantially the theory of restricted emergence without positing the necessity of special creative acts of God. This theory seems to be in close harmony with Augustine's *rationes seminales* (germinal causes).[13] Genesis 2:7 says that God "formed" man from the dust of the earth; such a "formation" could have been instantaneous or might have taken millions of years to complete.

Why should God have to intervene in the course of human events everytime a human sperm unites with a human ovum in order to create a human soul? Could He not have placed within the very essence of the gametes the ability, once united, to produce a human soul capable of intellection, volition, sensation, metabolism, growth, and reproduction (of the whole organism, both body and soul)? God cannot do what is metaphysically impossible; but we are speaking here of a *physical* possibility involving no contradiction in terms. These questions, of course, are academic and, we repeat, in no way substantially undermine the integrity of the Christian Faith.[14]

Matter and spirit: we use the terms glibly; yet physical science, with all of its epochal accomplishments, is unable to tell us basically what "matter" is (other than positive and negative charges of electricity — which doesn't really answer the question); philosophy, with all of its marvelous revelations of God, man, and the world by the light of reason, is unable to tell us basically what "spirit" is (other than substantial immateriality — which doesn't really answer the question). Both philosophy and theology should not be too smug in circumscribing the limits of spirit and matter, in making them so mutually exclusive. Perhaps Teilhard was right when he saw spirituality in all matter; it is, after all, one universe, with one first cause and one final end — the greater glory of God. Matter, life, consciousness, sensation, appetency, volition, intellection, soul, spirit: we have really only scratched the surface of these natural mysteries; there is nothing in the world of atoms, organisms, and man which does not end in mystery when pursued to its ultimate limits.

Man — "a composite of Heaven and mire" — was now ready to face the greatest challenge in human history.

Original Justice and Original Sin. The Church teaches that man was created in a state of Original Justice. God freely chose to bestow upon man certain supernatural gifts. (1) Man was given the gift of Sanctifying Grace, whereby he shared in the divine life, became an adopted child of God, became a temple of the Holy Spirit, and was given supernatural beatitude for his final end. (2) Man was also given preternatural gifts which preserved him from debilitating pain and suffering (impassibility); from bodily death (immortality); from concupiscence (integrity), whereby man was freed from the inordinate tendency of the sensuous appetite to violate reason; from ignorance, whereby the human intellect could attain knowledge with facility. And man was given strength of will to direct his actions toward the good.

In a so-called "state of pure nature," man would be subject to suffering and bodily death; his senses would tend to violate his rational nature; his intellect would attain truth only with much effort; his will would not always choose moral good. Man's nature does not intrinsically demand the indwelling of the Trinity, a share in the divine life, or a supernatural destiny. God could have created man in such a state of "pure nature"; but He chose to lavish supernatural gifts upon His prize creation, man — "the paragon of animals," "nature's finest clay." "Goodness tends to diffuse itself," and God is infinite goodness.

Many of the ancient traditions spoke of a Golden Age once enjoyed by man. Plato thought the human soul was imprisoned in a material body as a punishment for some primal sin. The Mazdistic religion of Zoroaster spoke of man eating forbidden fruit and polluting human nature at its source. The Judeo-Christian view of man has always seen him as more of a fallen king than a risen chimpanzee. Genesis, which Jews and Christians accept as divinely inspired, teaches that man was given a test, just as the angels had been tested. What test was man given? It could have been a simple matter, such as not eating a certain fruit. All sin has one essential ingredient: an enthronement of one's own ego. "You will be like God" (Gen. 3:5).

Man failed this primal test; the consequences of that failure affected all subsequent generations. By Original Sin man lost supernatural Grace: the right to Heaven, a share in the divine life, the indwelling of the Trinity. Man also lost the preternatural gifts: his body was now subject to suffering and death; the senses warred against reason; his intellect was darkened and his will weakened; man was under the captivity of Satan. Human nature was wounded, but not destroyed. Human nature did not become intrinsically corrupt, as Luther taught. Luther held that man's state before the Fall was *natural*. The Church insists that human nature has remained basically intact in spite of the Fall.

All men inherit Original Sin through the act of generation. Thomas Aquinas believed that had Original Sin not been committed, each person would have been able to commit his own "original sin," thus losing the supernatural and preternatural gifts for himself. There would conceivably be two races of men: one, a fallen race; the other, in the state of Original Justice.[15]

IV. THE INCARNATION AND REDEMPTION

The Incarnation. "All love tends toward an incarnation — even God's." Would the Incarnation have taken place if man had not sinned? Thomists, following the opinion of Thomas Aquinas, answer in the negative. Scotists, following the teaching of Duns Scotus, feel that God would still have become incarnate; they point to the Pauline doctrine of Christ as the center and final end of all creation.[16] Teilhard, with his doctrine of Christogenesis, certainly favored the Scotist view.

The Protoevangelium was uttered by God, following the Fall: "I will put enmity between you [Satan] and the woman, between your seed and her seed; He shall crush your head, and you shall lie in wait for His heel" (Gen. 3:15). This was the first good news since the Fall. Original Sin became the *felix culpa*; "O happy fault," cries the Church, "which merited to have so great a Redeemer!"

The problem of Christology occupied the attention of the early Church. Various heresies arose concerning the nature and person of Christ. *Nestorianism* taught that Christ was two distinct persons, one human and one divine. *Monophysitism* said Christ had only one nature, a blend of the divine and human. *Monotheletism* said Christ had only one will, a divine will. *Appolinariansim* taught that Christ had a sensitive, but not a rational, soul. *Monarchianism, Manicheism,* and *Docetism* taught that Christ was a manifestation of the Father and had only an apparent body. *Arianism* completely denied the divine nature of Christ; the heresy of Arius at one time claimed more adherents than did orthodox Christianity.

Various Councils of the Church defined the orthodox teaching concerning the nature and person of Christ. Jesus Christ was (and is) one, divine person, the Second Person of the Blessed

Trinity. Jesus Christ possessed two complete natures: one human, one divine. The human nature of Christ was real and complete: He had a real material body informed by a human, rational soul with powers of vegetation, sentiency, intellection, and volition.

The Greeks defined *hypostasis* as a complete, individual, self-acting substance; the Latins used the word *suppositum*. A person is an intelligent hypostasis. Christ was one hypostasis; His human nature and divine nature were hypostatically united. His human will was always in complete union with the divine will. His intellect always saw God face-to-face. Every act that Christ performed was the act of one person, the divine Son of God.

Christianity offers the supreme paradox. He Who built the cosmos was born in a cave and worked as a carpenter. He Who was omnipotence and omniscience became subject to Mary and Joseph and "advanced in wisdom and age and Grace before God and men" (Luke 2:52). The *Summum Bonum* experienced joy with the little children. He Who claimed to be the Resurrection and the Life wept over Jerusalem and the death of His friend, Lazarus. And He Who was eternal life suffered death on a cross.

The Eternal Galilean answered the yearnings of the pre-Christian world, the yearnings of Socrates, Buddha, Confucius, and the yearnings of Judaism. Heaven and earth were united for the first time by the Eternal Galilean — *eternal*, because one of the Trinity; *Galilean*, because one of us. Aristotle had said it would be foolish to pray to Zeus. This God, this Eternal Galilean, philosophers and theologians and all mankind could know, love, and serve![17]

The Redemption. The Master Composer of the cosmos had written a beautiful symphony with man as the principal player. Man had been given extraordinary gifts with which to play his part well. With the freedom God gave to man, he played a wrong note; the symphony became a cacophony. The misplayed note might have continued unredeemed. But the Divine Composer chose to take the misplayed note and make it the first note of a new symphony, with this new note being played by a God-Man.

Original Sin is a revealed truth; it is basically a mystery. The New Testament writers give us few specifics concerning the dogma's historical and anthropological aspects. St. Paul believed that it was the sin of one man that brought death into the world.

Christ never referred to "Original Sin" by that name; the term has been devised by theologians. Nor do the Gospels ever have Our Lord mentioning the names *Adam* and *Eve*. But almost every page of Scripture gives eloquent testimony of man's fallen condition and his need for redemption.

"For there is one God: and one mediator of God and men, the man Christ Jesus who gave himself a redemption for all," says St. Paul (1 Tim. 2:5-6). The dogma of the Redemption is thus defined by the Council of Trent: "If anyone say that this [Original] Sin of Adam is taken away by any other remedy than the merit of the one Mediator, Our Lord Jesus Christ, Who hath reconciled us to God in His own blood . . . let him be anathema." Christ Himself asserted His role as Redeemer: "Even as the Son of man is not come to be ministered unto, but to minister, and to give His life a redemption for many" (Matt. 20:28).

Original Sin offended infinite goodness and justice. A mere *fiat* of the divine will could have effected man's redemption. "It was necessary for the Son of God to assume a created nature, if God required condign satisfaction from man," writes W. Wilmers, S.J.[18] Both the offended, God, and the offender, man, were fully present in the Redemption effected by the God-Man, Jesus Christ.

The Redemption recovered the supernatural gifts lost in the Fall. The gates of Heaven were opened; Sanctifying Grace was restored and now flowed more abundantly; the Beatific Vision became possible for the just. Sanctifying Grace was given to the just even before the Incarnation, in anticipation of the Redemption; but only a natural happiness in "Abraham's bosom" was possible prior to the redemptive life of Christ. The Redemption freed man from the bondage of Satan. The moral order, disrupted by Original Sin, was redressed and divine justice satisfied. The preternatural gifts lost by Original Sin were not restored by the Redemption. Concupiscence, suffering, and death — all a part of man's nature — now exist as punishments for Original Sin.

In principle, all mankind has been saved and all sin conquered and forgiven; but each individual must appropriate for himself the fruits of the Redemption. Faith and good works are necessary for salvation; eternal damnation is still possible. Christ has put victory within the grasp of all who will come to Him in faith and love. "I have overcome the world" (John 16:33).

The Mother of God. Soteriology cannot ignore Mariology. God chose Mary to be the human mother of His divine Son's human nature. Since Christ was one Person, the Church has declared that Mary is rightfully called "the Mother of God." In this sense, Mary was a necessary part of God's plan of salvation.

The Church teaches that Mary was a perpetual virgin, that her divine Son was miraculously conceived by the Holy Spirit. The dogma of the Immaculate Conception, defined by Pope Pius IX on Dec. 8, 1854, states that Our Lady was preserved from Original Sin from the instant of her conception in the womb of St. Anne. Mary needed redemption, like the rest of mankind; but Christ's Redemption *prevented* her from being stained with Original Sin for even one instant.[19] Pope Pius XII, in 1950, defined the dogma of the Assumption, which states that Mary was taken up, body and soul, into Heaven; after Mary's death, her body was not to suffer corruption. Many theologians teach that Mary is the Mediatrix of all Graces. Because of her necessary role in God's plan of Redemption, she is also referred to as Co-Redemptrix. The latter two teachings have not been solemnly defined by the Church.

Adoration, or *cultus latriae*, belongs to God alone. Mary is given a special veneration, called *cultus hyperduliae*, which is given to no other creature. Protestants generally feel that Catholicism exaggerates the importance of Mary; Catholics feel that Protestantism understates the role of Mary in the economy of salvation. A true devotion to Mary, called by Wordsworth "our tainted nature's solitary boast," ought to lead one to a closer union with Christ; that is the way Mary wants it. She called herself "the handmaid of the Lord" and at Cana gave us her magnificent valedictory: "Do whatever He tells you" (John 2:5).[20]

V. THE MYSTICAL BODY OF CHRIST

The Doctrine in Scripture and Tradition. Just as soteriology cannot ignore Mariology, neither can the theological study of salvation ignore ecclesiology and God's plan for dispensing the fruits of the Redemption. We are not concerned here with the apologetical aspects of the Church of Christ;[21] our concern is with the dogma of the Church as contained in Sacred Scripture and sacred tradition.

Scripture reveals Christ's Church as His Mystical Body. Christ told His apostles, "I am the vine, you are the branches"

(John 15:5). Again, "He that hears you hears Me" (Luke 10:16). Christ was obviously identifying Himself with His followers in a most intimate union. St. Paul teaches the doctrine of the Mystical Body on a number of occasions. Our Lord identified Himself with the persecuted Church when He asked Paul, "Why do you persecute Me?" (Acts 9:4). Writing to the Corinthians, Paul tells them: "You are the body of Christ, and severally His members" (1 Cor. 12:27). St. Paul calls Christ "the Head of the Church" (Eph. 5:23).

Tradition affirms what Sacred Scripture teaches concerning the Church as Christ's Mystical Body. St. Irenaeus (c. 130-c. 200) spoke of "the great and glorious body of Christ," which Gnostics divide and seek to slay.[22] "The Catholic Church alone is the body of Christ," wrote St. Augustine; "outside that body the Holy Spirit gives life to no man . . . ."[23] Pope Pius XII issued his scholarly encyclical *Mystici Corporis*, on June 29, 1943.

Like a natural animal organism which has a head, a mind, a body, and a soul, so the Mystical Body of Christ has a visible head, which is the pope; an invisible head, or mind, which is Christ; a body, which is composed of all baptized persons; and a soul, which is the Holy Spirit. All who are in the state of Grace are members, or cells, of the Mystical Body.

The visible Church of Christ was not established until the coming of Christ "in the fullness of time"; yet, Grace was still possible for those who lived before the Incarnation. Hence, mankind shared in the life of the Mystical Body from the beginning of the human race following the Fall. Externally and legally, however, man belonged to the order of servitude prior to the redemptive life of Christ.

The Mystical Body of Christ exists in three states, as part of the doctrine of the Communion of Saints. (1) The Church Militant consists of cells of the Body still living on earth and working out their salvation. (2) The Church Suffering consists of the souls suffering in Purgatory, but whose salvation is assured. (3) The Church Triumphant consists of those angels and human souls that are enjoying eternal happiness in Heaven. The damned in Hell do not belong to the Mystical Body. There is a real "communion" among the cells of the Body in the various states. The Church Militant can pray for and help the Church Suffering; the Church Triumphant can intercede in behalf of the Church Militant. Just as man fell from God's Grace, not as an individual but as a race, so does mankind find corporate redemption and salvation in the Mystical Body, which can be described as the society of the redeemed.

From the brief outline we have presented, one can see that the doctrine of the Mystical Body of Christ is indeed a profound and sublime mystery of the Christian Faith. The doctrine is pregnant with spiritual significance. There are elements in the doctrine that appear to be in close harmony with some of the cosmological concepts of Pierre Teilhard de Chardin. It remains for future scholars to point out these agreements.

The Church on Earth. The claims of Roman Catholicism can best be understood in the context of the dogma of the Mystical Body. "He [Christ] conferred a triple power on His apostles and their successors, to teach, to govern, to lead men to holiness. This triple power ... He made the fundamental law of the whole Church."[24] Christ was pre-eminently a Teacher, the King of kings, and the eternal High Priest; He taught, He governed, and He sanctified. After His Ascension into Heaven, Christ took on a new Body, His Mystical Body, which would continue to teach, to govern, and to sanctify all men through the centuries.

First, the Church teaches. Before Pilate, Christ explicitly cited *truth* as the purpose for His coming: "This is why I was born, and why I have come into the world, to bear witness to the truth" (John 18:37). Just as Christ taught infallibly through His visible body, so does His Church today teach infallibly through its visible magisterium.

Secondly, the Church governs. Christ said that all power had been given to Him; He gave to Peter and his successors the power to bind and to loose, the power of authority and jurisdiction, as exemplified in the giving of the "keys of the Kingdom."

Thirdly, the Church sanctifies. Christ said, "I am come that they may have life, and may have it more abundantly" (John 10:10). He instituted the Sacraments that we might share more abundantly in the divine life of Grace. He bestowed the powers of the priesthood upon His apostles and their successors, to continue to the end of time.

In short, the Church on earth, Christ's Mystical Body, does now what Christ did during His brief time on this earth. Just as Christ was seen and heard and touched by means of His visible body, so is His Mystical Body, the Church, seen and heard and touched through a visible structure by the world today. Just as Christ's body was one, with one head, so is Christ's Church one,

with one visible head. Anything else would be a spiritual, as well
as a physical, monstrosity. Just as Christ was calumniated and
ridiculed and ultimately nailed to a cross, one should not be
surprised that His Mystical Body is slandered and persecuted.
The Church is presently undergoing a kind of internal Crucifixion; but the Church will emerge from the present crisis with a
mighty Resurrection — purified, strengthened, the salvation of
the world.

Frank Sheed has put it well:

... there is not an accusation hurled at Him that has not been hurled at
His Church. And notice that she is most bitterly hated not for what is
most human in her, the faults — sometimes the appalling faults — of
her members, but for what is most clearly the operation of Christ ....
She is hated for her claim to be unique, she is hated for being in fact
unique.[25]

A final point concerns the necessity of belonging to Christ's
Mystical Body. "No man comes to the Father, but by Me," de-
clared the Savior of the world (John 14:6). Since the Mystical
Body is Christ and the Redemption prolonged in time and space,
it clearly follows that one must be a part of the Mystical Body to
be saved. The constant teaching of the Church has been that
Baptism — of water, blood, or desire — incorporates one into
Christ's Mystical Body. Every individual in the state of Grace
belongs, in some way, to that Body. Obviously, not everyone in
Grace belongs to the visible structure of the Church. Many sincere, intelligent people simply do not recognize, or accept, the
Roman Catholic Church as being one with Christ's Mystical
Body. Insofar as one who is physically separated from the visible
Church is following his honestly formed conscience, he is said to
be "invincibly ignorant" of the true Chruch and is free of any
guilt. God gives everyone sufficient Grace to save his soul; separation from the Mystical Body occurs only by a deliberate,
culpable act, an act that involves the rejection of Christ
Himself.[26]

Ecclesiology Today. The Church of Christ is a mystery, affirmed Vatican II. The existence and nature of Christ's Church
cannot be fully explained by reason alone. The task of theology,
and ecclesiology in particular, is to shed as much light as possible
upon the revealed truth of Christ's Church on earth.

Father Avery Dulles, S.J., has made a significant contribution to modern ecclesiology with his valuable work *Models of the
Church.* He writes of five models:

(1) The Church as *institution* emphasizes the visible, hierarchical structure of the Church, which is recognizable by its unicity, holiness, catholicity, and apostolicity, as stated in the Nicene Creed. This substantialist model clearly points to the "one true Church of Christ," with an authentic magisterium teaching clearly defined and firmly held doctrines. This model has prevailed from post-Tridentine times to the advent of the Second Vatican Council, and is in the spirit of Pope Boniface VIII's *Unam Sanctam* (1302) and the writings of Cardinal Robert Bellarmine, S.J. (1542-1621). This model sees the Church as a "perfect society" and has tended toward "triumphalism," which makes the Church identical with the Kingdom of God. Membership in the institutional Church tends to be clear-cut.

(2) The Church as *mystical communion* sees the Church primarily as an invisible, spiritual reality in which all men of good will are united. The Church has its visible and material aspects, but these are all secondary to the mystical communion of the People of God. Membership is not so clearly defined as in the institutional model. Dualist models speak of an institutional and a Pentecostal Church, an "overground" and an "underground" Church, a parish-oriented and a communal Church. Andrew Greeley believes the Church of the future will be more communal in character. Karl Rahner sees the future Church as less structured, more decentralized, and more rightly described as Christ's "little flock."

(3) The Church as *sacrament* sees the Church as a visible sign and witness of Christ operating in the world today. As Christ is God's sacrament, so is the Church Christ's sacrament, signifying and containing in a historically tangible form the Grace of Christ.

(4) The Church as *herald* identifies the Church of Christ with the preaching of the word of God. The essential nature of the Church is *kerygmatic* — i.e., the Church exists to proclaim the good news of the Gospel. Actualist models see the Church more as an event than an institution. One should not ask, *What* is the Church? or *Where* is the Church? The important question is, *When* is the Church? When God's word is proclaimed and lived, there is the Church.

(5) The Church as *servant* defines the Church in terms of active service in the world. Creed and theory matter little. Praxis is all. The Church is not "over against" the world; rather, the Church is that part of the world destined to bring about the salvation of the world. If the Church does not mean social justice

and improvement of the human condition, it means nothing at all.

There is, of course, considerable overlapping of all five models, and no one model fully and exclusively states the reality of the Church of Christ. Each of the models reflects a facet of truth contained in the brilliant multifaceted jewel which is Christ's Church. The institutional and sacramental models are more oriented toward Catholic theology, whereas the communal and kerygmatic models are more Protestant in character. Many people with no particular religious stance or affiliation can readily identify with the Church as servant. Karl Barth was fully committed to the model of the Church as herald. Karl Rahner, Edward Schillebeeckx, and Yves Congar have directed much attention toward the Church as sacrament.

Vatican II taught that the Church of Christ, the "one true religion," *subsists in* the Catholic Church (cf. *Lumen Gentium*, n. 8; *Dignitatis Humanae*, n. 1). The first draft used the verb *is*; but the final draft replaced *is* with *subsists in* to allow for those elements of Grace and divine truth which can be found outside the visible structure of the Roman Catholic Church. Earlier in this section we cited a quotation of St. Augustine in which he identified the Body of Christ with the Catholic Church. Karl Rahner has cited another quotation from Augustine which apparently was ignored or neglected in subsequent centuries: "Many whom God has, the Church does not have; and many whom the Church has, God does not have." In *Humani Generis* (1950), Pope Pius XII wrote: ". . . the Mystical Body of Christ and the Catholic Church in communion with Rome are one and the same thing . . . ." Vatican II made a significant move away from this total identification. The reality of Christ's Body is not coterminous with the visible structure of the Roman Catholic Church.

The hierarchical, institutional model of the Church — which Cardinal Bellarmine thought is "as visible and palpable as the community of the Roman people, or the Kingdom of France, or the Republic of Venice" — is no longer sufficient in itself to define the full reality of the Body of Christ, the Church of Christ on earth. Significantly, and only after some debate, the Council Fathers of Vatican II treated the hierarchical structure of the Church *after* they first considered the Church as a "mystery" and the Church as "the People of God" (cf. *Lumen Gentium*). Father Richard P. McBrien, in *The Remaking of the Church*, defines the Church as "that part of the world which alone con-

fesses and celebrates the Lordship of Jesus Christ." The Church
is a sign (sacrament) of His presence and Grace in the world, and
is a promise of His final coming (*parousia*) to establish the Kingdom of God — the new Heaven and the new earth. The Church is
not yet the Kingdom of God, but is, according to Vatican II, "the
initial budding forth of that Kingdom" on earth (cf. *Lumen
Gentium*, n. 5).

The majority of the world's Christians do not accept an
exaggerated institutionalism and an exaggerated monarchicalism in the Church of Christ. Cardinal John Wright has
pointed out that Cardinal Newman ("the absent Council Father
of Vatican II") was a champion of the "infallibility of the total
Church believing." Newman recalled that the consensus of the
faithful as a whole resisted the heresy of Arianism, which shook
the Church to its foundations and found many bishops and
theological experts in its camp. Newman taught that there exists
in the Church of Christ an "infallibility in believing (*infallibilitas
in credendo*)" as well as an "infallibility in teaching" as exercised
by the magisterium. The ordinary teaching (*de fide Catholica*) of
the magisterium, apart from its solemn definitions, finds its
infallibility only in the acceptance of the whole Church — the
universitas fidelium. Thus did Vatican II teach: "The body of the
faithful as a whole, anointed as they are by the Holy One, cannot
err in matters of belief" (*Lumen Gentium*, n. 12).

The Roman Catholic Church, of course, is not about to get rid
of the papacy and the episcopacy. Indeed, the Catholic Church, in
so doing, would be unfaithful to its innermost consciousness and
conviction, and *ipso facto* would cease to exist. But the days for
regarding the pope as an absolute monarch, whose every utterance (whether in an encyclical, allocution, bull, declaration, *motu
proprio*, sermon, etc.) is regarded as God's infallible truth and
above all criticism and correction, are hopefully numbered and
few. Vatican I defined the special circumstances under which the
pope can teach infallibly; and a pope (Pius XII, 1950) has exercised this prerogative only once since the Council made its definition. Vatican I deferred considering the role of the bishops and
laity in the Church and the principle of collegiality. Hence, an
exaggerated monarchicalism in the Church followed Vatican I.
Vatican II has helped to restore a proper balance among the
elements of monarchicalism and collegiality and the "sense of
faith" of the entire People of God. Richard P. McBrien, in *Who Is a
Catholic?*, tells us the college of bishops is nothing without the

pope, and the pope is nothing without the college of bishops. We would add that both are nothing without the entire People of God.

As Father Henry Fehren has written in *U. S. Catholic*, to be above all criticism and correction is too great a burden for any man to bear, including the pope. Christ Himself did not hesitate to refer to the Prince of the Apostles as "Satan" (cf. Matt. 16:23) when he offered a "theological opinion" which would have lured Christ away from His Cross. St. Paul admits to differing openly with the Keeper of the Keys over a point of discipline and procedure (cf. Gal. 2:11).

Each model of the Church tells a truth. Christ's Church does have a visible hierarchy authorized by Christ to teach, govern, and sanctify the People of God. Christ's Church does have a mystical union of all its members in Grace. Christ's Church does allow for the principle of subsidiarity and personal religious experience within the parameters of Christian truth. Christ's Church does become real for a Christian in the actual existential events of Christian living: e.g., the preaching of the Word; the celebration of the Sacraments; the feeding of the hungry. Although Christ's Church is one, holy, catholic (with a lower case *c*), and apostolic, the Church is a Pilgrim Church in which each of these marks is yet to be fully realized, as Christ prayed "that all may be one." Christ's Church is in a real sense incomplete, flawed, imperfect, on a spiritual odyssey through human history in anticipation of and preparation for the coming Kingdom of God. Christ's Church is concerned with social justice and the temporal betterment of mankind — not simply as requirements of "pre-evangelization," but for the sake of human values *per se*. Vatican II counted it "among the more serious errors of our age" to divorce the Christian Faith from social involvement and daily living (cf. *Guadium et Spes*, n. 43).

The model of the Church as Christ's Mystical Body seems to incorporate the best features of the above-mentioned models, and has a firm foundation in Sacred Scripture. Christ's earthly body was visible and structured and governed by His mind and will — and so is His Mystical Body. Christ's earthly body was in intimate communion with the divine — and so is His Mystical Body. Christ's earthly body brought Grace and salvation, and was a sign *par excellence* of God's presence in the world — and so is His Mystical Body. Christ's earthly body proclaimed the saving word of God — and so does His Mystical Body. Christ's

earthly body went about doing good in a spirit of *diakonia*:
healing the sick, forgiving sinners, comforting the disturbed (and
disturbing the comfortable!) — and so does His Mystical Body.
As Christ's earthly body grew in wisdom and knowledge and
Grace before God and man, so does His Mystical Body grow in
wisdom and knowledge and Grace in its pilgrim mission on earth.
And just as Christ's earthly body underwent a Crucifixion followed by a glorious Resurrection, so does His Mystical Body
periodically undergo a crucifixion followed by a resurrection.

A study of the models of the Church makes the venerable
term "Holy Mother Church" more pregnant with meaning. May
the day come soon when all Christians, who "bear the name of
Christ on their foreheads," will find that unity for which Christ
prayed — a unity in spirit and in truth, inspired by the Holy
Spirit, and incorporated in "the great and glorious Body of
Christ."

VI. GRACE AND THE SACRAMENTS

The Life of Grace. Life exists on various levels. Vegetative
life is capable of nutrition, growth, and reproduction. Sentient
life, in addition to possessing vegetative powers, is capable of
locomotion, sense knowledge, and sensuous appetency. The rational life of man possesses the faculties of plant and animal life
as well as powers of intellection and volition.

The New Testament teaches that man has been raised to a
higher order of life, the life of Grace. Man has no intrinsic right to
this higher life. Grace (*gratia*, favor) is a unique gift from God
which enables man to have a real share in the divine life. As we
have noted, by Original Sin man had lost the supernatural life of
Grace; by the redemptive life of Christ, supernatural Grace was
restored to man.

Sanctifying Grace is a positive reality. We do not speak
metaphorically when we say that by Grace man becomes an
adopted son of God, as Christ is the natural Son of God. By Grace
man shares God's own nature and life, even though man's
human nature remains intact. "Grace builds upon nature and
presupposes nature." Luther erroneously believed that Grace
acted as a cloak that covered man's corrupt human nature. The
Pelagian heresy denied the necessity of Grace, believing that
unaided human nature could attain Heaven. Some today feel
that the tenets propounded by Teilhard de Chardin smack of
Pelagianism, which would reduce Christianity to naturalism.

The foremost opponent of Pelagianism was St. Augustine, *Doctor Gratiae*.

God naturally possesses the attribute of ubiquity: He is, and must be, everywhere. But by Sanctifying Grace the Trinity becomes present in man in a special way. God is present in a stone, but the nature of the stone is not thereby elevated. The indwelling of the Trinity makes man not only a temple of the Holy Spirit, but makes man a participator in the divine life, an heir of Heaven, with the Beatific Vision as his supernatural end.

Sanctifying Grace incorporates one into the Mystical Body of Christ. Just as every organism is capable of growth and maturity, so can one grow in Grace. All Grace has been merited by Christ; the possibility of knowing, loving, and serving Christ better always exists. Conversely, one can lose Grace to the extent that one fails to know, love, and serve the Lord. All natural life is characterized by processes of anabolism (building up) and katabolism (tearing down). Translating this biological truth to the supernatural order, we find that the life of Grace is built up by prayer, penance, good works, and reception of the Sacraments. Luther denied that Grace can be increased by good works. The life of Grace is lost by serious sin.

Actual Grace is necessary for avoiding sin and for every supernaturally meritorious act. Calvin's monstrous doctrine of predestination denies the efficacy of Actual Grace, since everyone has been predetermined for either Heaven or Hell. All who have the use of reason are given sufficient Grace to save their souls. Infants, idiots, and imbeciles who die without Baptism enjoy a state of natural happiness in Limbo, according to Thomas Aquinas.

The Seven Sacraments. Recent years have seen a considerable renewal in sacramental theology. The trend is away from a mechanical, *"ex opere operato"* (from the work done) concept of the Sacraments, which are now seen more as "actions of Christ," "divine encounters," and "signs of faith." Christ Himself is seen as "the Sacrament of God"; the Church, the Mystical Body, is seen as "the Sacrament of Christ." John A. O'Brien writes:

If these crucially important truths concerning the Sacraments along with the clarifying statement on the relation of faith to justification had been properly promulgated, preached and explained in the decades before the Reformation, one may well wonder whether the movement that shattered the unity of Christendom might not have been averted.[27]

A *signum*, or sign, is any expression apparent to the senses that carries an invisible meaning. A handshake, for example, is an outward way of expressing friendship. The Sacraments are outward signs instituted by Christ to give Grace; they are eminently in accord with man's nature, which is composed of matter and spirit. The universe itself is a great sacrament pointing the way to the divine.

The Seven Sacraments correspond to the seven essential needs of natural life. First, one must be born; Baptism gives one a supernatural birth. Secondly, one must grow and mature; Confirmation confirms and develops one in the Christian Faith. Thirdly, one must take nourishment to sustain life; the Holy Eucharist sustains and nourishes one in the life of Grace. Fourthly, one must be cured of disease and debility; Penance removes the spiritual disease of sin. Fifthly, one must have government and order; Holy Orders communicates the powers of the priesthood to those who are called. Sixthly, the human race must be propagated; Matrimony gives supernatural Grace to the conjugal state of Christian marriage. Lastly, one must be prepared to die; the Sacrament of the Anointing of the Sick prepares one's soul, and sometimes the body, to face death in Grace and Christian hope.[28]

(1) *Baptism*, the Sacrament of Faith, removes Original Sin, making one a participator in the divine life of Grace, a member of the Mystical Body of Christ, a temple of the Holy Spirit, and an heir of Heaven. Christ's words to Nicodemus indicate the necessity of Baptism (cf. John 3:5). The Sacrament is ordinarily administered by the pouring of water; but theologians teach that martyrdom for the Christian Faith constitutes Baptism of blood; and perfect charity and the desire to know, love, and serve the true God constitutes Baptism of desire for those not receiving Baptism of water. Some theologians believe that Baptism of desire was effected concomitantly with the rite of circumcision among the Jews.

(2) *Confirmation*, the Sacrament of maturity, strengthens one in the Faith, giving him the power to fulfill his public duty as a Christian. This Sacrament is not absolutely essential for salvation, as is Baptism. A bishop ordinarily administers the Sacrament, but in extraordinary circumstances any priest can be the minister.

(3) The *Holy Eucharist* is the Sacrament of Christ's body and blood, soul and divinity. Christ promised that He would give us His body and blood for our spiritual food (cf. John 6:52). Many

regarded this as "a hard saying" and thereafter refused to walk with Jesus. The doctrine is a hard saying for many today. Catholics accept the Holy Eucharist on Christ's own words at the Last Supper; Christ is worshipped in the bread and wine, which become truly and substantially the body and blood of Christ when consecrated by a priest. The consecration of the Eucharist is also a sacrifice, the perfect sacrifice to God the Father.

(4) *Penance,* the Sacrament of forgiveness and reconciliation, removes the guilt of sin, mortal and venial. Perfect contrition, of course, effects the remission of sin, even apart from this Sacrament. However, since Christ instituted the Sacrament of Penance, the desire to receive the Sacrament must be at least implicit in one's perfect act of contribution. Thus, contrition for sin and the Sacrament of Penance, though they may be physically separate, are morally one. The new Rite of Penance, introduced in 1976, allows for face-to-face confession and dialogue in a "reconciliation room" rather than the traditional confessional box.

(5) *Holy Orders,* the Sacrament of the priesthood, bestows the powers of orders and jurisdiction upon one who has been duly called. A priest is empowered to teach and govern (jurisdiction) and to sanctify (orders) in Christ's name. The constant tradition of the Church has been that the priesthood is a divine institution, that Christ's apostles were the first bishops, that the bishops today are the successors of the apostles, possessing "the fullness of the priesthood." Luther and other sixteenth-century reformers denied the special powers of the priesthood and taught a doctrine of "the priesthood of all believers." This doctrine follows from the general Protestant concept of the Church as essentially an invisible reality grounded in the faith of the individual believer.

We can only say that both Scripture and tradition favor the view that Christ did intend to establish a special priesthood, distinct from the priesthood of all believers. At the Last Supper He told His apostles to do what He had just done, viz., change bread and wine into His own body and blood and offer a perfect sacrifice to His heavenly Father. Christ spent three years training His apostles for their special work. Every indication is that Christ intended His apostles to teach, govern, and sanctify the cells of His Mystical Body: they would be preserved from error in their teaching as one moral body in union with the visible head and foundation of the Church, Peter the Rock, and his successors; they would be empowered to administer the Sacraments and thereby sanctify the cells of the Body. Such is the Catholic teaching on the priesthood.[29]

(6) *Matrimony*, the Sacrament of marriage, elevates what is a natural relationship between man and woman and makes it an occasion for a divine encounter and a special infusion of sacramental Grace. In the Christian view, marriage is seen as a type of Christ and His spouse, the Church — "two in one flesh." Far from depreciating the value of connubial love, the Church sees the state of matrimony as a source of many Graces, derived from the Sacrament received at the time of the nuptial contract.[30]

(7) The *Sacrament of the Anointing of the Sick*, formerly known as *Extreme Unction*, is administered to one in danger of death. The Sacrament remits mortal and venial sins in conjunction with the Sacrament of Penance. If the recipient is unable to confess, the Sacrament of the Sick is sufficient to remit sin, assuming the proper disposition of the ill person. The Sacrament also removes the "remnants" of sin, i.e., the temporal punishment due to sin. The power of the Sacrament to remove temporal punishment in Purgatory is greatly dependent upon both the habitual and immediate disposition of the recipient.

A not unusual effect of the Sacrament is a restoration of bodily health, if that be for the good of the soul. The Sacrament affords one strength of soul; vigor to ward off temptation; patience; and Christian hope, as one faces eternity.

In 1973 Pope Paul VI ruled that the Sacrament of the Anointing of the Sick, as it has been called since Vatican II, will henceforth be administered not only to those in imminent danger of death, but also to those who are seriously but not mortally ill. The new rite also allows for administering the Sacrament to "great gatherings of the faithful" during a Mass — for sick pilgrims at Lourdes, for example, or patients in a hospital.

Supernatural Grace and the Sacraments are basically mysteries; reason alone cannot establish their existence or explain their operation. We take them on faith, as taught by the Christian Revelation. There has always been a temptation to reduce Christianity to a purely natural level and thus "explain away" the doctrine of supernatural Grace. At the other extreme are those who would make Christianity a wholly mystical experience, shorn of its human and material elements. The sane position is to see Christianity as the embodiment of both nature and Grace, the meeting of the divine with the human.

How can the divine Life, which is one, infinite, and indivisible, be shared by Grace with a creature? How is this life of Grace communicated through the Sacraments? How can one grow in Grace? Why and how does serious sin destroy the life of Grace in one's soul? We do not have the answers, at least from reason alone. Faith supplies its own kind of answers. "For those who have the Faith, no explanation is necessary; for those who do not, no explanation is possible." The reward of faith is eternal life.

VII. JUDGMENT, HELL, HEAVEN

Death and the Particular Judgment. *Eschatology* is that branch of theology that treats of the last things: death, Judgment, Hell, Heaven. Death is a certainty; man alone is aware of this eventuality, which is a part of his animal nature. Since the Fall, death now exists as a punishment for Original Sin. Even if Adam had not sinned, according to Karl Rahner, Adam and his children would have undergone a kind of "death without dying" after attaining a consummation and fulfillment of their whole being. Death marks the end of one's spiritual progress.

Clinically and medically, death occurs when the brain dies. Philosophically, death occurs when the body is no longer a suitable and effective substantial co-principle with the human soul in constituting the human person. Theologically, death is that moment when one's earthly probation is ended, and one faces his Particular Judgment.

Gaea, Eros, and Thanatos; cosmogony and eschatology; birth and death; spring and fall; sunrise and sunset; health and sickness; joy and sorrow; triumph and tragedy — such is the rhythm of the cosmos. Katabolism must finally overtake anabolism. Thanatos must win over Eros and the daimonic. The shadow of the Cross must be present in the Stable of Bethlehem. Death is written into the very fabric of life.

Thanatopsis has become popular with many modern writers. A world that has been so preoccupied with technology has become intrigued with the idea of death. Stewart Alsop has written perceptively concerning his own impending death with cancer. Teilhard saw death as a kind of "hollowing out," a final paroxysm and purification enabling a human life to open to a higher life. Rollo May tells us that Cupid's arrows are poisoned. Francis Thompson saw Death and Birth as "mystical twins of Time inseparable," and wrote of the setting sun, "Thou dost thy dying so triumphally."

Sex proclaims life; yet sex is intimately connected with death, and is a reminder of one's own mortality. We are told that the male bee dies immediately after inseminating the queen bee. Salmon die soon after spawning. The female praying mantis bites the head off of the male during copulation. The male in the throes of death thus becomes a more effective inseminator. (One wonders about the so-called "weaker sex"!)

Birth must seem to the fetus as a kind of death as the organism leaves the life of the womb for a richer and fuller life in the world. Rollo May suggests that birth is the human organism's first experience of anxiety as it must labor to pass through the narrow confines of the mother's vagina, and finally catch its first breath. So too is death our great final anxiety as we pass from this world to the next. Some anxiety is necessary for human growth. Cows are contented; but human beings develop through anxiety. By passing through the jaws of death, a human life is opened to a fuller life with God.

The Christian view of death is one of hope and triumph. St. Paul could exclaim: "O death, where is thy victory? O death, where is thy sting?" "Life is changed, not taken away," sings the Church. The *white* vestments and *white* pall of the funeral rite proclaim victory and resurrection over death. The Church echoes David's poignant paean of trust: "My shepherd is the Lord; nothing indeed shall I want.... Though I should walk in a dark valley, I will fear no evils, because You are with me."

The Christian can face death bravely, confidently, and with equanimity. The Solitary Reaper may come expectedly or unexpectedly, like a thief in the night. But come he must. St. Francis of Assisi, who lived with Lady Poverty most of his life, gladly welcomed Sister Death. The early Christian martyrs faced death undaunted, knowing that death for the Holy Faith was their passport to eternal life. Even the ancient Greeks often portrayed Thanatos as an appealing young man who would transport one to Elysium. Job, who had more than his share of trials and suffering, could joyfully exclaim: "I know that my Redeemer lives, and in the last day I shall rise out of the earth. And I shall be clothed again with my skin, and in my flesh I shall see my God" (Job 19:25-26). "I am the Resurrection and the Life," said the Divine Master; "he who believes in Me, even if he die, shall live; and whoever lives and believes in Me shall never die" (John 11:25-26).

Euthanasia ("mercy killing" or literally, good death) is morally unacceptable because it is a usurpation of God's supreme dominion over life and death. Extraordinary means for extending one's life are not required; but one is obliged to use the ordinary means to preserve human life. What are ordinary and extraordinary means in a given case may be debatable; but the moral principles are clear. One who administers a lethal drug or withdraws the ordinary life supports becomes a murderer. The Fifth Commandment states simply: "Thou shalt not kill." It is not surprising that a society that condones abortion on demand will very readily accept euthanasia.

Albert Camus, the French existentialist, believed there is basically only one metaphysical question: is life worth living? He believed there is basically only one ethical question: should one commit suicide? For the Christian, life is a precious gift from God. Death is a physical evil, but a necessary condition to enter eternal life. The Christian places his life totally in God's hands, and says, with Job: "The Lord gives and the Lord takes away; blessed be the name of the Lord!"

The immortality of the human soul, which Kant considered to be one of the three great problems of speculative philosophy,[31] is known by reason, even apart from Revelation. The spiritual nature of man's soul demands immortality. One should note, however, that Aquinas taught the "personal survival" of man, but not "survival of the person," which will not take place until the separated soul is again united with the body after the General Judgment. Aquinas believed that the separated human soul will be even more conscious of itself.

The Particular Judgment takes place immediately following one's death. We shall die as we have lived. The soul has either lived the life of God through Grace or it hasn't. "Fear not that your life will come to an end," said Cardinal Newman; "rather fear that your life will never have a beginning." Life is the eternal decision; a soul destined for Hell could not be happy in Heaven, anymore than a soul destined for Heaven could be happy in Hell. We judge ourselves as much as God judges us; the Judgment is irrevocable.

Catholic tradition has consistently taught the existence of a state of Purgatory. The Old Testament says, "It is therefore a holy and wholesome thought to pray for the dead, that they may be loosed from sins" (2 Mach. 12:46). Such prayer would be meaningless if only Heaven and Hell existed. Purgatory exists for those souls needing to atone for temporal punishment due to their sins. Purgatory will cease to exist after the General Judgment. What about Limbo, where souls still in Original Sin exist? Opinions differ, but many theologians believe that these souls will be given an opportunity to enter Heaven. Others see Limbo as "the fringe of Hell" and believe Limbo will co-exist eternally with Hell. The Church has made no formal definition on the question. The question of *metempsychosis*, or the transmigration of souls — a common belief of Buddhist theology — is unaccept-able in the Christian view. St. Paul said, "It is appointed unto men to die once and after this comes the Judgment" (Heb. 9:27).

The General Judgment: the End of the World. Christ spoke of "the signs of the times" in rebuking the Pharisees. Billy Graham lists twelve signs of the end of the world, based on Scriptural texts:

(1) The mental state of the world; (2) the moral state of the world; (3) a falling away; (4) an increase in lawlessness; (5) the coming of scoffers; (6) widespread persecution; (7) affluence; (8) the preparation for Armageddon; (9) knowledge and travel; (10) peace conferences; (11) the coming of the world dictator; (12) worldwide evangelism.[32]

Mr. Graham feels that many of these signs are present in the world today.

The end will come; we know this even apart from Revelation. The Second Law of Thermodynamics and the Law of Entropy tell us that eventually all kinetic (available) energy of the uni-verse will be converted into potential (unavailable) energy. The universe is tending toward Absolute Zero; as presently consti-tuted, the cosmos must die an entropic death, a frozen mass in frozen space, devoid of life and light and motion. The principle of death is written into the very fabric of the universe.[33]

Revelation teaches that the end of the world will be catas-trophic in nature and that God alone knows when this event will occur. Scripture indicates that the physical world will be de-stroyed by fire; that the dead shall rise from the grave; that all men and angels shall be finally judged, with the good separated from the wicked. Christ, in both His divinity and humanity, shall judge the living and the dead in Heaven, in Purgatory, and in Hell.

The Resurrection of the Body is a revealed truth. The human soul is an incomplete substance tending toward union with the body for which it was made. Hence, philosophy *suggests* a reunion of body and soul, but such a reunion cannot be proved apodictically from reason alone. The Resurrection of the Body is truly miraculous, beyond the power of nature. Even the damned in Hell will be reunited with their bodies, which will only add to their punishment.

Theologians teach that the resurrected body of the just will possess the gifts of immortality (no death); incorruptibility (no disease); impassibility (no suffering); clarity (outward splendor); subtlety (ability to penetrate material objects); agility (ability to travel distances with ease and alacrity); dominance of the soul over the body and nature (no concupiscence or natural catastrophes). Most important of all, the glorified body will share in the complete enjoyment of the Beatific Vision.

There will be a "new Heaven and a new earth"; all things will be made new (cf. Apoc. 21:1-5). Paul tells us that all nature yearns for redemption. This world will not be annihilated, but will be remade for man in his glorified body.[34]

Hell. The most unpopular subject in all theology is Hell; people prefer stories with happy endings. Reason suggests (even if it does not apodictically demand) the existence of an eternal sanction of the moral law. The cosmos is governed by law, not the least of which is the moral law. All law has sanctions, in the sense that the violation of law incurs certain consequences. One cannot violate the law of gravity, for example, without experiencing the effects of that violation. Observance of the moral law is conditioned with sanctions that extend into eternity.

Divine Revelation teaches the existence of Hell. Christ referred to its existence in describing the Last Judgment: "Depart from Me, accursed ones, into the everlasting fire which was prepared for the Devil and his angels" (Matt. 25:41). Many find the doctrine hard to reconcile with the mercy, kindness, and love of Christ, which were manifested on so many occasions. One must not ignore the *justice* of God. We live in a teleological universe, one with purpose and design. The moral law carries sanctions of reward and punishment, and by Revelation we know these sanctions are everlasting. Origen (185-255) believed in "a restoration of all things," that the souls in Hell would eventually be freed. His doctrine was condemned by the Fifth General Council of Constantinople in 553 A.D.[35] Islamism teaches that Hell is not eternal for a Moslem. For Jean-Paul Sartre, "Hell is other people (*l'enfer est l'autre*)."[36]

Hell consists essentially in the loss of the Beatific Vision, in the separation from God. Along with the pain of loss and separation, the damned will suffer the pain of sense when their bodies are reunited with their souls after the Last Judgment. Theologians generally teach the existence of real fire in Hell. Thomas Aquinas believed that God gave fire, a material creature, the ability to "hem in" the soul, a spirit. Aquinas further teaches that Hell is a *locus*, a real place.[37]

Someone has said that he believes in an eternal Hell eternally empty. Scripture cites the Fall of the angels as the primary cause for the existence of Hell. Some believe that it is *de fide divina* that Judas is in Hell. Christ certainly had severe words for Judas, when He said it would have been better for him not to have been born (cf. Matt. 26:24); yet, the Church has never declared officially that there is a single human soul in Hell. History has had its procession of infamous characters who wrought considerable havoc and misery upon mankind. Yet, one would hope that even the most infamous had perfect contrition in his final moment. God alone knows. One thing is for sure: no one goes to Hell except through his own fault. God is not a capricious tyrant, sardonically damning souls to eternal punishment. As noted previously, one who has not lived the life of Grace could not be happy in Heaven. The possibility of Hell is intimately connected with that greatest of natural mysteries, human freedom. The choice of Heaven or Hell is wholly our own.[38]

Heaven. Christianity is primarily a religion of hope and victory. Christianity cannot be separated from the Crucifixion; but neither can the Crucifixion be separated from the Resurrection. Eternal happiness is the reward for living the Christian life.

Reason indicates that an extramundane reward exists as a sanction for the observance of the moral law. Viture is not its own reward, at least in terms of temporal security and monetary recompense. Living the Christian life gives no guarantee of temporal health, security, or success. The Christian must look to an extramundane reward for a life of virtue. A purely temporal sanction for the moral law would hardly be a sufficient motive for most men to live a life of virtue. We find peace of soul in this life in knowing that God will ultimately redress all grievances, that righteousness will ultimately be vindicated, that the virtuous will be happy with God forever.

Man might be destined for a purely natural beatitude; his nature demands no more. Divine Revelation tells us that God has prepared a supernatural end for man. "Beloved, now we are the children of God, and it has not yet appeared what we shall be. We know that, when He appears, we shall be like to Him, for we shall see Him just as He is" (1 John 3:2). To see God "just as He is" is above the natural power of man.

Christ spoke of man's eternal reward when He said: "Come, blessed of My Father, take possession of the Kingdom prepared for you from the foundation of the world" (Matt. 25:34).

The Beatific Vision is a mystery. Aristotle said that vision is the most spiritual of the senses; to "see" something is to make it a part of oneself. Man sees the universe, and in a sense possesses the entire cosmos in his mind. Both intellect and will — the intellect made for truth and the will made for goodness — will be completely satisfied in the Beatific Vision. ". . . in knowing Him Who is the fount of all truth we shall possess Him Who is the Infinite Good."[39]

The whole man — intellect and will, soul and (after the Last Judgment) body — will be perfectly, completely, and everlastingly satisfied. Sanctifying Grace, "the seed of glory," makes the Beatific Vision possible for man. There will be secondary sources of happiness in Heaven: Christ in His human nature; Mary in her glorified body; the angels, saints, and wonders of creation — all will be a part of man's eternal happiness. Heaven is both a Kingdom and a place; there are degrees of glory among the blessed. Faith and hope will no longer exist in the just, for now they see the Trinity (without comprehending the mystery) and now they possess Infinite Goodness (without exhausting the possibilities of love). Charity — love of God and fellow man — alone remains in Heaven.

The Christian doctrine of Heaven stands in contrast to the Buddhist concept of *Nirvana*: Heaven is fulfillment, completion, the fullness of life; *Nirvana* is extirpation, neutralization, the next thing to nonexistence. The Heaven of Islam is a sensual paradise. Both concepts of an afterlife are poles apart from the Christian teaching. So also are the doctrines of Karl Marx and materialistic philosophies which would convert this earth into an economic utopia, apart from any supernatural intervention. Every man senses deeply with St. Paul that this earth, as presently constituted, is not man's lasting city. Augustine summed it up best in his *Confessions* when he said: "You have made us for Yourself, O Lord, and our hearts are restless until they rest in You."

Fulton J. Sheen has written beautifully concerning the joys of Heaven:

Will Heaven surpass all the pleasures of the eye, and the ear, and the imagination? . . . I have seen a sunset on the Mediterranean when two clouds came down like pillars to form a brilliant red tabernacle for the sun and it glowing like a golden host . . . . I have seen, from the harbor, the towers and minarets of Constantinople pierce through the mist which hung over them like a silken veil . . . . I have heard of the beauties of the garden of Paradise where four-fold rivers flowed through lands rich with the gold and onyx . . . . I can imagine a world in which the winter would never come, and in which the flowers would never fade, and the sun would never set; I can imagine a world in which there would always be a peace and a quiet without idleness, a profound knowledge of things without research, a constant enjoyment without satiety . . . .

Will eternity be anything like what I have seen, or what I have heard, or what I can imagine? . . . Listen to the voice of God: 'Eye has not seen or ear heard, nor has it entered into the heart of man, what things God has prepared for those who love Him' (1 Cor. 2:9).[40]

Theology, according to John L. McKenzie, is "God-talk." Man can put his mind to no higher endeavor. Theology must ever strive to relate to the realities of the world. The world is impregnated with God; and theology's task is to help the world find God. The poet William Blake has put it beautifully:

> To see the world in a grain of sand
> And a Heaven in a wild flower;
> Hold infinity in the palm of your hand,
> And eternity in an hour.
>
> "Auguries of Innocence"

CHAPTER III

CATHOLICISM AND MORAL THEOLOGY

Living the Christian Life

If you love Me, keep My Commandments.

— John 14:15

Not everyone who says to Me, 'Lord, Lord,' shall enter the Kingdom of Heaven; but he who does the will of My Father in Heaven shall enter the Kingdom of Heaven.

— Matt. 7:21

Do you not know that the unjust will not possess the Kingdom of God? Do not err: neither fornicators, nor idolaters, nor adulterers, nor the effeminate, nor sodomites, nor theives, nor the covetous, nor drunkards, nor the evil-tongued, nor the greedy will possess the Kingdom of God.

— 1 Cor. 6:9-10

Man is the only animal that blushes – or needs to.

— Mark Twain

Much of our moral freedom is good: it is pleasant to be relieved of theological terrors, to enjoy without qualm the pleasures that harm neither others nor ourselves, and to feel the tang of the open air upon our liberated flesh . . . .[1] We frolic in our emancipation from theology, but have we developed a natural ethic – a moral code independent of religion – strong enough to keep our instincts of acquisition, pugnacity, and sex from debasing our civilization into a mire of greed, crime, and promiscuity?[2]

— Will and Ariel Durant

I will not recant anything, for to go against my conscience is neither right nor safe. Here I stand; I can do no other.

— Martin Luther

I can resist everything except temptation.

— Oscar Wilde

"EVERY art and every inquiry, and similarly every action and pursuit, is thought to aim at some good; and for this reason the good has rightly been declared to be that

71

at which all things aim"; so states the opening line of Aristotle's *Nicomachean Ethics*.[3] Moral theology is directed toward the good, the supreme good, the *Summum Bonum*. Moral theology differs from moral philosophy, or ethics, in that the former is directed toward a supernatural end; moral theology also relies upon Divine Revelation as well as the light of reason, thus providing divine certitude. The Church rightly considers itself to be the teacher and guardian of moral theology inasmuch as its truths form a part of Divine Revelation and are necessary for man to attain his supernatural end.

In this chapter we shall survey the general aspects of the moral law, the theological virtues, and the Ten Commandments.

I. THE MORAL LAW

The Concept and Kinds of Law. *Law*, like time and space, is an elusive concept; Augustine said he knew what time is if no one asked him.[4] In the widest sense, law can be defined as "the rule or norm according to which something is drawn toward an action or restrained from an action."[5] Law is an *ens rationis* (logical being) *cum fundamento in re* (with a foundation in reality). The entire universe, and every creature in it, is governed by law, by its own internal mode of operation and by its external relations with other creatures. In a narrower sense, law was defined by Thomas Aquinas as "an ordinance of reason directed toward the common good and promulgated by the one who has the care of the community."[6]

The *eternal law*, according to Aquinas, is "the plan of God's wisdom directing all actions and movements"; thus, all creatures are able to achieve their natural end and purpose. Every true and valid law must trace its origin ultimately to the eternal law. The eternal law is manifested in time and space by the natural law and by positive law.

The *natural law* is defined as a participation of creatural beings in the eternal law insofar as a creature is directed by its nature to achieve its proper end. Nonintelligent creatures follow the natural law blindly and necessarily; even the physical and biological functions of man are necessarily subject to *natural physical law*. The entire cosmos — from the smallest atom to the largest star, from the simple amoeba to the body of man — is necessarily subject to the natural physical law, ordained by God Himself. The natural moral law guides the free acts of free creatures. Angels are free creatures and are also subject to natural law; but angels will not violate the natural moral law inasmuch as they are in full union with God through the Beatific Vision. The *natural moral law* is defined as "the moral law, manifested by the natural light of reason, demanding the preservation of the natural order and forbidding its violation."[7] Man, being a free creature, is psychologically, or physically, free to observe or not to observe the natural moral law; man, however, is *morally bound* to observe the natural moral law.[8]

The most fundamental postulate of the natural moral law is: do good and avoid evil. Other general precepts pertain to the most general situations and objects. Man's habitual knowledge of these fundamental postulates of the moral law was given the name *synderesis* by Aquinas. Secondary precepts of the natural moral law pertain to immediate applications of the primary precepts; all of the Commandments of the Decalogue but the Third fall into this category. Tertiary precepts pertain to specific and more remote applications of the moral law as discovered and deduced by reason.

Positive law is a specific statement made by either divine or human authority in applying the natural moral law to the needs of a given situation. The *divine positive law* is contained in Sacred Scripture; one should note that the ceremonial and judicial laws of the Mosaic Code have been abrogated.[9] All other moral precepts contained in the Bible form the divine positive law.[10] *Human positive law* contains those precepts promulgated by legitimate human authority for the good of the community. Human positive law may be *ecclesiastical*, i.e., promulgated by legitimate Church authority concerning a matter of faith, morals, or discipline; *civil law* is enacted by the authority of the state to ensure the common good.

The Norms of Morality. A *norm* is a rule, a guide, a standard of measurement, or a criterion relating to a given act, condition, or situation. The *objective norm of morality* is law, whether conceived of as God's will, the divine law, the eternal law, the natural law, or positive law. The proximate objective norm of morality is human nature and reason relating to the good of the whole man. Divine positive law has its source in the word of God revealing through Sacred Scripture and through sacred tradition.

The *subjective norm of morality* is one's conscience, which is a practical judgment of the intellect in terms of the "rightness" or "wrongness" — the moral quality — of a given act. The moral quality of a free, human act *(actus humanus)* is determined by three factors: (1) the object, or the inherent nature of the act itself; (2) the circumstances that attend the act (such as time, place, manner, etc.);[11] and (3) the end or intention of the agent of the human act. A good intention (factor 3) cannot make an objectively evil act a good act (factor 1); neither can a good intention (factor 3) justify the use of immoral means to obtain a good object (factor 1).

One's own conscience must be regarded as the final norm and the supreme arbiter of morality; such is the teaching of Aquinas. A given act might be objectively evil in itself (suicide, for example); but if one's own conscience, honestly and sincerely formed, is not cognizant of the immorality of a given act, the act is not sinful for *this* individual in *this* existential situation. Conversely, one might regard an objectively good act as being morally wrong; the individual must follow his subjectively certain conscience in refraining from the objectively good act. To act against one's own conscience — though it be objectively erroneous — is the same as committing sin.[12]

What we have said about conscience is in one sense a concession to existentialism, which stresses the priority of existence over essence; the subjective, free existent over the objective, determined existent. To say this is not to minimize the importance of objective morality; on the contrary, the finality of conscience, *a fortiori*, makes it imperative that one's conscience be rightly formed, that a sincere and adequate effort be made to know moral truth, and that one's motives be inspired with a good will. One has a moral duty to form a right conscience; the omniscient God sees the mind and heart of each of us and will judge us accordingly.

A number of erroneous and inadequate norms of morality can be cited. We reject the tenets of *Stoicism*, which says that virtue, or reason, is the only good. The doctrine is one-sided and incomplete in rejecting the value of feeling and emotion in human life. The *formalism* of Immanuel Kant, which makes the will the author of its own laws ("the categorical imperative") is to be rejected. *Public opinion,* or "everyone is doing it," is not in itself an adequate norm of morality; everyone was doing it in Sodom and Gomorrah. Neither is *feeling, instinct,* or *emotion* an adequate norm of morality. Animals are governed by their blind feelings and instincts; man has a higher faculty of rationality which must govern his conduct. The philosophy of *hedonism*, making pleasure the final norm of human conduct, is an inadequate norm, since it prescinds from the dictates of reason. Pleasure is indeed a human good, but its use needs a valid rationale.

Situation ethics, as proposed by Joseph Fletcher, declares that no moral principle is absolute; anything is all right as long as it is done from a motive of love, which alone is immutable and intrinsically good.[13] In one sense, love is the fundamental norm of morality. Christ gave as the two great commandments to love God and to love one's neighbor as oneself. "Love, and do what you will," said St. Augustine. Martin Luther made faith the ultimate norm when he said, "Sin boldly, but believe more boldly." A genuine faith and love will not ignore law, which ultimately has its source in Love Itself, which is God. "If you love Me, keep My Commandments," Our Lord reminded us (John 14:15).[14]

Modern existentialism has its roots in the philosophical systems of René Descartes (1596-1650) and Immanuel Kant (1724-1804). The impact of existentialism and personalism on moral theology should not be underestimated. The trend is away from an ultralegal, antipersonal, computer-style concept of morality and sin. The thrust is upon individual responsibility, as witnessed by the relaxation of fast and abstinence laws. Existentialists, like Sartre, Camus, Heidegger, and Marcel, speak much of the "authentic life." Much of this personal emphasis has been good for moral theology, so long as balance is maintained and the importance of objective morality is not minimized.[15]

Mortal Sin. The nature and possibility of mortal sin have been the topics of considerable discussion among moral theologians in the last decade. Traditionally, *mortal sin* has been defined as "the transgression of a divine law in a grievous matter with full knowledge and consent."[16] The law transgressed must be a *divine law*, in the sense that either a natural law or a divine positive law (or both) has been transgressed; the transgression of human law involves a serious matter insofar as it violates either the natural or divine positive law (or both). The matter of the transgression may be serious in itself (e.g., blasphemy); or the matter may be serious because of the circumstances or because of the intention of the transgressor. Mortal sin requires full knowledge of the serious nature of an act and full consent of the will. The influence of passion, coercion, deception, fear, etc., diminishes — and sometimes entirely eradicates — the imputation of guilt. Conscience is the final arbiter.

Mortal sin, fundamentally, involves a rejection of God and the loss of Sanctifying Grace. Some students of moral theology have questioned whether one, single act can truly separate oneself from God, from His love and Grace. Thus, James Kavanaugh writes:

How can a single act send him [man] to Hell? Love is not a single act, nor is its loss. The moral theology that handed us our view of mortal sin and forced us to run trembling to confession was based upon a medieval vision of man. Such a vision has passed, as should our archaic description of sin.[17]

Reflecting the impact of existentialism and personalism, some writers speak of mortal sin only in terms of one's general "life-orientation" and "life-style." One grows in God's love by a series of good acts, by a lifetime of perseverance and dedication, by one's general orientation toward God. One does not prove he is a child of God and is in Grace by a single act; neither does one lose God's love and Grace by a single act. So goes the rationale.

We can only say that the traditional view of mortal sin seems valid, despite the new values and emphases of personalism. An act is either good or it isn't; one's conscience is either satisfied or it isn't. The ultrapersonalist view tends to erase the distinction. Granted that one's general orientation is significant; one who is generally oriented toward God will not remain long in mortal sin. We find it difficult, however, to deny the possibility of seriously offending God in a single act which is *unrepented*. The last word is important: after all, it is not so much the act itself which constitutes mortal sin as *what the act does to the sinner;* one unrepented act *can* reverse one's life-orientation. Civil law certainly assumes that one act is sufficient to put a man in jail.

Personalism is right in stressing life-orientation. Ordinarily, one will die as he has lived. Miracles of Grace can, and no doubt do, happen on one's deathbed; but one should not be presumptuous of God's Grace. Augustine's prayer, "I want to be chaste, Lord, but not yet," ought not to be our own. It is inconceivable to us that one who has lived a consistently moral life should lose his soul in his final moments because of a single act. Divine Providence does not operate that way. God would at least give such a person the opportunity for repentance.

We believe the scope of mortal sin might have been unnecessarily extensive in the past. To deliberately eat meat on Friday, for example — insofar as the act involved a rejection of Church authority and indirectly the divine command to do penance — was considered to be a mortal sin. One might be sent to Hell for eating meat on Friday just as surely as if one poisoned his mother-in-law. Presumably, one would receive a hotter place in Hell for the latter. Laws of fasting were binding under pain of mortal sin. We feel that moral theology in general and human positive law in particular need to be very careful as to what is called a mortal sin; the term should not be stretched thin. It is presently considered to be a mortal sin to deliberately and without a sufficient reason miss Mass on Sunday (or Saturday evening in place of Sunday) and Holy Days of obligation. At this writing, the Code of Canon Law is undergoing an extensive revision, the first since 1917.

As Fulton J. Sheen has pointed out many times in his writings, sin must be seen, not as simply the breaking of a law, but the severance of a relationship with a Person. Sin injures either oneself, or one's neighbor, or the good of society. This injury involves a "fundamental option" which severs one from the divine purposes and, hence, from God Himself. In this context, sin is the most serious business in the world.

Perhaps the Church has been ultralegalistic in some instances in the past. The Church feels the weighty responsibility for guiding souls to their eternal salvation; if the Church must "sin" by either excess or defect in moral theology, the Church has opted for excess in the past. We see a moderating trend within the Church in moral theology. Christ excoriated the Scribes and Pharisees for placing heavy burdens on men's shoulders (cf. Matt. 23:4). The Church is now lifting more than "a finger" to ease the burden.

II. THE THEOLOGICAL VIRTUES

The word *virtue* comes from a Latin word, *vir*, meaning *man*. Aristotle defined virtue as "the state of character which makes a man good and which makes him do his own work well."[18] Plato and Aristotle both spoke of the four cardinal virtues: prudence, justice, temperance, and fortitude. The Book of Wisdom (8:7) refers to these four virtues. The *theological virtues* are three: faith, hope, and charity; they differ from the natural virtues in that they are a free gift of God, supernaturally infused, leading man to his supernatural destiny.

Faith. That man does not live by bread alone is no cliché; faith is a fundamental and profound fact of human existence. *Faith* means belief on the word of another. Faith is essential even in the natural order. I have faith (and hope), for example, that the breakfast cereal I ate this morning is free of poison; I have faith that the producer of the product is competent and trustworthy. That the Vatican is in Rome I believe on faith, on the testimony of others. I have not been to Rome personally; I have no *intrinsic evidence* that the Vatican is in Rome. Astronomers tell me that the sun is over ninety million miles from the earth; I cannot prove this fact for myself. I know that 2 times 2 equals 4; I have intellectual evidence of this truth. But I take on the *testimony* of chemists that water is composed of two atoms of hydrogen and one atom of oxygen.

If one is to take the word of other human beings concerning natural facts of human existence, then, *a fortiori*, one should be willing to accept the testimony of God Himself concerning truths of the supernatural order. That God has revealed Himself to man in a supernatural manner and has revealed supernatural truths was established in Chapter I. Faith can be defined as "a divinely infused virtue, whereby we firmly hold as true whatever God has revealed, because He, the all-truthful, has revealed it."[19] St. Paul tells us that faith is "the substance of things to be hoped for, the evidence of things that are not seen" (Heb. 11:1).

Supernatural faith is necessary for salvation. St. Paul teaches that "without faith it is impossible to please God" (Heb. 11:6). Christ said, "He that does not believe shall be condemned" (Mark 16:16). The necessary truths of salvation are given to every man who desires them. Thomas Aquinas said that God would send an angel, if that were necessary.

Faith is necessarily one and complete; there cannot be two or more "faiths"; nor can one accept some truths of faith and reject others. Faith is the perfection of reason, as reason is the perfection of the senses.. Faith preserves freedom and answers the fundamental questions of human existence. Faith does not destroy reason, anymore than a telescope destroys vision; faith enlarges and perfects knowledge. Faith preserves quality and gives one "the mind of Christ." Faith is received at Baptism, incorporating one into the Mystical Body of Christ. Faith is steadfast; "a thousand difficulties do not make one doubt," in the words of Cardinal Newman.

The sins against faith are infidelity, apostasy, and heresy. An *infidel* is one who has been presented the truths of Revelation but rejects them. An *apostate* is one who has accepted the truths of Revelation but later rejects them. A *heretic* is one who holds doctrinal error. The subjective guilt of infidelity, apostasy, and heresy depends upon the state of one's conscience, which God alone can judge.

The Christian Faith is the most precious of human possessions, "the pearl of great price." It would seem that some would sell this treasure "for a mess of pottage." Faith can be lost — through egotism, materialism, secularism, sin, indifferentism, rationalism, positivism, scientism, and empiricism. Faith, like a mustard seed, must be nurtured.[20]

Hope. "*Hope* is a supernatural, infused virtue by which, with reliance on God's omnipotence, goodness and fidelity, we look forward to eternal salvation and the necessary means to obtain it."[21] The theological virtue of hope is necessary for all who have sufficiently recognized eternal happiness with God to be man's last end.

One sins against hope by having no desire for the possession of God as the *Summum Bonum.* Placing material creatures and temporal goals above the goal of everlasting salvation is a sin against hope. *Despair,* or giving up all hope of salvation and the means to attain it, is a serious affront to the goodness, mercy, and power of the Almighty. "Hope springs eternal"; till man becomes intrinsically wicked and God ceases to be infinitely good (neither of which can happen), there is always hope. "A contrite and humbled heart, O God, You will not despise" (Psalms 50:19).

Presumption sins against hope by assuming that one can attain salvation through his own power alone or by assuming that God will grant salvation regardless of what one does. It is presumptuous to expect the merits of Christ exclusive of all good works to effect salvation. The "faith alone" theory is simply not compatible with the virtues of hope and charity.

Some find a great obstacle to the virtue of hope in the existence of evil in the world. Evil is basically a negative reality, the absence or deprivation of a good that ought to be present. The problem of evil has perplexed philosophers for centuries.[22] No finite creature can absolutely demand every perfection of its nature at all times; hence, the possibility of evil. Evil should present no insuperable obstacle to the virtue of hope; in the plan of Divine Providence, evil can be turned to good. "It is an ill wind that blows no good"; man can rise above physical and moral evils and use them as steppingstones to union with God.

Charity. Centuries before Newton enunciated the laws of gravity and motion, St. Augustine spoke of a spiritual law of gravitation. *"Pondus meum, amor meus* (my weight, my love)," said the Bishop of Hippo. From the lowliest atom to the highest angel, all creatures tend toward their end through the medium of love, the "bond of perfection."

Charity is "a supernatural, infused virtue by which we love God as the highest good for His own sake and ourselves and our neighbor for God's sake."[23] A perfect love of God takes away mortal sin and includes justification insofar as no other means (e.g., Baptism or Penance) is available; hence, the pre-eminence of the virtue of charity.

A Christian self-love is based upon both a natural and supernatural necessity. One has a duty to grow in virtue, to learn more about his Christian Faith, and to take reasonable care of his body and soul. One must love his neighbor as himself, regardless of race, creed, ethnic origin, or socioeconomic status. "By this will all men know that you are My disciples, if you have love for one another," said Our Lord (John 13:35). Persons are not to be *tolerated;* they are to be *loved.* In the total giving of oneself, one fully recovers himself in the love of God: "He who loses his life for My sake, will find it" (Matt. 10:39).

Every sin is an offense against charity. Especially opposed to charity are hatred of God and religion; egotism, or an inordinate love of self; seduction; scandal; and discrimination against one's neighbor. Charity commands that we foster the virtue of religion, humility, meekness (which is not *weakness*), forgiveness, and fraternal correction. One must be willing to give of his superflous goods to help the impoverished.[24]

Loving a person is not necessarily the same as *liking* a person. Liking depends on taste; loving is grounded in the theological virtue and the love of God. *"De gustibus non disputandi* (concerning taste there is no disputing)," said Augustine. We cannot like everyone (Will Rogers notwithstanding); we can love everyone.

In Heaven faith will no longer be necessary, for now we know; hope will no longer be needed, for now we possess; only charity will remain. Philosophy studies *ens* (being); theology studies *caritas* (love). The greatest revelation of all is that God is Love: *"Deus est caritas"* (1 John 4:16).

III. THE TEN COMMANDMENTS

"Man has never reconciled himself to the Ten Commandments," write Will and Ariel Durant.[25] The Ten Commandments have been around for a long time; but greed, war, killing, deceit, adultery, injustice, and hatred continue in the hearts of men. Ours is a planet in rebellion.

The Decalogue was given to Moses by God on Mount Sinai through a special Revelation.[26] The Commandments are positive laws having their foundation in the natural law. The Third Commandment prescribes that the Sabbath day be kept holy; reason, while not positing any certain day, does suggest that man set aside a certain time for rest and divine worship. The first three Commandments regulate man's relations with God; the last seven regulate man's relations with his fellow man.

(1) "I, the Lord, am your God .... You shall not have other gods besides Me" (Ex. 20:2-3). Vatican Council I paid reason its highest compliment when the Council stated that reason alone can know of God's existence with certainty. Both reason and the First Commandment require that man should give God His due; God and His holy will must be "number one" in human affairs. Atheism, religious indifferentism, agnosticism, superstition, materialism, and secularism are all opposed to this Commandment.

The world has its own "gods": fame, security, pleasure, power, science (apart from God), sex, wealth, etc. All of these have their proper place, but they must never become a misplaced infinity. They must not take the place of God, Who is "a jealous God" (Ex. 20:5).

(2) "You shall not take the name of the Lord, your God, in vain" (Ex. 20:7). Surely this Commandment is frequently violated today. The name of God is used as a term of exclamation, of emphasis, or simply as an expletive. God's name deserves better; one ordinarily would not use the names of his parents in such a manner. Why abuse the name of God, the infinite Creator of the universe?

The thoughtless use of God's name ordinarily would involve venial sin at most; however, insofar as contempt, ridicule, or blasphemy is involved, one could sin mortally. Man is commanded to revere God's name and those things associated with religion. Oaths and vows are binding under this Commandment. Sceptics, cynics, and scoffers of religion are in violation of God's Second Commandment.

(3) **"Remember to keep holy the Sabbath day"** (Ex. 20:8). This is the only Commandment to be prefaced by the word *remember*. God seems to be indicating that man might easily gloss over his obligation to set aside time for divine worship. The world is too much with us; the temptation to make more money, to "beat the competition" is so strong. Why set aside a day for the Lord?

God in His wisdom knows that man needs at least one day out of the week for rest, detachment from worldly cares, recreation, and participation in divine worship in communion with his fellow man. Lately, the world has professed a superior wisdom, with grocery stores, department stores, and other commercial enterprises remaining open on Sunday. We suggest that by a common agreement, one day of the week — acceptable to people of all faiths — be set aside for rest and divine worship, with only necessary enterprises involving health, welfare, or recreation being allowed to function. Our society will be happier and healthier for having observed the Third Commandment.[27]

(4) **"Honor your father and your mother ..."** (Ex. 20:12). All legitimate authority comes from God, be it the authority of the Church, the state, or the family. No society can function normally without authority. The question, therefore, is not whether there should be authority; rather, the problem is that authority be exercised responsibly and that those who are subject to authority be obedient to its legitimate demands.

The Fourth Commandment prescribes that children honor and obey their parents in all that is good; parents have the duty to provide for the spiritual and material needs of their children. Citizens of a state are obliged to obey all civil laws that are not immoral. Patriotism is a virtue; chauvinism is not. Likewise, members of Christ's Mystical Body must respect and obey ecclesiastical authority in all that is not immoral and contrary to one's own conscience.

We live in a time characterized by a general breakdown of authority. Perhaps our understanding of what legitimate authority is and how it should function in modern society is undergoing radical change. A natural tension has always existed between authority and freedom, between the governor and the governed. Democratic principles have become permanently ingrained in the Western mind. Democracy is not anarchy; nor is absolutism necessarily from God. We can only hope that modern society, both Church and state, will find the most salubrious balance between authority and freedom, a balance which will work most effectively for the common good.

(5) "You shall not kill" (Ex. 20:13). Human life possesses a sacred character, inasmuch as the body is informed by a spiritual, immortal soul; inasmuch as God is the Author of human life; and inasmuch as man has been redeemed by the precious blood of Christ. Human life must be taken seriously; hence, the Fifth Commandment forbids the deliberate and direct taking of a human life, either one's own life or the life of another.

As corollaries to the Fifth Commandment, one is obliged to take reasonable care of his health and to use the ordinary means to do so; one is obliged to observe moderation in food and drink;[28] and one must refrain from the use of hard drugs which substantially alter one's physical and mental condition. Immoderate anger (as distinguished from "righteous indignation") and mutilation of the body without a sufficient reason are also forbidden by the Fifth Commandment.

Moral theologians have generally maintained the position that one may defend himself against an unjust aggressor even to the extent of taking the life of the unjust aggressor if this be the only means available for saving one's own life. Certainly the life of the innocent party must take precedence over the life of the unjust aggressor if a desperate situation is reduced to this alternative. A defensive war is morally justified by this same rationale.[29] Some moral theologians question whether it is ever morally justifiable to use atomic or nuclear weapons, since the good to be achieved is not proportionate to the evil effect of the means used.

Capital punishment has been traditionally defended as the state's right to defend itself from pernicious criminals; the casuistry here is not quite so convincing, and the question continues to be debated. Some states have, in fact, outlawed capital punishment.[30] It is by no means self-evident that capital punishment acts as an effective deterrent to serious felonies.

The question of abortion has taken on special significance in contemporary society. Because of the importance of this topic, we have devoted an entire chapter to the biological, philosophical, and sociological aspects of abortion (see Chap. IV).

(6) **"You shall not commit adultery"** (Ex. 20:14). Chastity, as defined by Aquinas, is a virtue that *controls* "the tendencies of sex."[31] Notice that Aquinas does not limit chastity to total sexual abstinence; the married can, and should, practice the virtue of chastity. The term *a vow of chastity* — meaning total sexual abstinence — does not totally coincide with the Thomistic definition of chastity.

The Sixth Commandment specifically forbids the act of adultery, or coitus performed by a married person with another who is not the former's lawful spouse. Other passages in the Bible specifically condemn fornication (sexual intercourse between two unmarried persons) and sodomy (homosexual relations). Contraception presents a special problem to moral theology; the morality of artificially regulating conception has been briskly debated in the last decade. Nowhere does the Bible clearly condemn the practice. The Bible does condemn "unnatural" sex acts; but whether or not contraception is strictly unnatural is precisely the crux of the problem. Because of the special significance of the morality of contraception in particular and of human sexuality in general, we have devoted a special chapter to these topics (see Chap. VI).

There can be no doubt that we live in a period of sexual laxity. Norman Vincent Peale cites statistics showing that 1 out of 6 brides is pregnant; a poll of the senior class at Columbia revealed that 83 percent favored premarital relations; venereal disease among adolescents rose 130 percent between 1956 and 1961.[32] The urgency for clear thinking, of distinguishing between what is and what is not sinful in the area of human sexuality cannot be overestimated.

(7) **"You shall not steal"** (Ex. 20:15). The right to private ownership is grounded in the nature of man and the nature of the universe. Material possessions are an extension of one's person; the human person, as a composit of matter and spirit, requires the use of the goods of this earth. But man's personality is best served if he has the exclusive right to control and dispose of certain temporal goods, which is the meaning of *ownership*. Hence, private property has its foundation in the nature of man and in the natural law.

The Seventh Commandment assumes the right of private property. Statism, or absolute socialism, which denies the right of private property, is immoral. Communism, which theoretically holds that eventually the governmental ownership of all property will be unnecessary, with all government "withering away," is highly unrealistic and basically immoral in its denial of private property and its overemphasis on the material.[33]

Private property, of course, presents problems. Greed, class injustice and strife are always ready to rear their ugly heads. Socialism and communism are right in decrying the injustices which can, and do, occur in a capitalistic, free enterprise system; but socialism and communism offer no acceptable solutions. The Seventh and Tenth Commandments are the only true solution to greed and social injustice: do not take what is not yours; give to others in their need. The *right* to property is personal; the *use* of property is socially conditioned.

The right to private ownership need not be exercised by all people at all times and places. There is nothing intrinsically evil about the common ownership of material goods if there is a sufficient reason for such common ownership. Members of religious communities, for example, renounce their right to ownership, for a spiritual purpose. Public, tax-supported property is held in common. An analogy is seen in the elementary right to marry which belongs to mankind in general, but need not be exercised by every individual in all circumstances; the right to marry may be lawfully renounced for a spiritual purpose or for some other good reason. Christ *counseled voluntary* poverty and virginity as steps to Christian perfection; He obviously was not establishing a norm for mankind in general. Thomas Aquinas believed that all property would have been held in common in the state of Original Justice.

(8) **"You shall not bear false witness against your neighbor"** (Ex. 20:16). The gift of reason and speech distinguishes man from the rest of creation. Man alone has spiritual ideas and universal concepts and is able to express his ideas to others by means of words, either oral or written. The Eighth Commandment forbids one to abuse the gift of speech by knowingly uttering a falsehood so as to deceive or mislead another who has a right to know.[34] Veracity is a virtue; lying is a vice.

Lies can take various forms: one can bear false witness concerning the good name and character of another, which is *calumny.* Oral calumny is called *slander;* written calumny is called *libel. Contumely* is unjustly dishonoring a person by insult in words or gestures. *Hypocrisy* can be defined as a lie expressed in action. Christ had harsh words for the Scribes and Pharisees·· in this regard, calling them "whited sepulchres" (cf. Matt. 23:27). *Detraction* is unnecessarily disclosing what is true about a person so as to cause the person harm. Gossip columnists, take heed!

(9) **"You shall not covet your neighbor's wife . . ."** (Ex. 20:17). Whereas the Sixth Commandment forbids immoral sexual *acts*, the Ninth Commandment forbids immoral sexual *thoughts*. Obviously, if it is immoral to perform a certain act, it is also immoral to consciously and deliberately entertain the thought of committing the act. If adultery is wrong, then one may not even covet another partner other than one's spouse. Christ warned that "anyone who so much as looks with lust at a woman has already committed adultery with her in his heart" (Matt. 5:28).

Scrupulosity, of course, is always possible in the area of one's thoughts. There is no guilt in being attracted to the goods of this earth, be it sex, a shiny automobile, etc. Guilt can be imputed to one only to the extent that he deliberately entertains thoughts of immorality; one is not required, ostrichlike, to bury his head in the sand. Everything in this world is good; only the *misuse* of material things is evil.

(10) **"You shall not covet your neighbor's house . . ., nor his male or female slave, nor his ox or ass, nor anything else that belongs to him"** (Ex. 20:17). As the Ninth Commandment reverts to the Sixth Commandment in forbidding even the willful thought of committing sexual immorality, so does the Tenth Commandment revert to the Seventh Commandment in forbidding avarice, greed, and the immoderate *desire* to possess material goods.

"God saw that all He had made was very good," Genesis tells us (1:31). Opinions as to the relative goodness of the material world have ranged from the ultradualism of Zoroastrianism and the Manichean view that all matter is intrinsically evil to materialistic and pantheistic philosophies which make matter and the goods of this earth tantamount to God Himself. Between these extremes, various nuances are possible. For example, one cannot read the great spiritual classic *The Imitation of Christ,* attributed to Thomas á Kempis, without getting the distinct impression that there is something basically suspect — if not downright evil — about the material goods of this world. "As often as I have been amongst men, said one, I have returned less a man."[35] These views do not seem to be in the spirit of Vatican II, which called for *koinonia* (fellowship) for the salvation of the world.

The Seventh and Tenth Commandments give us the true perspective concerning the material goods of this world: they are from God and, as such, are good in themselves. Larceny and avarice are to be condemned; the virtue of detachment, which keeps material goods in their proper place and order, is to be practiced. Material things are to lead man *toward* God, not away from Him.

"A man's character is his fate," said the Greek philosopher Heraclitus. Morality gets at the very roots of human existence. Inscribed over the grave of Immanuel Kant in Königsberg are his famous words: "The starry heavens above me; the moral law within me." The great German philosopher was supremely aware of the ultimate realities: God, the universe, and the free human spirit. George Washington likewise expressed his concern for morality in his *Farewell Address:* ". . . reason and experience both forbid us to expect that national morality can prevail in exclusion of religious principles." True religion and true morality are basically inseparable; God is the Underwriter and Guarantor of the moral law. And it is by living the Christian life that we shall be with God for all eternity.

There is an oxymoronic quality to Christian morality. Christ never promised His followers euphoria, fame, or material wealth. He asks us to take up our crosses daily and follow Him. Christ did promise His peace to those who live the Christian life: an abiding joy and peace of soul which the world alone, in its traitorous trueness, cannot give. We are not in agreement with those who would simplistically reduce the Christian religion to a matter of "good psychology" and "good business." Christian morality can never be divorced from asceticism and a life of the Cross; but by "losing one's life," by a life of self-discipline and mortification (words infrequently heard in Catholicism today), one shall have affirmed life to the fullest and shall find life everlasting. Such is the Christian paradox.

St. Francis of Assisi expressed it beautifully:

Lord, make me an instrument of Your peace. Where there is hatred, let me sow love; where there is injury, pardon; where there is doubt, faith; where there is despair, hope; where there is darkness, light; and where there is sadness, joy. O Divine Master, grant that I may not so much seek to be consoled as to console; to be understood as to understand; to be loved as to love. For it is in giving that we receive; · it is in pardoning that we are pardoned; and it is in dying that we are born to eternal life.

— "Peace Prayer"

PART II

CATHOLICISM AND ABORTION

Let the little children come to Me, and do not hinder them, for of such is the Kingdom of God.
— Mark 10:14

AMERICA AND ABORTION

Guidelines from Philosophy, Science, and History

Thou shalt not kill.
— Fifth Commandment of the Decalogue

See that you do not despise one of these little ones; for I tell you, their angels in Heaven always behold the face of My Father in Heaven.
— Matt. 18:10

... nor shall any State deprive any person of life, liberty, or property without due process of law ....
— Fourteenth Amendment to the Constitution of the United States

I will give no deadly drug to any, though it be asked of me, nor will I counsel such, and especially I will not aid a woman to procure abortion.
— Hippocratic Oath

From the moment of its conception life must be guarded with the greatest care, while abortion and infanticide are unspeakable crimes.
— Vatican II, *Gaudium et Spes*, n. 51

DANIEL Callahan, former editor of *Commonweal*, sees the fetus as "potential human life." Our position in this chapter will be that there are only human beings with potential, but no "potential human beings."

I. PHILOSOPHY AND ABORTION

What did Thomas Aquinas say on the subject of the unborn fetus? Robert Edward Brennan, the noted Dominican scholar, in his work *Thomistic Psychology*, explains that Aquinas subscribed to a theory of "ensoulment" whereby the material substrate which eventually becomes a human body is previously informed by infrahuman souls before the organism actually becomes human. Thus, a human being first exists as a simple vegetative organism, then as an animal, and finally becomes human by the infusion of a spiritual soul created by God.[1]

Opposed to the polymorphic theory of Aquinas is the position of *monomorphism* which states that the human soul, and it alone, is present in the organism from the instant of conception. Proponents of polymorphism object that the monomorphic theory does violence to a principle of proportion which demands a certain ratio between matter and form in the genesis of a living being. Monomorphists answer that, even in the zygotic stage of human ontogenesis, the fertilized ovum has all the potentialities of a perfect human body. The human soul is present, they say, operationally supplying the principle of human epigenesis. In the final analysis, the union of sperm and ovum is brought about by a reproductive act that is wholly human in all of its elements so that the material receptacle of the rational soul is always aptly disposed.

Celestine N. Bittle, O.F.M. Cap., points out in *Man and Morals* that, philosophically and medically, the exact time when the rational soul enters the fetus, making it a human person, is unknown. Both the polymorphic and monomorphic theories may be considered probable. Father Bittle states further that in a question of such importance, we must accept the view that the body of the fetus is animated by the rational soul at the moment of conception, since one is obliged to follow the safer side when the morality of an act is involved.[2]

The Thomistic doctrine of a succession of infrahuman souls during gestation fails to give a sufficient reason why the zygote develops into an animal and why the animal develops sufficiently to be an apt material substrate for a rational soul. Aquinas alludes to a "formative virtue" present in the semen; yet, modern medical science knows of no such "formative virtue" present in the fluid containing the reproductive cells. A more logical explanation of why the zygote develops into a human being is that the human, spiritual soul is present from the first moment of conception, guiding the organism as its vital principle along the various stages of human development.

That sometime during gestation a rational soul is infused by God, making the fetus a rational human being, is unacceptable to this writer, mainly because we do not conceive of God making numerous special interventions in the course of natural processes. Augustine, the learned Bishop of Hippo, uttered a profound truth many centuries ago when he spoke of *"rationes seminales,"* or germinal causes, implanted in matter by the Creator at the first moment of creation, to be developed and ramified according to His divine plan during the course of time. So also, a human being begins life as a one-celled zygote, containing the genes and "germinal causes" that will require many years to develop and become manifest.

Simply because man in his embryonic and fetal stages of life does not manifest rational, intelligent behavior is no sufficient reason to assume that the embryo and fetus are not *persons*, defined as creatures possessing at least the latent capacity for intellectual and volitional activity, depending upon the apt development of the organism. There is an old Scholastic axiom that says, "What is first in intention is last in execution." Thus, the corporeal universe existed millions of years before algae and invertebrates appeared in Pre-Cambrian times, some 620 million years ago. More millions of years elapsed before man finally appeared in the Pleistocene epoch, about a million years ago. Man was actually "first in intention" in the purposes of the Creator but "last in execution." Any product of evolution and growth is best evaluated, not in its primitive condition, but in its final development. We should not be deceived, therefore, by considering a human organism in a primitive stage of development as anything less than human.

Who would suspect, upon examining a chrysalis, that from it will emerge a fleet-winged butterfly with gorgeous coloring and tremulous beauty? Who would suspect, upon examining a tiny fecundated ovum, that from it would develop a Plato, a Michelangelo, a Shakespeare, or an Einstein? A principle laid down by Aristotle is pertinent to any discussion concerning the morality of abortion: "We judge the nature and the worth of a being, not by its origin, but by the goal at which it finally arrives." Aquinas taught: "The potency of a cause is greater, the more remote the effects to which it extends."[3]

II. BIOLOGY AND ABORTION

What does biology say about the status of the unborn fetus? Leo J. Hombach, S.J., of the University of Santa Clara, says:

As a biologist, one doesn't have much of a choice when asked to state when human life begins. The character of any animal depends on its chromosomal content. When you have any organism with forty-six chromosomes and the genes proper to a human being — then you have a human being.

Dr. Peter Amenta, of Hahnemann Medical School, puts it succinctly: "When the sperm and egg fuse, the newly formed cell has conferred upon it the degree of H.S. *(homo sapiens)* with all the rights and privileges pertaining."

There is nothing magical about a fetus passing through the birth canal which suddenly makes it an actual, no longer a potential, human being. A mother's vagina has no special power to confer upon her newborn infant the right to life which was not already possessed by the unborn fetus. Birth, in the final analysis, is but one event — albeit a most important event — in the total spectrum of human ontogenesis.

Even after birth it is some time before the infant will manifest rational behavior. Yet, some would deny that a real human being exists prior to birth, but would not think of denying life to a newborn child on the grounds that the child is not yet manifesting rational behavior associated with a person. The logic breaks down. Some consider the fact that the fetus is totally dependent upon the mother militates against considering it a real person. Who can deny that the newborn infant is totally dependent upon its mother, or other human beings, for its continued existence? *Viability* is a relative term. Manifestation of rationality and independence cannot be considered a real criterion for judging whether or not a human being exists.

One can logically conclude from the biological facts that at no time in the process of human development — from zygote to morula, to blastocyst, to embryo, to fetus, to infant, to youth, to adult, and finally to "senior citizen" — is the individual known as *homo sapiens* anything less than a real human being with an immortal soul destined for eternity. Nature knows no interruption from fertilized ovum to old age, from a physiological standpoint. Why should one attempt to make an arbitrary division in human development in terms of being actually or potentially human? Where make such a division? On what iron-clad foundation?

The argument has been advanced, mainly by advocates of women's liberation, that a woman has a right to control her own body, including the right to have an abortion. The argument is fallacious for two reasons: (1) A fetus cannot biologically be totally identified with the mother's body. The mother provides nourishment and a suitable environment for the unborn child; but the fetus alone directs the pregnancy during the various stages of gestation. The fetus maintains a biological autonomy, self-direction and self-preservation. (2) The rights that one has over his or her own body are relative, not absolute: they are relative to ethical norms, to the moral law, to the welfare of others and the good of society.

Nature has its say. One may rightfully question the moral acceptability of behavior that is harmful to one's own health or the health of another. Good morals and good health ought to be highly compatible. For example, promiscuous sexual relations can result in venereal disease; here nature has its say in proscribing sexual relations outside of marriage. A report published in London cited some 75 scientific papers from 12 countries which indicate that induced abortion can have deleterious effects upon a woman's ability to reproduce healthy children. The research indicates that between 2 and 5 percent of women having induced abortions become sterile; between 30 and 40 percent have miscarriages; still-births double; premature births increase by 40 percent. Some cases of cerebral palsy, epilepsy, deafness, blindness, and autism were linked to complications of pregnancy resulting from previously induced abortion.

Woman has a unique vocation in sharing with the Creator the production of a human life. This vocation should not be taken lightly. Woman is the divinely appointed custodian of embryonic and fetal human life. To deliberately abort that life for any reason short of the preservation of her own life is to renounce an essential part of her own nature and to denigrate her unique calling for motherhood. The fetus may be the result of an illegitimate relationship; but to commit the crime of feticide to cover up a previous mistake is to be guilty of two sins instead of one.

The plight of an unwed mother is admittedly an unhappy situation; but life and society in general teach that individuals are responsible for their actions. The responsibility of the male in an unwanted pregnancy is not to be overlooked or downplayed. Nor should the need for pastoral help and counseling concerning appropriate alternatives to abortion be neglected. Abortion on demand seems to erase individual responsibility for the procreation of life. A study at Johns Hopkins University revealed that 46 percent of single American girls become nonvirgins by the time they are 20. It is estimated that more than 100,000 unmarried teenagers had legal abortions from mid-1971 to mid-1972, and probably another 100,000 teenage girls underwent cirminal abortions during the same period. The availability of abortion on demand, now declared legal in America, weakens the sanction against extramarital and premarital sex relations; such a weakening is an affront and a menace to the institution and sanctity of marriage.

Biology is all on the side of the fetus. To abort a fetus at any stage of development is to be responsible for a human life. We can see no other acceptable conclusion, so far as biology is concerned. Consider some significant stages of pregnancy:

By the beginning of the third week of gestation, the embryo is barely visible to the naked eye.

By the fourth week the head forms and the heart is visible.

By the end of the fourth week, the beginnings of arms and legs appear.

By the sixth week eyes can be seen in the embryo, which is now about a half inch in length.

In the sixth week face and ears form.

By the end of the third month, EKG tracings can be made of the fetus' heartbeat and the fetus' sex can be determined.

By the end of the fourth month, fetal movements may be felt by the mother.

By the end of the fifth month, hair appears on the head of the fetus, which is now about a foot long.

By the end of the seventh month, a child born alive has a better than 50 percent chance for survival; by the end of the eighth month, a better than 90 percent chance for survival; and by the end of the ninth month, the fetus has reached "full term," with a 99 percent chance for survival.

The foregoing sketch indicates that gestation is a continuous process. At every stage we are considering a human being — not a potato or a chimpanzee. We cannot escape the irrefragable conclusion from biology that to abort an embryo or fetus at any stage of development is to be responsible for taking a human life. Abortion is therefore to be considered a morally unacceptable form of birth control.

III. CATHOLICISM AND ABORTION

Most Scholastic philosophers today reject the Thomistic theory of polymorphism. The Catholic Church assumes the presence of an immortal soul from the moment of conception, as reflected in the Church's practice of baptizing a fetus in danger of death.

Heribert Jone, O.F.M. Cap., in his *Moral Theology*, states that whoever procures an abortion or is an accomplice to an abortion incurs excommunication, reserved to the Ordinary, according to Canon 2350.[4] Father Jone also points out that an indirect abortion produced by treatment of a diseased organ of the body, such as a diseased uterus or Fallopian tube, is morally permissible.[5] He further notes that the amniotic fluid is not considered valid matter for the Sacrament of Baptism.[6]

William C. McCready and Andrew M. Greeley report that 80 percent of American Catholics interviewed in 1972 believe that a legal abortion may be obtained when a woman's health is seriously endangered by her pregnancy; in 1965, 61 percent so believed.

In *Morality Is for Persons*, Bernard Haring, C.SS.R., tells of a case published by a famous Austrian gynecologist.[7] A pregnant woman was experiencing dangerous bleeding in her womb. The bleeding could not be stopped by ordinary means. The doctor decided to remove the live embryo and compress the womb. The bleeding was stopped; the mother's life was saved; and she was able to subsequently bear several healthy children.

The ultralegalist, of course, would say that the doctor should have removed the entire uterus; then the abortion would have been indirect. The child was doomed to die by circumstances, independent of any decision by the doctor or mother. Although the child had no chance to live, the mother's life and future fertility might be preserved. Father Haring feels that in this case an abortion was performed only in a medical sense, not in a moral sense.

Aristotle spoke of *epikeia* as the special virtue of prudence and of realism in the lawgiver, who recognizes that no man-made law can be applied mechanically and without exception in all cases. St. Thomas Aquinas, in his *Summa Theologica*,[8] agreed with Aristotle that it is vicious to apply human laws mechanically, without respect to the dignity of man and the common good. St. Alphonsus Liguori, patron of moral theologians, went a step beyond Aristotle and St. Thomas and said that *epikeia* applies to secondary formulations of the natural law as well as to man-made laws.[9] It would seem that *epikeia*, or the sense of exception, would apply to the conduct of the Austrian gynecologist in the above-mentioned case: in the existential situation in which he found himself, he acted as the interpreter of the moral law, and not simply as a programmed automaton that would rigidly enforce an abstract moral precept.

IV. LESSONS FROM HISTORY

Any society that condones wholesale murder of unborn, innocent life simply on the grounds that the individual is unwanted is surely not far away from condoning the murder of the retarded, the psychotic, or the aged and infirmed, on the grounds that they also are "unwanted." The 1971 Florida legislature, in fact, considered (and rejected) a bill to provide "death with dignity" to those suffering needlessly, to the incurably ill, and to the nonproductively retarded.

The Jews of Nazi Germany were "unwanted" by Adolf Hitler; he proceeded to have some 5,750,000 of them exterminated in concentration camps on the grounds that he was ensuring a pure Aryan race, a race of supermen.[10] Surely this was the most heinously outrageous crime of human history (excepting the crucifixion of Christ), a sin crying to Heaven for vengeance. Yet, one wonders if the genocide perpetrated by the Third Reich might have to take second place to the outrageous crime, perpetrated quietly and without headlines in hospitals and clinics throughout the world today, of murdering innocent life *in utero*. These hapless victims are the Holy Innocents of the Twentieth Century.

The foundation of modern Western democracy is built upon the dignity, the sacredness, and the inviolability of human life. We see the practice of abortion corroding and undermining this foundation, just as an irresponsible expenditure of human life in warfare eats away at the cornerstone of our democracy. Furthermore, such wanton killing of human life represents a gross usurpation as well as a grotesque caricature of a right that belongs to God alone.

America, take heed! With the increase in pornography, drug abuse, legal abortion, divorce, promiscuity, and venereal disease in our beloved country, listen to these wise voices of the past: Socrates said the corruption of a society can be measured to the degree that virtues are called vices and vices, virtues. Thus, in the nineteenth century, Nietzsche could say, "Evil, be thou my good!" Alexis Charles de Tocqueville, after coming from France to study democracy in America in the early nineteenth century, said America is great because America is good; he then gave the ominous warning that when America ceases to be good, she will cease to be great. Abraham Lincoln said: "I do not fear that America will ever be destroyed from without, but I fear that it will be destroyed from within."

Will Durant, author of the monumental, eleven-volume *The Story of Civilization*, observes that nations are born Stoic, die Epicurean.[11] In *The Lessons of History*, Dr. Durant and his wife, Ariel, tell us: "The only real revolution is in the enlightenment of the mind and the improvement of character, the only real emancipation is individual, and the only real revolutionists are philosophers and saints."[12]

Arnold J. Toynbee, eminent British historian and author of the twelve-volume *A Study of History*, shows us that most of the twenty-six civilizations of recorded history have fallen from internal decay rather than from external conquest.[13]

Is there hope for America? "Western civilization with its Christian roots is not perishing; it is beginning to come into its own," writes Archbishop Fulton J. Sheen in *Footprints in a Darkened Forest*.[14] The potential for goodness and greatness in Western society is tremendous, based on our Judeo-Christian, Greek, and Roman heritage. Lincoln called America the last, best hope of mankind.

America will not fail: the America that insists that all men are created equal; that all men have the right to life, liberty, and happiness; the America that has spilled its treasure in two world wars in the defense of freedom; the America that has fed the hungry, clothed the naked, and harbored the harborless; the America that protects freedom of speech and freedom of religion; the America with the national motto, "In God we trust"; the America that is "one nation under God." No, *that* America cannot fail.

The only America that can fail is the America that has forgotten its origin and its destiny; the America that has pulled up its roots and withdrawn its antennae; the America absorbed in materialism and expediency; the America that has declared its independence of God, of the family of nations, of moral restraint, of spiritual purpose and the duty to exercise power responsibly — such an America could fail!

We ask God to "stand beside her and guide her through the night with a light from above." We pray that America shall not be weighed in the balance and found wanting.

V. THE SUPREME COURT DECISION OF 1973

On January 22, 1973, the U.S. Supreme Court, by a vote of 7 to 2 (a Catholic Justice voted with the majority), ruled that states may not forbid abortion during the first six months of pregnancy. John Cardinal Krol, President of the National Conference of Catholic Bishops, decried the decision:

The Supreme Court's decision today is an unspeakable tragedy for the nation. It is hard to think of any decision in the 200 years of our history which has had more disastrous implications for our stability as a civilized society. The ruling drastically diminishes the constitutional guarantee of right to life, and in doing so, sets in motion developments which are terrifying to contemplate.

The majority opinion of the Court, written by Associate Justice Blackmun, distinguished between a viable and a non-viable fetus. A state may legislate for the protection of a viable fetus (one that can survive outside of the mother's womb); but a state may not interfere with a woman's and her doctor's decision to abort a nonviable fetus. What, we ask, makes viability the deciding factor? Viability has no direct bearing upon the nature of the fetus. Either a fetus is human or it isn't, regardless of its viability. Is not the state being recreant in its duty to protect the right of a nonviable fetus to develop into a viable fetus? We are mystified at the logic, or lack of it, exhibited by the highest court in the land. Surely, to kill a human fetus that is presently in a state of nonviability is as much of a crime as killing a viable fetus.

The lessons of history cry out that human life in all stages of development, from zygote to old age, is to be respected. Some oriental customs require that one compute his age from the time of conception, not from the time of birth. Perhaps we of the West have unjustly downplayed the prenatal existence of a human being. The quality of life is important; but the quality of life will never be improved by a wanton disregard for the right to life. Civil society has no right to abscond from its duty to protect human life in all of its many forms. It is both ironic and inconsistent that the same Supreme Court that declared capital punishment to be an unconstitutional option for a jury has declared state laws to protect the nonviable fetus — which has committed no crime — to be unlawful. Our Constitution guarantees the protection of human life; no distinction is made between viability and nonviability. Our Declaration of Independence states that life is a right bestowed by the Creator. A fetus has sometimes been recognized by state law as a legal person with the right of inheritance.

More than eleven million people of Indochina have been killed, wounded, or left homeless, mostly by U.S. bombing. About

a half million legal abortions were estimated to have been performed in America in 1972; an estimated million illegal abortions
were performed during the same period. Our country must return to a respect for life; and this respect for life must begin with
life *in utero*.

In his written opinion, Justice Harry A. Blackmun went to
great length to show that abortion laws are of relatively recent
vintage; that their prime intent seemed to be to protect the
health of the mother when abortion procedures were much more
dangerous; that Greek, Roman, and Jewish tradition by no
means was unanimous in condemning abortion; that there is not
today a conclusive philosophical, theological, or medical proof of
when human life actually begins; that various criteria — for
example, the 40 (male)-80 (female)-days-after-conception ensoulment theory of Aristotle and Aquinas, "quickening," and
viability — have been used to determine the start of human life;[15]
that the Constitution does not clearly indicate that the unborn
are to be legally regarded as persons, as the term is used in the
Fourteenth Amendment; that laws proscribing abortion during
the first and second trimesters of pregnancy must be constitutionally regarded as an unlawful invasion of a woman's right to
privacy.

We submit that none of the points made by Justice Blackmun are sufficiently cogent to legalize abortion on demand.
Some of his arguments are purely pragmatic in character and do
not come to grips with the essential question at hand. Unanimity
of history, philosophy, and science is not required in determining
the morality of a given form of human behavior. The Court has
decided upon viability as the determining norm for the beginning of a human person. Where does the Constitution give the
Court the right to decide and, in effect, legislate when a human
life begins? Rightly did Justice Byron White call the decision "an
exercise of raw judicial power," smacking of judicial legislation.
Why does not "quickening," or the power of movement by the
fetus (occurring by the end of the fourth month) qualify as the
deciding norm? We must revert to the central theme of this
chapter that any point after conception for determining the
beginning of a human life will necessarily be arbitrary and inadequate. Again we say that human life begins when the pro-
nuclei of sperm and ovum fuse to form the individual zygote — a
biological event commonly known as conception. The newly
formed zygote has its own special chromosomal character. Con-

ception is an *event*, not a prolonged process; though Justice Blackmun mentions a current theory to the contrary, embryology continues to define conception in terms of the union of sperm and ovum. All of the human potentialities are present in the zygote from the first moment of its existence. Nothing the Supreme Court has said can alter the conclusion we arrived at earlier: to deliberately abort prenatal human life at any stage of development is to be responsible for a human life.

Justice William Rehnquist, in his dissenting opinion, noted that when the Fourteenth Amendment was adopted in 1868, there were at least thirty-six laws enacted by state or territorial legislatures which limited abortion. The drafters of the Amendment and the legislatures evidently saw no contradiction between the Amendment and the existing laws proscribing abortion. At this writing, there is a movement underway to amend the Constitution so as to define a legal person as including the unborn at all stages of gestation. The states could thus overrule the Supreme Court's decision on abortion. By so doing, our nation could lead the way for other nations — such as Japan, India, the Soviet Union, and most Eastern European countries — to rescind their liberal abortion laws and reaffirm the sacredness and inviolability of human life.

While there is an honest difference of opinion within Catholicism today concerning the morality of contraception, there seems to be an overwhelming consensus among Catholic theologians and scholars that abortion is a morally unacceptable form of birth control. Following the announcement of the Supreme Court's decision on abortion, sixty prominent Catholic theologians signed a statement authored by Father Charles E. Curran of Catholic University. Among the signers were Father William Bassett of Catholic University, Father Richard P. McBrien of Boston College, Msgr. John Tracy Ellis of the University of San Francisco, Father John L. McKenzie of DePaul University, Chicago, and Father John Wright, president of the Catholic Theological Society of America.

Father Curran stated:

In the light of the recent decision of the Supreme Court on abortion laws we Roman Catholic scholars, many of whom disagreed with some of the practical conclusions of the papal encyclical *Humanae Vitae* on artificial contraception, affirm our conviction that individual human life is present before the time of the viability of the fetus. We therefore strongly urge others to accept this understanding and act in accord with it.[16]

John T. Noonan, Jr., writing in the *National Catholic Reporter*, proposes a "Human Life Amendment" to the Constitution which would not only protect the life of the unborn, but the lives of the retarded and senile as well. Noonan notes that the Supreme Court decision on abortion spoke of "persons in the whole sense" and human beings with the "capability of meaningful life" as being protected by the Constitution. The Court seems not far away from denying constitutional rights to the retarded, the psychotic, the senile, and the incurably ill.

Noonan, who has extensively researched the question of contraception and edited a book on abortion, cites the infamous Dred Scott decision rendered by the Supreme Court prior to the Civil War. Striking parallels exist between *Dred Scott v. Sanford*, *Doe v. Bolton*, and *Roe v. Wade*. Chief Justice Roger B. Taney (a Catholic), speaking for seven Democratic justices, decided that Negroes who were of the African race and the descendents of slaves were not and could not become citizens of a state, as the word *citizen* was used by the framers of the Constitution. Negro slaves were then commonly regarded, according to Taney, as an inferior order of beings possessing no rights that a white man need respect. The intervening years had made no change in this constitutional understanding of the term *citizen*, said the Chief Justice. The Missouri Compromise and numerous state laws proscribing slavery were declared unconstitutional. The Court attempted, unsuccessfully, to resolve forever a deep moral issue agitating the American people. The Dred Scott decision was ultimately overruled by a constitutional amendment, and then only after a bloody civil war.

Again, in the twentieth century, the Supreme Court has restricted the meaning of *citizen* and *person* as used in the Constitution to exclude a particular class of human beings, namely, the unborn. In so doing, the Court invalidates laws in all fifty states. While not specifically advocating abortion, *Wade* and *Bolton* make abortion legal, just as *Dred Scott* in effect legalized slavery. Sexual liberty is taken as "given"; "Victorian social concern" is derided. Prostitution can be handily legalized by the rationale provided by the Court. As with *Dred Scott*, pragmatism reigns supreme. In 1867 the Supreme Court had an important opportunity to exercise moral leadership; though five of the justices were Southerners, one wonders if the Court might possibly have averted a civil war through responsible moral persuasion. The Supreme Court in 1973 missed an important opportun-

ity to provide moral leadership for our country and for the world
by affirming respect for human life in all of its stages and conditions. *Time* magazine reports that more than half the world's
population live in countries that permit abortion for social as well
as medical reasons. The Soviet Union passed its first open abortion law in 1920.

One should note that even the viable fetus is not guaranteed
the right to life, since states are not *compelled* to enact such laws.
The Supreme Court held that in the last trimester of pregnancy,
the state has no right to prefer the fetus' life to the health of the
mother— with "health" being defined in physical, emotional,
psychological, familial, and chronological terms. Thus, what
America has at this writing is a blanket, legal approbation of the
destruction of the unborn at any stage of pregnancy for any
reason, or no reason at all; just as in 1857 it was legal in America
to hold a certain class of human beings in slavery. The New York
Times predicts 1.8 million abortions within the year (1974) — all
legal. One further wonders if the newly born infant can find
protection under the Constitution as interpreted by the Supreme
Court. Is a tiny baby a "person in the whole sense" and "capable
of meaningful life" prior to its socialization? One can see how
tragically inadequate and unjust are the criteria imposed by the
Supreme Court upon American society in evaluating a human
life.

In November, 1972, North Dakota and Michigan defeated
proposed liberalization of abortion laws, the people voting in
referendums. Perhaps a national referendum on the issue of
abortion is in order. The American people, the U.S. Congress, and
the state legislatures must have their say on this vital issue. As
with *Dred Scott*, a constitutional amendment may be the only
answer. Such is the lesson of history.[17]

Life is immanent activity, say the philosophers. Only human
immanent activity, along with the life of the angels, has the
power of knowing, loving, and freely serving Almighty God. As
such, human life is sacred, redeemed by the Blood of Christ,
destined for immortality, and of more value than the entire
universe.

PART III

CATHOLICISM AND REFORM

*They bind together heavy and oppressive burdens,
and lay them on men's shoulders; but not with one
finger of their own do they choose to move them.*

— Matt. 23:4

C H A P T E R   V

CATHOLICISM AND CHANGE

Religious Truth in a Changing World

To live is to change; and to be perfect is to have changed often.
— Cardinal Newman

Let them blend modern science and its theories and the understanding of the most recent discoveries with Christian morality and doctrine. Thus their religious practice and morality can keep pace with their scientific knowledge and with an ever-advancing technology.
— Vatican II, *Gaudium et Spes*, n. 62

To identify the new knowledge with heresy is to make orthodoxy synonymous with ignorance.
— Desiderius Erasmus (1466-1536)

To know how to say what other people only think is what makes men poets and sages; and to dare to say what others only dare to think makes men martyrs or reformers.
— Elizabeth Rundle Charles

The old order changeth, yielding place to new;
And God fulfills Himself in many ways,
Lest one good custom should corrupt the world.
— Alfred, Lord Tennyson

When one has no doubt that in fundamentals one is right and secure, one shrinks the less from complete candor. One does not tremble lest to face a new fact may mean to dissolve one's faith.
— Wilfrid Ward

WE live in an age of ferment. Change seems to be the order of the day, the one thing that doesn't change. Some changes are for the better; some are not. All change needs order, direction, insight, and purpose; otherwise change becomes chaos and retrogression. Sexual morality in particular has taken a decided turn for the worse. There is an increased interest in the occult and in Devil worship. "The literature of our time," write Will and Ariel Durant in *Interpretations of Life*, "reeks with the ruins of men who presumed that the Ten Commandments had been

107

abrogated by the reputed death of their reputed Author."[1] Every change needs a valid rationale; no purely human custom ought to be considered sacrosanct and exempt from revision and improvement.

"The new knowledge and the old Faith" has always been a moot topic in the history of the Church. Some felt that the heliocentric theory of Copernicus and the evolutionary theories of Lamarck and Darwin were anti-Biblical and inimical to the Christian Faith. That the earth revolves around the sun is taken pretty much for granted nowadays; evolution as a highly probable explanation of organic development is generally accepted today — with no serious harm done to the Christian Faith. After all, the truths of science and the truths of religion cannot be incompatible when both are rightly understood, since all truth comes from the one Author of the universe. The Bible is not a textbook of natural science; many centuries ago, Augustine observed that the Bible teaches how to go to Heaven, not how the heavens go.

It is of paramount importance, then, that a clear distinction be made between changeable and unchangeable elements in our Christian Faith.

I. THE PHILOSOPHY OF CHANGE

Aristotle (384-322 B.C.), described by Dante as "the master of them who know,"[2] made some profound observations concerning change. He defined the ontological concept of *motus* (loosely translated as *change* or *movement*) as the act of a being in potency while still in potency. Three elements are involved in every change: (1) a starting point (*terminus a quo*); (2) a goal or ending point (*terminus ad quem*); and (3) a transition (*transitus*) from one to the other.

Cardinal Leo Suenens of Belgium, who is best described as a moderate progressive, makes the point that human beings achieve forward movement by keeping one foot on the ground and one foot in the air. The "one foot on the ground" represents one's ties with tradition and essential principles; the "one foot in the air" represents one's openness to newer insights and meaningful change.

All finite, contingent creatures are subject to change, which involves a movement from potency to act. No finite being can be said to necessarily demand a perfection (act) of its nature. God alone is the necessary being Whose essence demands every perfection. God is not in potency to become anything else but what He already is. Hence, there is no change in God. An "extrinsic" change is sometimes ascribed to God in terms of His relationship to changeable creatures.

The "principle of change" was stated by the medieval Scholastics: *quidquid movetur, ab alio movetur;* i.e., whatever is moved is moved by another. No change can be effected except under the influence of another being which is already in act. Every change requires an efficient cause, a final cause, a material cause, and a formal cuase. God alone is the unmoved prime mover, the uncaused efficient and final cause of all creation.

In contrast to the Aristotelian-Scholastic concepts of *a priori* truth and a prime mover unmoved are the doctrines of "process theology." Aristotelianism emphasizes the *a priori*, the unchanging, the static, the universal, the essential. Process thought, based on the philosophy of science expounded by Alfred North Whitehead (1861-1947), sees *essence* as *change*. For Aristotle, essence is being; for process thought, one's very essence is to change.

The immutable God of classical theology becomes "He who can surpass Himself" in process theology. God can become more and more God; mankind can become more and more human, thus enriching God's life so that He surpasses Himself in His own reality. God is part of time, which is infinite and synonymous with the whole becoming process. God "doesn't have a plan," and knows the future only in an indeterminate way. Sin is a failure to grow, to develop and advance the process. Sin is whatever fails to enrich God, and consequently fails to enrich man who can become a part of God. In process theology, the Church isn't an immutable institution "dropped from Heaven" two thousand years ago.

A detailed critique of process thought would carry us considerably beyond the scope and purpose of this study. Process thought admits of many nuances and variations. We can only say that the question of being and becoming, of the static and dynamic, of the changeless and the changing is an ancient philosophical problem. Every important Greek philosopher grappled with it. Aristotle alone, in our judgment, provided the best solution with his doctrines of substance and accident, act and potency, cause and effect, and God as the prime mover unmoved. Aristotle's philosophy gives an adequate explanation for both the changing and the unchanging, for being and becoming. The universe is both in act (*in actu*) and in potency (*in potentia*). Ultimate reality cannot be eternally and infinitely changing and unfixed. If there were change in God, there would have to be a sufficient cause *beyond God* (a contradiction in terms) to account for His change. "Whatever is moved is moved by another."

While we must reject process theology in its extreme form, we can readily accept some of the insights and thrusts provided by process thought. Truth does have a dynamic and developmental quality which the classicist worldview at times has ignored or downplayed. Many Christian theologians today utilize concepts of process theology in explaining Christian doctrine. Teilhard and Hans Kung can certainly be considered process thinkers, in the broad sense of the term. A balance must be maintained between downplaying the importance of change and making change the very essence of all reality. Aristotle's philosophy, we submit, maintains such a balance.

Traditional Scholasticism maintains that God is *transcendent* to the universe because His essence is totally and necessarily distinct and separate from the universe as its efficient and final cause; yet God is *immanent* in the universe by virtue of His knowledge and wisdom, His power and governance, and His essence which demands ubiquity. The universe *has* being, whereas God *is* being. The Old Testament defined God for philosophers when God told Moses, "I am Who am" (Ex. 3:14). The New Testament defined God for theologians when St. John said, "God is Love" (1 John 4:8).

The Mystical Body of Christ is very much a part of God's creation and is subject, therefore, to elements of change. The Church is an integral part of cosmological evolution, which is change or movement on a universal scale. Teilhard de Chardin, S.J., has done pioneering work on the relation of Christianity to cosmological evolution.[3] The Church is *in* the world, hence, is subject to the laws of the universe; the Church is not *of* the world because the essential character and purpose of the Church transcend the universe.

II. TRUTH AND CHANGE

"What is truth?" asked Pilate, the first pragmatist of the Christian era. *Truth* is defined as the conformity between mind and thing. The definition assumes two realities: an objective order to be known and a subject capable of knowing.

Truth is found in the judgment of the human intellect, either affirming or denying some predicate as belonging to a subject. The human intellect is intrinsically capable of knowing reality; the contrary philosophy is that of scepticism, which is intellectual suicide. The mind cannot perceive essences directly, but only indirectly by way of the appearances and accidents of a substance.

According to Thomas Aquinas, the intellect can never know essences completely; we know *that* essences exist but we cannot know *what* they are. God's knowledge alone exhausts all the potentialities of essences. The human grasp of truth is always partial and imperfect, always subject to re-examination, always capable of being expanded, deepened, and qualified.

Essences, as such, are immutable in the sense that another essential element added to or taken from an existing essence destroys the essence itself. What is true, therefore, is eternally and immutably true. Truth can be developed, expanded, deepened, qualified, but not contradicted or reversed; otherwise, no truth existed in the first place.

Mankind once commonly believed that the earth was flat and the sun revolved around the earth. The sense information received by ancient man was accurate and essentially the same as modern man receives. The earth *is* flat, in terms of one's immediate surroundings; the sun *does* move from east to west, if the earth is considered as a fixed frame of reference. Ancient man was not in error, strictly speaking, concerning the earth and the sun; his knowledge, true as far as it went, was incomplete and subject to expansion, qualification, and reinterpretation.

We conclude that truth, while essentially immutable, is not static, rigid, or sterile, but is capable of amplification, development, and qualification. What we have said applies to both natural and divinely revealed truth.

Modern philosophy finds itself in a quagmire of epistemology, phenomenology, and existentialism, mainly because of a denial of the fundamental Aristotelian concept of *substance*. Truth becomes nebulous, undefined, and ultrasubjective. Modern philosophy would do well to return to the great verities expounded by the ancient Greek philosopher.

III. RELIGIOUS TRUTH AND CHANGE

Christ commissioned His Church to teach all nations (cf. Matt. 28:18-20). The Church is infallible in the discharge of its office as teacher of Christ's doctrine and the truths of Revelation. The magisterium exercises its doctrinal authority in diverse ways: (1) through papal documents, such as encyclicals, pastorals, allocutions, bulls, decrees, etc.; (2) through the ordinary teaching of bishops and theologians dispersed throughout the world but united with the pope; (3) through ecumenical councils in union with the pope; and (4) through the pope alone teaching *ex cathedra*.

A particular doctrine can be said to be "of faith" (*de fide*) in any of three ways: (1) a doctrine is of defined faith (*de fide definita*) inasmuch as the doctrine has been explicitly defined either by an ecumenical council and approved by the pope, or by an *ex cathedra* pronouncement of the pope alone; (2) a doctrine is of divine faith (*de fide divina*) inasmuch as the doctrine is contained in Sacred Scripture; and (3) a doctrine is of Catholic faith (*de fide Catholica*) inasmuch as the doctrine is taught by the whole Church and believed by the general consensus of the faithful.

The Christian Revelation ended with the Apocalypse of St. John. The Church has no power to set aside or reject a truth of Revelation or to invent a new doctrine; but Christian doctrine does not exist in a vacuum. Infallibility guarantees that the Church may think about doctrine, develop it, and apply it to each new age and do so without fear of error.

John Henry Newman (1801-1890) — scholar of Oxford, convert to Catholicism, and cardinal of the Church — concluded that the laws of historical development apply to Christian society; that the early Church developed into the modern Roman Catholic Church; and that Protestantism represented a break in this development, both in doctrine and devotion. Cardinal Newman expressed his ideas in his *Essay on the Development of Christian Doctrine.*[4]

One can scarcely overestimate the impact that the existentialism of the nineteenth and twentieth centuries has had upon philosophy and theology. Of course, the problems of the objective and the subjective, matter and mind, the substantial and the accidental or phenomenal, and the static and the dynamic have been with philosophy for a long time. Socrates waged war with the Sophists of his day who were subjectivists. Heraclitus

(530-470 B.C.) taught that all is becoming; nothing is stable. Traditional Greco-Scholastic philosophy has tended to emphasize the stable, the immutable, the *a priori*. All the truth of the Aristotelian syllogism is somehow locked up in the major premise; all that remains is to deduce the truth from that premise.

A number of modern writers — such as Soren Kierkegaard, Henri Bergson, Lloyd Morgan, Martin Buber, Karl Barth, Karl Jaspers, Maurice Blondel, Nicolas Berdyaev, Pierre Teilhard de Chardin, Gabriel Marcel, Paul Tillich, Edward Schillebeeckx, Marc Oraison, Karl Rahner, Hans Kung, Leslie Dewart, and Charles E. Curran — have stressed the dynamic, the developmental, and the historical character of truth. Dewart, for example, prefers to define truth as "the fidelity of consciousness to being." Such a definition has more dynamic and developmental overtones than does the Scholastic definition of truth as consisting in the conformity, the correspondence, or the adequation of the mind to a thing. The latter definition might be described as the "snap shot" or "card file" theory of truth. Kung's theories on the infallibility of the Church reflect a dynamic, historical approach.

Aristotle considered *relation* to be an accidental property of being. Perhaps Greco-Scholastic thought has underestimated the importance of relation in the hierarchy of being. All essences relate to each other and can be thus substantially affected by that relation. Fire put to paper effects a substantial change in the paper. There is ample room, we submit, for an adequate philosophy of change stated in Greco-Scholastic terms.

In his discerning book *The Future of Belief*, Dewart shows the developmental character of the Christian Revelation. There is but one, complete Christian Revelation which ended with the apostles; but man's understanding and consciousness of the import of that Revelation continues to grow, ramify, and intensify in the course of history. Thomas Aquinas noted that there were more articles of faith in his day than in apostolic times; but there was not more Christian truth. The one Christian Revelation continues to reveal and renew itself throughout history. In 1907 the Inquisition condemned the proposition that "the chief articles of the Apostles' Creed did not have the same sense for the Christians of the first ages as they have for the Christians of our time." The condemnation seems to make no allowance for a real development and growth in Christian understanding and consciousness.

An articulate spokesman for the newer insights into the dynamic and historical character of Christian truth is Charles E. Curran of Catholic University of America. In a book of great significance for Catholicism today, *A New Look at Christian Morality*, Father Curran does not discard the traditional Greco-Scholastic concepts; but he does make ample room for the newer insights derived from personalism and contextual moral theology. He denies the existence of an immutable, absolute, self-contained "natural law" which forbids certain actions defined in purely biological, physical, or mechanical terms. He does not deny the existence of moral absolutes; certain forms of human behavior will always be incompatible with the Christian life. But he believes the number of such moral absolutes is considerably less than was once supposed. Curran proposes "Christian experience" as a valid norm of morality.

Scholastic moral philosophy, of course, has always been aware that circumstances may substantially affect the moral character of any act; in this respect Scholasticism can agree with the situational theories of Joseph Fletcher. What is unacceptable to modern situationists is the Scholastic contention that certain acts are intrinsically and always wrong in themselves — prescinding from attendant circumstances. The problem can be graphically illustrated by a consideration of the moral theology of a lie.

Scholasticism defines a *lie (mendacium)* as a deliberate expression, oral or otherwise, contrary to one's own mind (*deliberata locutio contra mentem*). A lie, as defined, is intrinsically and always evil (*omne mendacium, etiam officiosum et jocosum, est intrinsece malum*). The prohibition has been somewhat softened, as we mentioned in Chapter III, by allowing the use of a broad mental reservation (*late restrictio mentalis*) where one has no right to know the truth. Francis J. Connell, C.SS.R., probably the pre-eminent moral theologian in America in the 1950s, distinguished between a lie and a falsehood. The latter consists in the simple disconformity between what one says and what one knows or believes, whereas a lie consists in the uttering of a falsehood to one who has a right to know the truth.

During World War II American prisoners of war gave false information to their Nazi captors; to have told the truth under torture would have cost the lives of thousands of innocent people. The strict moral legalist would say that the Americans used an immoral means (lying) to obtain a good end (the saving of many innocent lives). Father Connell was of the opinion that the formal element of a lie is directly related to one's right to know. Therefore, the mere uttering of a falsehood should not be considered an intrinsically evil act.

Father Curran has provided a valuable insight for moral theology by pointing out that sometimes one finds himself trapped in an evil situation which is not of his own doing. The American prisoners of war did the best they could in the evil situation in which they were involuntarily placed. Even if one wishes to retain the intrinsic evil of uttering a falsehood, the Americans surely chose the lesser of two evils. Who can reasonably say that the prisoners were obliged to tell the truth, or even remain silent and divulge the truth under torture?

A woman whose pregnancy seriously threatens to take her own life as well as the life of the unborn child finds herself involuntarily placed in an evil situation. Is nature so inviolable that the life of the fetus may not be taken earlier than nature has determined so that the mother's life might be saved? May she not save her own life, though the means used in this evil situation is less than perfect? Surely if the fetus could speak, it would say "yes," knowing its own life cannot be saved under any circumstances. The fetus is most certainly not an unjust aggressor, as some maintain; but one surely has a right to defend himself even from an innocent aggressor.

Similarly with contraception: is nature so inviolable and unalterable that physical means may not be used to prevent conception when circumstances in some cases not only warrant but require such prevention? There is no cogent reason why the physical act of contraception — or any other human act considered solely in its physical aspects — ought to be considered intrinsically evil and therefore never morally permissible.

The principle that no act in itself is intrinsically evil will have a profound and widespread effect upon moral theology; the principle is already becoming more widely recognized and accepted. The thrust of morality will turn away from physical acts considered in themselves and instead will focus upon the circumstances — the situation or context, if you will — that attend the physical act. Thus, the highly regarded moral theologian Bernard Haring has stated that it is "probable" that a semen specimen obtained by masturbation for a sufficient medical purpose is morally licit, statements by Pius XII to the contrary notwithstanding. Father Curran believes that masturbation should no longer be regarded as objectively grave matter; and he offers many good reasons to support his view. Even if one is not ready to deny that some human physical acts are intrinsically evil, the well-known Scholastic principle, *ex duobus malis minus eligi debet* (one ought to choose the lesser of two evils) should be given a wider application than has heretofore been the case.

In addition to significant changes occurring in moral theology, one can also cite examples of change and development in dogmatic teaching. Sacramental theology offers a capital example. It was not until the twelfth century that all Seven Sacraments were listed together and treated systematically. Recent scholarship, as we have mentioned in Chapter II, has developed the understanding of the Sacraments as signs of faith, divine encounters, etc., with less emphasis on their *ex opere operato* character. One looks in vain in the Bible for such terms as Sacrament, Trinity, Original Sin, or even *mortal* or *venial* sin. All of these terms developed in later centuries.

It has been said that if St. Peter — reckoned by Catholics as the first pope — were alive today, he would not be able to pass a third grade exam in religion (or in math, science, geography, or history, for that matter). Such terms as "'transubstantiation," "papal infallibility," *"imprimatur,"* "indulgences," the "Immaculate Conception" would simply be beyond him. All of these concepts represent a development, a delineation, an increase in consciousness and discipline in terms of the Christian Revelation.

A final example of doctrinal change and development in the light of Christian experience concerns the Church's attitude toward religious liberty. Popes Gregory XVI, Pius IX, and Leo XIII all condemned in encyclicals the principle that an individual's right to worship God in the light of his own conscience should take precedence over the duty to worship in the one, true Church established by Christ for all men — the Roman Catholic Church. Gregory XVI referred to freedom of conscience as "a false and absurd maxim, or rather madness . . ., the most contagious of errors." Pius IX, in his *Syllabus of Errors*, condemned the proposition: "Every man is free to embrace and profess the religion he considers to be the true one by the light of reason."

Pope Boniface VIII (1235-1303), in his bull *Unam Sanctam*, declared, defined, and pronounced that "it is absolutely necessary for the salvation of every human creature to be subject to the Roman pontiff." The Council of Florence, in the fifteenth century, declared that salvation is impossible for anyone who is separated from the unity of the Roman Catholic Church. The Fifth Council of the Lateran (1512-17) declared: *"Nulla salus extra Ecclesiam* (outside the Church there is no salvation)." With the coming of the Protestant Reformation, which divided Christendom almost in half, the Church had to make finer distinctions concerning invincible ignorance, following one's sincere conscience, and salvific Grace being available to all — distinctions and clarifications missing from the papal and conciliar statements cited above. These statements were not objectively in error, but were incomplete and subject to development and refinement. Although "error has no rights," *persons* in error do have rights. Writing in *Concilium*, Gregory Baum puts it bluntly, but truthfully, when he states that "concretely and actually the Church of Christ may be realized less, equally, or more in a Church separated from Rome than in a Church in communion with Rome."

Christian enlightenment and experience finally taught the Church that the individual's subjective right and duty to follow his own conscience in matters of religion must supersede the objective obligation to belong to and profess the one, true Church of Christ, the Catholic Church. Thus did Vatican II declare that religious liberty is a right belonging to every individual and that coercion has no rightful place in matters religious.

The Church today presents itself to the world, not as an institution with all the answers, not as a force "over against" the world, but as the *Pilgrim Church* — a phrase frequently employed by Vatican II — with a mission in the world to be the salvation of the world. The Church learns with and from the world and from Christian experience; sometimes errs in its choices; sometimes falters; sometimes is less than adequate in coping with world poverty (which is basically a moral problem), with war, injustice, and discrimination (both inside and outside of the Church). Christianity does have all the answers, at least those that have supernatural significance; but these answers are hammered out on the anvils of time, historical development, and Christian experience. As Chesterton noted, Christianity has not failed the world; Christianity has not been really tried.

The Church on Earth is not the Church Triumphant; the Church Militant makes its pilgrim way through human history in fear and trembling. A rich, powerful, supercilious Church, luxuriating in triumphalism, will never be the salvation of the world. But a poor and humble Church that grows, learns, and develops within the human family, rejoicing in human successes and commiserating in human failures, becoming ever more relevant to human needs and aspirations — *this* is the Church which Christ promised to be with all days unto the consummation of the world.

We conclude that the Christian Faith is not sterile, inert, and irrelevant to a particular age and culture. On the contrary, our Christian Faith is alive and well and supremely pertinent to our times.

IV. THE DOCTRINE OF INFALLIBILITY

A violent thunderstorm raged over Rome on Monday, July 18, 1870, as 533 Council Fathers voted "*placet*" (it pleases) for the decree *Pastor Aeternus*, which stated that the pope is preserved from error when defining *ex cathedra* a doctrine of faith or morals. Two bishops voted "*non placet*," one being Bishop Edward Fitzgerald of Little Rock, Arkansas.

The Second Vatican Council reaffirmed the teaching of the First Vatican Council regarding papal infallibility (cf. *Lumen Gentium*, n. 25). The college of bishops is likewise regarded as infallible: "This is so, even when they are dispersed around the world, provided that while maintaining the bond of unity among themselves and with Peter's successor, and while teaching authentically on a matter of faith and morals, they concur in a single viewpoint as the one which must be held conclusively" (*Lumen Gentium*, n. 25). So also, the body of the faithful as a whole will not err in matters of belief (cf. *Lumen Gentium*, n. 12).

On June 24, 1973, the Sacred Congregation for the Doctrine of the Faith issued a *Declaration in Defense of the Catholic Doctrine on the Church Against Certain Errors of the Present Day*. The document taught that the Church shares in the infallibility of God by a special charism. The infallibility of the Church resides in the entire People of God inasmuch as a truth of Revelation is held universally and uniformly by the faithful. The infallibility of the Church, as willed by Christ, is especially exercised by the Church's magisterium — by the bishops teaching as a collegial body with the pope or by the pope alone teaching *ex cathedra*. The magisterium does not function merely as a body of theological experts; nor is it the function of the magisterium to merely ratify the assent of the faithful. The magisterium teaches infallibly in its own right, and its teachings are binding upon the entire People of God.

The document recognized that Divine Revelation remains concealed by the veil of faith; that dogmatic formulas are to some extent historically conditioned and limited by human language; that dogmatic truth may be more perfectly and fully expressed at a later date. However, the document stressed that the *meaning* of dogmatic formulas remains ever constant and true in the Church, even when that meaning is expressed with greater clarity or is more developed. One may not hold that theological formulas defined by the Church signify the truth only in an indeterminate way, that truth is a goal constantly being sought by such formulations. Such an opinion, declared the document, does not avoid dogmatic relativism and corrupts the concept of the Church's infallibility. "There is no doubt that . . . the meaning of dogmas which is declared by the Church is determinate and unalterable."

The New Testament does not explicitly teach the doctrine of infallibility; but a number of passages are intelligible only in the light of an infallible magisterium. Christ promised to be with His Church all days (cf. Matt. 28:20). He promised to send the Paraclete (helper, advocate), the Spirit of truth (cf. John 14:16-17) Who will teach all truth (cf. John 16:13). Christ promised to preserve His Church from "the gates of Hell" and to bind in Heaven what His Church bound on earth (cf. Matt. 16:18). St. Paul regarded the Church as "the pillar and ground of truth" (cf. 1 Tim. 3:15). The apostles recognized and claimed the assistance of the Holy Spirit in their teaching: "It has pleased the Holy Spirit and us. . ." (Acts 15:28). By a special charism of infallibility, the deposit of Divine Revelation is correctly taught by the magisterium and understood with "the sense of faith" by the faithful as a whole. Such has been the constant tradition of the Church.

In his candid book *Did I Say That?*, John L. McKenzie writes about "the infallibility syndrome." Magisterial documents and decrees are generally written in a turgid style that exudes an air of infallibility and finality even in matters which ought to be candidly recognized as doubtful or probable or outside the domain of Divine Revelation. The magisterium of the Church is authorized to proclaim the Gospel, "the good news" of salvation and Divine Revelation. The "overworked" magisterium has no authority to teach logic, metaphysics, moral philosophy, science, or literary criticism. The scope of the Church's infallibility encompasses the content of Divine Revelation and those "dogmatic facts" and "theological conclusions" which are so intimately related to a revealed doctrine that error regarding the one would necessarily involve error regarding the other.

The encyclical *Humanae Vitae*, which condemned artificial contraception, was so poorly received because it contravened the consensus of most Christians and most Catholics. Further, it spoke with an air of infallibility on a matter of moral philosophy not clearly contained in Divine Revelation nor necessarily related to a revealed doctrine. The encyclical makes no claim to be teaching a divinely revealed truth; nor does the letter make a strong case from the standpoint of philosophical reasoning. *Humanae Vitae* bases its case mainly on the citation of earlier authorities in the Church. Aquinas regarded "the appeal to authority" as the weakest of all arguments. Andrew Greeley sees a positive correlation between the issuance of *Humanae Vitae* in 1968 and the subsequent decline in Catholic school enrollment and weekly Mass attendance in America.

The issuance of *Humanae Vitae* and its subsequent poor reception point up the lack of an adequate theology of the ordinary magisterium in the Church today. Vatican press secretary Msgr. Ferdinando Lambruschini, in releasing *Humanae Vitae* in 1968, noted that the letter was not an infallible document and that its proscription was "not unreformable." Catholics are asked to give "an internal religious assent" to such pronouncements of the ordinary magisterium. The possibility that one might have grave reasons of conscience to withhold such assent is simply not considered as a viable option; the individual conscience ought to be always in agreement with magisterial doctrine. Yet we know that freedom is a necessary corollary of conscience; where there is no freedom, there can hardly be conscience. F. J. Sheed noted in *Is It the Same Church?* that Vatican II failed to adequately come to grips with the possibility of serious objections by an individual conscience in accepting a magisterial teaching. There is room, we submit, for a legitimate and constructive dissent within Catholicism; and Vatican II never explicitly excluded such a possibility.

There is no mechanism in the Catholic Church today which would define limits and check abuses of the ordinary teaching office. Magisterial documents never retract or acknowledge error in previous magisterial statements. There has never been a formal magisterial acknowledgment of error in the Galileo case. The infamous and inhumane tactics of the medieval Inquisition have never been formally confessed by the magisterium. The Church once forbade interest, and the Crusades made war in the name of religion acceptable ("God wills it!"). The Pontifical Biblical Commission in the early 1900s issued decrees concerning literary criticism of the Bible that are honored by no reputable Catholic exegete today. None of these pronouncements have ever been formally retracted.

Why cannot the magisterium admit error when error has been committed? Why cannot the magisterium acknowledge the existence of doubt and probability when only doubt and probability actually exist? Why must "the infallibility syndrome" permeate every magisterial utterance? Father McKenzie is not totally happy with the term *infallibility*, but he is hard put to find a better term. Hans Kung has proposed the term *indefectibility*. The human, fallible judgments of the Church are bound in Heaven in such a way that the Holy Spirit will guide the Church ultimately to the truth. The Church will never "defect" from this path of Christ's truth.

We submit that *infallibility* is indeed the correct and accurate term for the *ex cathedra* definitions of the pope, the definitions of ecumenical councils, and the uniform teaching of the pope and bishops regarding a doctrine of faith or morals contained in the Christian Revelation. We further submit that *infallibility* is the correct term for the belief of the whole Church regarding a doctrine of the Christian Revelation. Infallibility resides essentially in the whole Church. The pope alone is uniquely empowered to speak for the whole Church and to infallibly pronounce what the whole Church believes.

The magisterium has gotten into trouble in the past when it ventured outside the domain of Divine Revelation. We do not say that the Church should never comment on philosophy, science, sociology, etc. After all, free speech is a right belonging to the magisterium as much as to anyone else. But prudence requires that such statements will be promulgated as opinion; and prudence will many times proscribe saying anything at all. By a more restrained and humble posture, the credibility of the magisterium can be restored.

St. Thomas Aquinas (1225-1274) is a brilliant light in the history of Catholic thought. Better than anyone else, the Angelic

Doctor succeeded in harmonizing philosophy and theology; he built the Faith on the firm foundation of reason. Aquinas always gave science and the human body their due place, sometimes to the dismay of his contemporaries; this great thinker was considered to be avant-garde. Where is our Thomas of the Twentieth Century, to write a *summa* for our times, to harmonize and synthesize philosophy, theology, and science as the Angelic Doctor did in the thirteenth century?

St. Francis of Assisi (1182-1226), better than anyone else, renewed a Church that was growing cold and indifferent to the demands of the Gospel. Where is our Francis of the Twentieth Century, to enkindle the fires of love for God, for Christ, for the Church, for all creation as the Poverello did for Christendom in the thirteenth century?

The Church learns as well as teaches, just as Christ gained human knowledge through His human nature. The Church can learn from the world; truth is where one finds it. Where there is truth, there also is the Holy Spirit.

One of the prime characteristics of a living organism is the ability to grow, to adapt, to change when necessary for the good of the whole organism. The Church is a supernatural organism, the Mystical Body of Christ. Fulton J. Sheen has written: "Like a mighty oak tree which has stood for twenty centuries, [the Church] bears fresh green foliage for each new age . . . . She is therefore not behind the times, but beyond the times, always fresh while the age is dying."[5]

Motus is written into the very warp and woof of the cosmos. The restlessness of cosmic evolution pushes on; and God alone knows where it will all end. "Nothing is certain but uncertainty," says the cynic. But the man of Faith knows that "God's in His Heaven" and all change will ultimately fulfill the divine purposes.

CHAPTER VI

CATHOLICISM AND HUMAN SEXUALITY

A Rationale for Reform

O how beautiful is the chaste generation with glory; for the meaning thereof is immortal, because it is known both with God and with men.
— Wisdom 4:1

Blessed are the clean of heart, for they shall see God.
— Matt. 5:8

There seems to be an emerging consensus that we need to develop a more adequate understanding of man's sexuality in its human wholeness and totality. Sex is indeed such a fundamental dimension of human existence that we cannot long avoid clarifying our stance in its regard . . . .
— John L. Thomas, S.J.

. . . there has always been an underlying tendency to consider everything connected with sexuality . . . as at least suspect.
— Marc Oraison

I lose my respect for the man who can make the mystery of sex the subject of a coarse jest, yet when you speak earnestly and seriously on the subject, is silent.
— Henry David Thoreau

There is no sin of matrimonial copulation.
— St. Albert the Great, *Summa Theologica*

. . . non-Catholic observers must wonder what kind of a natural law it is that is discernible only by Roman Catholics . . . .
— Archbishop Thomas D. Roberts, S.J.

I would deny the existence of negative moral absolutes when the act is described only in terms of its physical structure.
— Charles E. Curran

LAWRENCE Losoncy, Director of the Division of Adult Education, U.S. Catholic Conference, is typical of the newer emphases being employed in sex education today. Writing in *Sign* magazine, Losoncy observes that misconceptions concerning sex can easily block religious growth. The Bible and Christianity teach that sex is identified with life; is good and beautiful; is a sign of love; makes men and women beautiful; makes flowers; makes seeds from which crops grow; inspires poems, art, and drama; produces symbols in the liturgy; is a great source of happiness; is *rarely* an occasion of sin and is never identified with sin.

Losoncy points out, by contrast, how misconstrued ideas can distort the true Christian concept of human sexuality within the parameters of Christian morality. Some wrong attitudes would include the following: sex is dirty, shameful, animal-like, sinful, a curse; is a matter for perverts; is done secretly so no one ever knows; is for the weak; is risen above by all those who really love God. Losoncy concludes that we are not destroying religion when we affirm the value of sex in its myriad forms within the human condition. He writes: "Underneath all that we say about sex, there is the deeper point to be made: It is good to be a human being."

I. SEXUAL MORALITY IN SCRIPTURE AND TRADITION[1]

Scripture and Sexual Morality. The Old Testament generally extols marriage and procreation; bachelorhood is not held in high esteem. Genesis teaches "be fruitful and multiply" (1:28) and "it is not good that the man is alone" (2:18). Thus, the twofold purpose of marriage, to propagate the species and to provide personal fulfillment and completion, is set forth. The Book of Wisdom lauds "the chaste generation"; the Decalogue forbids adultery and unchaste thoughts. The inhabitants of Sodom and Gomorrah were punished with fire and brimstone for committing sins of homosexuality.

The sin of Onan, recorded in Genesis 38:8-10, presents something of a problem for exegesis. Onan allowed his seed to fall on the ground rather than to inseminate his brother's widow. The Levirate law required that one should marry his brother's widow who had begotten no offspring. Was Onan slain by God for performing an act of contraception (in this case, *coitus interruptus*) or for refusing to fulfill the requirement of the Levirate law?

Augustine believed that Onan was slain for contraception. Augustine's view was cited by Pope Pius XI in *Casti Connubii*. Neither Jerome, Aquinas, Albert, nor Alphonsus Liguori used Gen. 38:8-10 to condemn contraception. André Snoeck, writing in

1953, said flatly that the sin of Onan "obviously consisted in the fact that he did not observe the Levirate law." One should note that in translating Gen. 38:8-10 into Latin, Jerome imposed his own view concerning contraception. The original Hebrew said Onan "did not please God"; Jerome said Onan "did a detestable thing" (*rem detestabilem*), thus focusing attention on the act. *Detestable* is a harsh word, harsher than the original Hebrew; Jerome used the word nowhere else in his translation of the Bible, the Vulgate.

"That contraception as such is condemned [in the Old Testament] seems unlikely," writes John T. Noonan. "There is no commandment against contraception in any of the codes of law.²

The New Testament counsels virginity for the sake of the Kingdom of God. Marriage is good, but consecrated celibacy is better. Chastity is upheld; unchastity, adultery, fornication, sodomy are condemned. There is no specific condemnation of contraception, though the practice was certainly known in New Testament times.

In St. Paul's famous list of sinners who will not possess the Kingdom of God (cf. 1 Cor. 6:9-10), he named the *effeminate*. Some commentators understand the term to refer to those who commit autoerotic acts. "Effeminate" can mean simply softness, laxity, or acting like a woman. If Paul wished to condemn autoeroticism, he had available a more precise term than effeminate. Furthermore, the term cannot be applied to females, who are certainly capable of autoeroticism.

In short, the Bible upholds the virtue of chastity, or the proper ordering of the sexual faculty.

Tradition and Sexual Morality: a Historical Sketch. To provide a background and a perspective for making conclusions concerning human sexuality, we here give some significant personalities, doctrines, and events that have shaped the Church's present teaching on sexuality. No doctrine exists in a vacuum; theological, philosophical, scientific, and sociological influences are constantly operating in the development of doctrine.

(1) St. Ambrose (340-397) applied the term *parricide* (the killing of a close relative) to users of potions preventing life. Ambrose probably made no clear distinction between an *abortifacient* (that which effects an abortion) and a contraceptive potion.

(2) Eusebius Hiernonymus Sophronius, better known as St. Jerome (340-420), spent a licentious youth, according to one biographer. He denounced contraception, intercourse during pregnancy, and any separation of sexuality from procreation. Jerome's translation of Gen. 38:8-10 offered the strongest text in the Bible against contraception; his translation would be used by the Church until recent times.

(3) St. Augustine (354-430), from his eighteenth to twenty-ninth year, was a Manichean and lived with an unnamed mistress with whom he fathered one child. Presumably, Augustine practiced some form of contraception during this relationship.

Mani was a third-century Persian, strongly influenced by Zoroastrianism. He claimed to have a final revelation which superseded Christianity. Mani taught a bizarre doctrine concerning the origin of matter and man: all matter and procreation are evil; contraception is preferable to procreation.

After Augustine converted to Christianity, he reacted to his former Manicheism by teaching that coitus ought to be always attended by a procreative purpose, which was the primary and essential justification for the act. The three "goods" of marriage are *proles* (offspring); *fides* (fidelity to one's spouse); and *sacramentum* (sacramental Grace, stability, and indissolubility). Augustine accepted the Stoic belief that coitus for pleasure is debasing and would be at least venially sinful. He said he had never met anyone who *always* had a procreative intent in coitus. Augustine made no specific reference to love or personal fulfillment as a purpose for coitus. Contraception is mortally sinful. The doctrine of Augustine, more than any other man, would profoundly influence Church teaching on sexuality for more than a thousand years.

(4) St. John Chrysostom (345-407) said virginity renders "mortals like angels." Marriage is a nest for birds who cannot fly. Who can make the journey to Heaven encumbered by a wife and family? He opposed contraception, not so much because nature is violated, but because God has attached a sacral character to coitus.

(5) St. John Damascene, an eighth-century Greek, repeated the doctrine of Chrysostom; he justified marriage to avoid fornication, thus eliminating a procreative requirement. He opposed any interference with coitus, regarding the act as sacral.

(6) Bishop Ivo of Chartres agreed with Augustine that "to act against nature is always unlawful and beyond doubt more

flagrant and shameful than to sin by a natural use in fornication or adultery."

(7) Peter Lombard's *Sentences* became the common theological textbook of the Middle Ages; it was the subject of some twelve hundred commentaries. Lombard (1100-1160?), Bishop of Paris, reaffirmed Augustine's *proles, fides, sacramentum* formula as the goods of marriage; of the three, only the seeking of the good of offspring is sufficient to excuse intercourse. Lombard condemned contraception thusly: "Those who indeed procure poisons of sterility [Augustine's term for contraceptives] are not spouses but fornicators."

(8) The Cathars and Albanians, reviving the Manichean doctrine in the Middle Ages, opposed procreation as being evil.

(9) Peter Abélard (1079-1142) was the most brilliant and incisive thinker of his day. Like Augustine, Abélard had a tempestuous sexual experience. He seduced his pupil Heloise and then married her. Heloise finally was sent to a convent; Abélard was involuntarily castrated by Fulbert, the uncle of Heloise. Abélard became a monk and Heloise took the veil.

Abélard believed that if marriage is entered with the intention of procreating children, it excuses "those acts of intercourse which occur without this intention." Intercourse is justifiable as "a remedy for their incontinence." Abélard, who tended toward rationalism, was the first married man in the Western Church to contribute to the theology of marriage.

(10) Bishop Huguccio supported the teaching of Pope St. Gregory the Great (540?-604) that sexual pleasure is evil. Marital intercourse "in order to sate one's lust or satisfy one's pleasure [*voluptas*] is mortal sin." Since some degree of concupiscence is always present, coitus "can never be without sin . . . ." Unnatural acts are grounds for dismissal. Huguccio defended *coitus reservatus* (or *amplexus reservatus*) as being lawful.

(11) Pope Innocent III (1161-1216), a pupil of Huguccio, agreed that coitus is inevitably accompanied by "at least a very small venial sin."

(12) According to her biographer and confessor, Catherine of Siena in a vision of Hell noted only one distinct class of sinners: those who sinned in the married state. They were punished more severely because "they do not have as much conscience about it, and consequently not as much contrition. . . ."

(13) By the thirteenth century no ecumenical council had spoken on contraception. No pope had issued a formal condemnation. The prestige of Augustine remained enormous.

(14) St. Thomas Aquinas (1225-1274) condemned any unnatural or artificial means of thwarting the natural effect of
sexual intercourse. He defined *lust* as the vice of indulging in
unlawful sexual pleasure. He cited six species (or parts) of lust:
fornication, adultery, incest, seduction, rape, and unnatural vice.
There are four kinds of "sins against nature": (1) autoerotic acts
(*mollities*); (2) bestiality, or coitus with an animal; (3) sodomy, or
unisexuality; (4) unnatural methods of copulation.

Thomas agreed with earlier writers that unnatural vice is
the worst of all sins of lust, worse than adultery (which is far
worse than fornication). He did not condemn the use of potions
causing sterility as a sin against *nature*, but as a sin against
marriage and the purpose of procreation. Thomas made a prime
distinction between *the order of nature* and *the order of reason*.
Similarly, fornication and adultery are condemned, not as being
against the order of nature, but against the order of reason. Sins
against "the order of nature" do injury to God, if to no one else.

As a young man, commenting on Lombard's *Sentences*,
Thomas took his stand with Augustine that only a procreative
purpose freed marital intercourse from sin. Coitus is naturally
ordained for procreation, and nothing else, not even for one's
good health. To seek pleasure in the marital act is venial sin; yet,
inconsistently, he held that God placed pleasure in the act of
coition as an inducement to perform it.

Later, in his *Summa Contra Gentiles*, Thomas wrote: ". . . if,
per accidens, generation cannot follow from emission of the seed,
this is not against nature, nor a sin, as if it happens that the
woman is sterile." In justifying mutilation of the body when
necessary for the good of the whole person, Thomas recognized
that a natural function may be sacrificed for a rational good — a
rationale that is basic to contemporary thinking on contraception.

Thomas acknowledged that matrimony has two ends, a personal end and an objective end. Yet he would not admit that
intercourse had a sacramental value. Thomas thought that sins
against nature in marriage were grounds for divorce. Thomas
was steeped in Augustine; he repeated the latter's epigram that
in coitus man "becomes all flesh." His formulas on concupiscence
are Augustine's. For man as an individual, "it cannot be said
good to touch woman."

It is an irony of history that Aquinas did not complete his
masterpiece, the *Summa Theologica*, beyond the Sacrament of

Penance. Thus, posterity was denied Thomas' final, mature statement on the objective and subjective ends of matrimony.

(15) St. Albert the Great (1193-1280), teacher of Thomas Aquinas, felt that to desert the "natural position" in coitus was to assume "that of brute animals." Here, *animal* becomes a dirty word. Theologians following Albert and Thomas said that any way but woman beneath the man was mortal sin.

Albert made one statement that came like a clap of thunder on a clear day: "There is no sin of matrimonial copulation." The line was written in Albert's last years. What did he mean by this somewhat cryptic observation? He did not immediately explain himself, but from other writings one can infer his meaning: intercourse is a *matrimonial* act when the *sacramental good* is recalled. "Most important of all in the long history of doctrine," writes John T. Noonan, "Albert had adumbrated an analysis of intercourse which freed it from service to procreation and tied it to the Sacrament."[3] Thomas had said that it was possible to have coitus without sin.

(16) Twelfth-century rigorists held that coitus for delight or pleasure or lust was a mortal sin. The milder Augustinian view, held by most, labeled the intent to seek pleasure as venial. This view was held by Alexander of Hales, Thomas, Bonaventure, and Peter de Palude. Immoderation in coitus was a mortal sin; as for Jerome, the too ardent lover was an adulterer. No category of *moderate love* was recognized as a purpose in intercourse.[4]

Thomas, Raymond, and Scotus believed intercourse during menstruation was a mortal sin. Almost all held that intercourse during pregnancy was a mortal sin because of the supposed danger of abortion. The sanction against contraception was mortal sin.[5] Most felt that intercourse when sterility was known was a venial sin. Anaphrodisiacs were generally not criticized as being unnatural.

(17) Richard Middleton was an English Franciscan. Writing about 1272, he cited the theory of "some theologians" that moderate pleasure in coitus is good and that the good of the Sacrament justifies the marital act. He did not call the theory his own; neither did he refute it. He agreed that "to satiate concupiscence and to will moderate delight are not the same." Augustine is explained away; a ray of light had pierced the mist.

(18) Impotency was considered an impediment to a valid marriage; the possibility of insemination was necessary. But sterility did not invalidate a marriage. The inconsistent position

of requiring a procreative intent, even in a sterile marriage, was maintained. Again, the sacral character of insemination was stressed in the above regulations, even apart from the possibility of conception. Augustinianism inconsistently incorporated in St. Thomas continued to prevail.

(19) Denis the Carthusian (1402-1471) said: "The married can mutually love each other because of the mutual pleasure they have in the marital act." The principle introduced by Albert and Middleton was gaining impetus.

(20) St. Bridget said a man was damned for loving his wife too carnally.

(21) Martin Le Maistre (1432-1481), in his *Moral Questions*, rendered "the most independent critique of the Christian sexual ethic ever undertaken by an orthodox critic."[6] Like Augustine and Aquinas, Le Maistre was a teacher; but he was not jaundiced by a Manichean background, as was Augustine, nor restricted by a contemplative asceticism, as was Aquinas. Le Maistre's writing was marked by a cool professorial outlook.

"Not every copulation of spouses not performed to generate offspring is an act opposed to conjugal chastity." The break from Augustinianism is firm. Pleasure can be sought and used for an honest end: to avoid tedium, for health, for one's general well-being. Le Maistre cited Aristotle, who permitted the use of the pleasurable when it aided "health and the good condition of body and soul." Only excess was sinful in coition.

Le Maistre, writing in 1480, saw only a hedonistic motive for practicing contraception. He upheld the traditional rationale against unnatural sins.

(22) Desiderius Erasmus (1464-1536) said the marriages of the old or sterile were not true marriages.

(23) John Major (1470-1550) was a Scottish theologian. He maintained that it is no more a sin to copulate for pleasure than "to eat a handsome apple for the pleasure of it." He quoted Aristotle, and said that nowhere does the Bible forbid seeking pleasure in intercourse. Major called the twelfth-century opinion of Huguccio, that coition always involves at least venial sin, "most absurd."

(24) Thomas de Vio, Cardinal Cajetan (1469-1534), repeated the Augustinian dictum that intercourse for pleasure was venially sinful; but Cajetan accepted a weakened Augustinianism on other matters.

(25) John Calvin (1509-1564) adhered closely to the old Catholic doctrines on sexuality. Martin Luther (1483-1546) es-

poused the Augustinian view on sexuality (although he is supposed to have once said, "Chastity is impossible").

(26) Robert Bellarmine (1542-1611) separated concupiscence from the transmission of Original Sin. A modified view on concupiscence and Original Sin was evolving, a view which had heretofore connected the two with sexuality.

(27) Jansenism, originating in France, maintained ultra-rigorous views on sexuality.

(28) Pope Sixtus V, an overzealous Franciscan reformer, issued the bull *Effraenatam* on Oct. 29, 1588. The giving or taking of contraceptives was to be treated literally as murder, incurring the death penalty. The bull was in force for two and one-half years.

(29) Thomas Sanchez (1550-1610) was a Spanish Jesuit who specialized on the theology of marriage. There is no sin in spouses who intend "only to copulate as spouses." Pleasure can be a lawful purpose in coition, but not pleasure *alone*. Sanchez said a woman who is raped may expel the seed. Here he puts "the order of reason" above "the order of nature."

(30) Charles Billuart (1685-1757) approved of marriage for the sterile, but still demanded a procreative intent to justify coitus. He made no reply to the objection that such a rationale "makes marriage a continual occasion for venial sin."

(31) Alphonsus Liguori (1697-1787) was a successful lawyer before he became a priest. The Church has named him the patron saint of moral theologians. He founded the Redemptorist Order.

Liguori, realizing that mortal sin means eternal damnation, was always careful as to what he called a mortal sin. He recognized a nonprocreative purpose in marriage. Liguori condemned contraception; but he added that ignorance of the sinfulness of contraception was not ignorance about a necessary means of salvation. He would not categorically condemn the Church practice of sometimes requiring choir boys to submit to castration for the purpose of keeping their voices high. Concerning abortion, Liguori preferred the teaching of Aquinas that ensoulment takes place forty days after conception for males, eighty days for females.

(32) John of St. Thomas (1589-1644), a Spanish Thomist, said that autoerotic ejaculation was "an abuse of the seed."

(33) In 1661, Paul Zacchias, physician to Pope Innocent X, taught that the human soul is infused at the moment of conception. Thomas Roncaglia, in 1736, was the first theologian to defend the thesis of Zacchias.

(34) Simon André Tissot (1728-1797), a personal physician to the pope, published a medical monograph in 1774 entitled *Onanism, or the Treatment of the Diseases That Result from Self-Abuse*. Tissot believed that autosexual acts could cause "impotence, epilepsy, consumption, blindness, imbecility," and even death. Tissot's work is important because it marked the beginning of an effort to submit autosexuality to scientific investigation.

(35) Thomas Malthus, in 1798, said that the population doubles every twenty-five years in a geometrical ratio, whereas the food supply increases arithmetically.

(36) John Gury (1801-1866), a French Jesuit, authored *Compendium of Moral Theology*, which was used in most nineteenth-century seminaries. Gury cited conjugal affection as a lawful purpose for intercourse.

(37) Pope Pius IX, by means of the Inquisition, on May 21, 1851, reaffirmed the condemnation of Innocent XI of the laxist proposition, "An autoerotic act (*mollities*) is not prohibited by natural law. Whence, if God had not forbidden it, it would often be good, sometimes obligatory under mortal penalty."

(38) In 1827, Karl Ernst von Baer published his discovery of the human ovum. August Joseph Lecomte (1824-1881) made the first attempt to take theological account of the physiology of ovulation.

(39) The so-called Comstock law of March 3, 1873, forbade sending contraceptives through the U.S. mail. The Congress of the United States had gone farther than any pope since Sixtus V in penalizing the possession of contraceptives. Massachusetts categorically prohibited the sale of contraceptives; Connecticut made it a criminal misdemeanor to use a drug, article or instrument to prevent conception. The Connecticut law was only recently declared unconstitutional.

(40) Pope Leo XIII issued *Arcanum Divinae Sapientiae* on Feb. 10, 1880. The full-length encyclical on marriage was directed toward civil divorce in France; not a single word was said about contraception.

(41) The Penitentiary, on June 16, 1880, said the sterile period could be used as a remedy for Onanism.

(42) Indiana, in 1903, became the first state to permit the sterilization of the feebleminded and insane.

(43) Margaret Sanger organized a birth control movement in 1913 in the United States.

(44) On Aug. 20, 1913, the German bishops met at Fulda and declared that Catholics practicing contraception could not receive the Sacraments. A pastoral letter promulgated by the bishops of the United States on Sept. 26, 1919, condemned "the selfishness which leads to race suicide" and "the fraudulent prudence that would improve upon nature by defeating its obvious purpose, and would purify life by defiling its source."

(45) The joint role of sperm and ovum was discovered in 1875; that fecundation is possible only a brief period of the female cycle was discovered in 1923.

(46) Edmund Husserl and Max Scheler evolved a system of phenomenology in the 1920s. Gabriel Marcel evolved existentialist personalism and a personalist conception of natural law.

(47) Dominikus Lindner published *Der Usus Matrimonii* in 1929, a pioneering work in the history of sexual ethics.

(48) By 1930 the birth control movement had overcome most restraints in most countries. By 1933 a majority of better medical schools in the United States, not under Catholic auspices, gave instructions in techniques of contraception, which was no longer considered suspect by the medical profession.

(49) The Lambeth Conference of 1930, by a vote of 193 to 67, agreed that "other methods" besides complete abstinence might be used to control conception. The Anglican bishops had previously, in 1908 and 1920, condemned contraception.

(50) Pope Pius XI, on Dec. 31, 1930, promulgated *Casti Connubii*. Three reasons can be cited for the encyclical: (1) a reaction to the Lambeth Conference of Aug. 1930; (2) a call for the revision of the teaching contained in the German periodical *Hochland* of June 1930, which advocated a liberal view on contraception; (3) an uneasiness that priests were not enforcing the ban on contraception. The encyclical was the strongest papal statement against contraception since *Effraenatam* of Sixtus V.[7] Ford and Kelly (1963) believed the encyclical put forth its teaching as infallibly true.

(51) Arthur Vermeersch (1858-1936) was the most influential moral theologian of the early twentieth century. He probably had a hand in composing *Casti Connubii*. Vermeersch said a wife sinned by cooperating even passively in the use of contraceptives.

(52) Dietrich von Hildebrand was the first married layman to make a substantial contribution to the theology of marriage. Love is a requirement for lawful coition; love is part of *fides*. Von

Hildebrand rejected a purely biological approach to the understanding of coitus. In his celebrated *In Defense of Purity* (1931), love is made the central meaning of coitus.

(53) **Havelock Ellis (1859-1939)** and **Sigmund Freud (1856-1939)** made valuable contributions to a better understanding of the psychology of sex. Wilhelm Stekel did pioneering work in the scientific understanding of autoeroticism in the early twentieth century.

(54) Herbert Doms was the most influential writer of the personalist school. In *The Meaning and End of Marriage* (1935), Doms said that coitus is an ontological act of persons, involving personal fulfillment. The "primary" and "secondary" ends of marriage are discarded. In their place Doms posited an "immanent" and a "procreative" end; "conjugal love is the first end of marriage."

(55) Msgr. John A. Ryan (1869-1945) said he had confidence that American Catholics, if properly instructed, would desist from contraception; he approved of rhythm for any serious reason.

(56) The Holy Office, on Feb. 21, 1940, said direct sterilization is forbidden by the law of nature.

(57) Alfred C. Kinsey, W. B. Pomeroy, and C. E. Martin published *Sexual Behavior in the Human Male* in 1948 and *Sexual Behavior in the Human Female* in 1953. These works represented the most scientific investigation into human sexual behavior yet undertaken. Among other findings, Kinsey and his associates found autoerotic behavior to be a common phenomenon among both men and women.

(58) Pope Pius XII, on Oct. 29, 1951, in an allocution to the Italian Catholic Society of Midwives, said rhythm is a method for regulating conception that is open to all Christian couples. This was the fullest statement on the subject of birth control since *Casti Connubii*. For the first time a pope had approved of birth regulation in a formal statement. In the same address, Pius XII cited pleasure as lawful in the marriage act. "They [couples] accept that which the Creator has given them."

(59) In 1953 Karl Rahner published a pioneering work, *Free Speech in the Church*. He discussed the role of public opinion in the Church and distinguished between "the Church teaching" and "the Church taught." Rahner cited John Henry Newman, the outstanding Catholic theologian of the nineteenth century (a century with a dearth of outstanding theologians); Newman, in

his essay *On Consulting the Faithful in Matters of Doctrine* (1859), noted that in the fourth century the laity preserved the doctrine on the Trinity against the Arians. Most bishops had turned Arian. Newman's essay was given a cool reception in Rome.

(60) Bernard Haring, in *The Law of Christ* (1954), said that conjugal love is "the accomplishment of a sacramental mission in virtue of a sacramental Grace"; he cited Gen. 38:8-10 to condemn contraception.

(61) Writing in July, 1957, Francis Connell said the anovulant pill could be used to regulate the female cycle; to use the pill directly as a contraceptive, however, would be "a grave sin."

(62) The World Council of Churches allowed contraception in 1959. By this time most non-Catholic Christian denominations had approved of the use of artificial contraceptives. Karl Barth, regarded as pre-eminent among Protestant theologians, made no absolute prohibition of contraception.

(63) M. G. Plattel, writing in 1962, said it has become more difficult to insist that biological norms dominate human acts.

(64) Demographers showed that a 2 percent annual growth rate would result in one square yard of land per person in 600 years; the world population has been doubling about every thirty years.

(65) Before 1963 no Catholic writer had said that the prohibition of contraception was wrong.

(66) In 1963 John Rock published *The Time Has Come*. Rock, a Catholic gynecologist living in Boston, had a major role in developing the progesterone pill. He argued that anovulants do not destroy the integrity of the conjugal act; rather, they employ a method used by nature itself in preventing conception during pregnancy. He urged the approval of the Church for the use of anovulants as a contraceptive technique based on nature.

(67) On Aug. 10, 1963, the Dutch hierarchy agreed that the use of the pill might be an open question, and possibly licit in special situations.

(68) In 1963 Joseph Mary Reuss, Auxiliary Bishop of Mainz, defended the use of the anovulant pill; he also defended sterilization in certain cases.

(69) *Contraception and Holiness* appeared in 1964. Archbishop Thomas D. Roberts, S.J., and others, cited reasons why contraception should be allowed by the Church.

(70) Also in 1964, a number of other significant studies appeared: *Contraception and Catholics: A New Appraisal*, by Louis

Dupré; *The Experience of Marriage*, edited by Michael Novak; *What Modern Catholics Think About Birth Control*, edited by William Birmingham. The last two books are significant because they mark the first time in twenty centuries that a married Catholic woman voiced her opinion on the subject of contraception.

(71) Also in 1964, Germain G. Grisez, in *Contraception and the Natural Law*, defended the ban on contraception. His central thesis was: to act against life and procreation is always wrong.

(72) The Second Vatican Council taught that "sons of the Church may not undertake methods of regulating procreation which are found blameworthy by the teaching authority of the Church in its unfolding of the divine law" (*Gaudium et Spes*, n. 51). A footnote cited *Casti Connubii* of Pius XI (1930); Pius XII's allocution of Oct. 29, 1951; and an address to a group of cardinals by Paul VI on June 23, 1964. The footnote further stated:

Certain questions which need further and more careful investigation have been handed over, at the command of the Supreme Pontiff, to a commission for the study of population, family, and births, in order that, after it fulfills its function, the Supreme Pontiff may pass judgment. With the doctrine of the magisterium in this state, this holy Synod does not intend to propose immediately concrete solutions.

According to the *National Catholic Reporter*, the Commission voted 70 to 14 in favor of permitting any harmless, medically approved method of contraception.

(73) In 1965 John T. Noonan, Jr., of the Notre Dame Law School, published *Contraception*, one of the most thorough investigations ever undertaken into the history of Catholic thought on human sexuality. The work showed an unmistakable evolution in the attitudes of moral theologians, canonists, and popes concerning the function of sexuality in human life.

(74) Dr. William H. Masters and Mrs. Virginia E. Johnson, of the Reproductive Biology Research Foundation in St. Louis, published *Human Sexual Response* in April 1966. The work continued the Kinsey tradition.

(75) On July 29, 1968, Pope Paul VI issued *Humanae Vitae*. The encyclical reaffirmed the teaching of *Casti Connubii:*

... we must once again declare that the direct interruption of the generative process already begun, and, above all, directly willed and procured abortion ... are to be absolutely excluded as licit means of regulating birth .... The Church teaches ... that each and every marriage act must remain open to the transmission of life.

(76) The American bishops, meeting in Washington, D.C., in Nov. 1968, stated in their pastoral letter: "No one following the teaching of the Church can deny the objective evil of contraception itself." But U.S. Catholics who practice contraception will not be barred from the Sacraments. The French and Canadian hierarchies took an even more lenient view, the former stating that contraception as "the lesser of two evils" might be conscientiously chosen in a given case.

(77) John A. O'Brien, who had done outstanding work in gaining converts to Catholicism and was one of the foremost popularizers of the rhythm method in the 1930s, authored an article appearing in the Jan., 1969, issue of the *Reader's Digest* in which he disagreed with the teaching of *Humanae Vitae*. O'Brien maintained that Catholic couples are free, and even obliged, to follow their own enlightened consciences concerning contraception. O'Brien and others stated their views in *Family Planning in an Exploding Population* (1968).

(78) James P. Shannon, Auxiliary Bishop of St. Paul-Minneapolis since 1965, resigned in 1969, saying he could not conscientiously accept the teaching of *Humanae Vitae* or conscientiously counsel its teaching to others.

(79) On Jan. 15, 1976, the Holy See issued a *Declaration on Certain Questions Concerning Sexual Ethics*. It was the most significant statement by the Vatican on human sexuality since *Humanae Vitae* in 1968. In addition to condemning premarital sex and all homosexual acts, the document taught that masturbation is "an intrinsically and seriously disordered act."

II. NATURAL LAW AND THE PHILOSOPHY OF PLEASURE

Natural Law Theory: a Critique. The doctrine of natural law has had a venerable history. The doctrine can be traced, at least, to the Greek philosopher Heraclitus (536-470 B.C.), who held that all things are in a constant state of flux and change; nothing abides. There must be an ultramundane *logos*, unchangeable, and the source of all human laws. The Sophists and Epicureans said that all laws are merely human conventions.

Socrates, Plato, and Aristotle — that illustrious philosophic trio — all posited an objective norm of morality. There is an objective order written into the nature of things. They opposed the extreme individualism of the Sophists and justified human positive laws as being grounded in the natural law.

The Stoics staunchly defended the existence of an immutable natural law. Men like Seneca, Epictetus, Marcus Aurelius, and Cicero defended the thesis that "true law is right reason in agreement with nature; it is of universal application, unchanging and everlasting. . . ."[8]

St. Paul referred to the natural law written by God in the hearts of men (cf. Rom. 2:14-15). Augustine incorporated natural law doctrine into the framework of Christian ethics. The medieval Scholastics expounded the doctrine with depth and brilliance. Modern Scholasticism accepts the doctrine, but recently it has been subjected to a much more thorough scrutiny in the face of existential and personalist criticism.

Modern science assumes the existence of natural physical laws. Science works on the assumption that there is an established teleology, order, design, and predictability within nature. For every natural effect there is a sufficient natural cause to explain that effect, which is another way of saying that the universe is governed by law. Man can discover these laws by the use of his senses and reason. Laws are not capricious; they are stable, fixed, and universally applicable.

The doctrine of "the natural moral law" states that there is an established moral order, grounded in the nature of things and discovered by human reason, which should govern the free acts of all men at all times and places. Every finite creature has written within itself its own mode of operation. Subhuman creatures follow their own internal law necessarily. Only man is free to violate his own nature or misuse other creatures. It is always wrong to act "against nature," to violate the obvious and natural purpose of a creatural being. Such is the rationale for the existence of natural law that has held sway for more than two thousand years.

Some modern students of natural law (we henceforth use the term to mean the natural *moral* law) are now asking these questions: Just how inviolable is "the order of nature"? Does "the order of nature" have an absolute or a relative value? Can any natural function of the human body be considered absolutely sacrosanct, not subject to modification, even if such modification were to minister to the well-being of the whole man? When can "the order of reason" justifiably overrule "the order of nature"?

Consider these examples: (1) Moralists have generally conceded the right to correct defects of nature and to remove diseased organs of the body. The good of the part may be sacrificed for the good of the whole. Yet, to remove an organ or to correct a defect is, in a real sense, to "act against nature" as nature has functioned in a given case.

(2) Damming a river, to harness its power for a human purpose, has never been called immoral. Yet, to dam a river is to act against the nature of a river, to interfere with its natural function.

(3) An airplane, in a real sense, can be considered a testimony to "acting against nature." Man is not naturally endowed with the ability to fly. By the use of his intelligence, man has devised a means of overcoming gravity and making flight possible. Yet, in the early days of the airplane it was common to hear, "If God intended man to fly, He would have given him wings." The airplane assumes gravity. Gravity is not denied; it is overcome.

(4) Glasses, hearing aids, dentures, toupees, etc., act to correct defects of nature. They are not provided by nature, but man uses them to minister to his total well-being. Even the wearing of warm clothing in the winter is an artificial method of protection from the cold, a protection not naturally provided by the human body. Hardly anyone has called these techniques an unnatural interference with "the order of nature."

Many more examples could be cited. The few we have given should suffice to justify the following conclusion: No act of nature, no natural function ought to be considered absolutely, and without exception, unalterable, not subject to modification and interference *as long as* such modification can be clearly and cogently shown to minister to the total well-being of the whole man and the good of society.

Are some acts "intrinsically evil"? Peter Abélard denied it, saying the moral quality of every act will ultimately be determined by the intention of the agent. One mother deliberately procures an abortion; another mother, while nursing her child, accidentally smothers the child to death. In both cases a life was taken, but only the first case was murder. Abélard thought it was meaningless to speak of an act being "evil in itself."

If intrinsically evil acts exist, surely the taking of a human life would be most elementary. Yet, moralists have generally admitted that a life may be taken in one's own defense or in the defense of the common good. If killing were intrinsically evil absolutely, it would admit of no exceptions. Again, to steal is generally considered an intrinsically evil act. Yet, moralists have

generally agreed that one who is seriously in need of another's
goods may take what he needs to preserve his own life. In this
case, the act is not "stealing," as in the former case self-defense is
not "killing." Again, lying is regarded as intrinsically evil; yet
moralists have approved of the use of "a broad mental reservation," even though what one says is not true as stated.

We cite these examples to show that "the order of reason"
must always take precedence over "the order of nature." Abélard
was right in denying the existence of acts that are wrong in
themselves. Father Charles E. Curran takes the same position
today. In the final analysis the moral quality of any human act is
determined by circumstances attending that act and/or the intention of the agent. Scholastic philosophy has always denied the
possibility of ontological evil; to say an act is evil *in itself,* apart
from extrinsic circumstances and/or the intention of the agent,
seems to posit the possibility of ontological evil.

Blasphemy, for example, is regarded as objectively, absolutely, and intrinsically evil in itself; yet a blasphemous act
derives its moral quality *entirely* from the intention of the agent,
not from the nature of any given act in itself. One might perform
an objective act regarded as blasphemous with no intention or
awareness of blasphemy. In such a case, *blasphemy would simply
not have occurred,* in either an objective or subjective sense. One
can easily get lost here in semantics; but it seems clear that no
act should be regarded as objectively and intrinsically evil in
itself *apart from* the intention of the agent and/or circumstances
of time, place, person, etc. One may rightfully speak of an act
being intrinsically evil and always morally wrong only in the
context of certain circumstances attendant to that act.

From the foregoing it follows that a natural function or
condition should not be considered so absolute as to admit of no
exceptions, as long as the order of reason has not been violated.
Genesis implies this truth by teaching that man was given
dominion over all creation (cf. 1:28).

We can no longer accept the *a priori* condemnation of certain
acts as mortally sinful simply because they are "against nature"
— with no further rationale being provided. Isn't it against the
nature of knees for a Carmelite nun to remain on them for one
hour before the Blessed Sacrament? To glibly condemn an act as
being against nature and therefore immoral carries no weight
unless the act can also be shown to violate reason. The Carmelite
nun has a good *reason* for remaining on her knees for one hour.

Contraception is called morally wrong because it is "against nature" and destroys the integrity of an act regarded as sacral. We need better reasons than these; human reason shows that contraception can be a supremely rational and beneficial form of human behavior.

Charles E. Curran has written lucidly concerning the philosophical basis of natural law theory.[9] He has provided an adequate rationale for refinements in the traditional doctrine and pointed the way to newer approaches in coming to grips with contemporary problems in moral theology. Father Curran's teaching can be paraphrased and summarized as follows:

Traditional natural law theory suffers from three major defects: (1) There is really no such thing as *the* natural law, understood as a monolithic, self-contained, immutable, universally agreed upon body of ethical doctrine existing since the beginning of time. The term *natural law* has meant different things to different people. Cicero, the Stoic philosopher; Ulpian, the Roman jurist; St. Isidore of Seville; and Gratian, the monk who first codified canon law — all proposed divergent theories of natural law. The Stoics appealed to natural law in defending behavior, such as slavery and suicide, that is presently condemned by ethicists. Usury (the taking of interest) was once condemned by the Church from *a priori* premises. The term is now reserved only for the taking of exorbitant interest. Christian theologians have generally held that a source of ethical wisdom does exist apart from Revelation and Scripture. Protestant thinking tends to minimize the value of ethical teaching apart from Sacred Scripture. Bonhoeffer spoke of "divine mandates"; Niebuhr, "love and justice"; Bennett, "common ground morality." One cannot rightly say that Catholicism is irrevocably committed to a natural law theory which brands certain physical acts as being intrinsically evil and always wrong.

(2) Traditional natural law theory has too long been dominated by "physicism," which tends to define the moral quality of a human act solely in terms of its physical, biological, or mechanical properties. Aquinas was careful to distinguish between the order of nature and the order of reason; but he was inclined to identify the requirements of natural law with physical and biological processes. A major influence upon Thomas and Scholasticism in general was the teaching of the third-century Roman lawyer Ulpian, who defined natural law (*ius naturale*) as

"that which is common to all animals." (Albert rejected this definition.) "Natural" thus became synonymous with "animal" or "biological." The animal nature of man retains its own finalities, independent of the demands of rationality. The "order of nature" became somewhat sacrosanct. A prescientific, non-technical culture tended to conform to nature; modern culture, with its technology, makes nature conform to man. Man is a maker, as well as a responder and citizen of the world. There are few today who would say that man has no right to interfere with natural processes, provided there is a sufficient reason to do so.

(3) A third major weakness of natural law theory, according to Curran, is derived from its classicist worldview which emphasizes the static, the abstract, the unchangeable, the eternal, and the universal. A more historical worldview accents the changing, the developing, the dynamic, the concrete, the histori-cal, and the experiential. Two methodologies result from the two worldviews: the classicist methodology which tends to be ab-stract, *a priori*, and deductive; the historical methodology which tends to be concrete, *a posteriori*, and inductive. The two worldviews and methodologies need not be mutually exclusive in all respects. The differences pertain more to emphases and a total view of the human person. A historically conscious methodology must avoid the pitfalls of complete relativism and subjectivism. There is an ontological foundation for historical development. The classicist methodology must avoid a naive realism that defines morality solely in terms of man's animality and biological processes, ignoring the total person in his existen-tial situation. Rationality is not simply a discrete layer on top of animality, each with its separate finalities; man is one, integral organism. The classicist methodology has not adequately come to grips with all moral issues, especially in the area of medical and sexual ethics. Karl Rahner, Bernard Lonergan, and others, have proposed a "transcendental methodology" which examines the conditions and structure in the subject which are necessary for the subject to know reality.

John Courtney Murray has pointed out that it was a classi-cist, *a priori* methodology that denied the principle of religious freedom; the Council Fathers of Vatican II recognized, *de facto*, the existence of religious pluralism in declaring the principle of religious freedom to be an essential part of the Christian Faith. The methodology employed was inductive, *a posteriori*, and his-torical. Vatican II espoused no particular worldview or methodology. The Council was regarded as primarily "pastoral," not in opposition to "doctrinal," but to indicate its concern for the concrete, existential needs of mankind. The "Pilgrim Church" was emphasized, a Church that is finding its way in a world blighted with the effects of Original Sin. Vatican II did not proclaim a Church with all the answers, with a *priori* solutions to every human problem. There was no appeal to a self-contained "natural law" which inexorably and with absolute certitude decides every moral issue. The Council spoke much of the human person and his total orientation toward God.

Natural law theory, based on a classicist worldview and methodology (which permeate the manuals of moral theology), has simply not come to grips with the major moral problems of today. Contraception; direct sterilization; direct therapeutic abortion to save the mother's life; all deliberate sexual actuation outside of marriage; artificial insemination — all are condemned by a physicist natural law theory as being "against nature" and intrinsically evil. A personalist, relational anthropology would not regard these physical acts as immoral, since there is essentially no violation of the order of reason.

Father Curran proposes a "theology of compromise": one sometimes finds himself in a sinful, evil situation which is not of his own making. The effects of Original Sin are very much with every Christian in his ethical decisions. In such "conflict situations" one can choose the lesser of two evils when not to act at all would allow a greater evil than the act committed. Such a rationale would apply to therapeutic abortion to save the mother's life.

In Chapter III we reflected the traditional classicist view by defining the natural moral law as "the moral law, manifested by the natural light of reason, demanding the preservation of the natural order and forbidding its violation." The "natural order" should not be understood in a totally physical or biological sense. In the final analysis, human reason belongs to the "natural order" and decides what is and what is not consonant with the natural order. Man in his ethical decisions is seen as a maker, as well as a responder. There is no reason why physical processes must predominate a theory of natural law. Most philosophers and theologians today will not accept an ethical theory that subordinates the whole man and his well-being and progress to the integrity of a physical or biological process.

The personalist approach is being increasingly recognized and accepted within Catholicism today. Neither Vatican II nor

Humanae Vitae, for example, made any mention of the "primary" and "secondary" ends of marriage, distinctions which subordinate the personal to the biological. Personalism does not deny the importance of physical acts; such acts must always be considered in their effects upon oneself and one's fellow man. Personalism simply states that the total person and his well-being, along with the well-being of others and the good of society in general, ought to pre-empt any consideration of the mere physical aspects of a human act. The personalist anthropology sees mortal sin less in terms of the commission of discrete physical acts and more in terms of "fundamental options" involving the very core of one's being and orientation.

Father Curran has pointed out some inadequate approaches in moral theology. Catholic theology has traditionally emphasized the *a priori,* the importance of works, the validity of reason and natural theology, and the goodness of natural man. Such an approach, though not without value, has at times tended toward Pelagianism, legalism, and an exaggerated trust in the ability of reason, especially as authoritatively interpreted by the Church. Protestantism, on the other hand, has accentuated the transcendence and complete freedom of God, faith over reason and works, and the Scriptures as the sole norm of religious truth. The ethical theories of Barth, Bonhoeffer, Lehmenn, Sittler, and others, lead to a dangerous theological "actualism" which unduly stresses the concrete, the particular, and the existential apart from general norms. "Consequentialism" is another simplistic approach which says that morality is ultimately determined by weighing the results of one's actions. Catholic theology erred by identifying the moral object with the physical structure of the act; but some modern pragmatic and situationist approaches would not pay enough attention to the object, giving too much importance to circumstances and the end of the agent. No simplistic answer is possible to the question, What determines the morality of human acts?

The concept of "the teaching Church" is undergoing development. Curran does not believe that the Church has ever made an infallible pronouncement concerning a specific moral matter; he further believes that the very nature of specific moral actions makes infallible pronouncements in this area impossible. Vatican II was careful to state that the Mystical Body of Christ *subsists* in the Roman Catholic Church; *subsists* connotes something less than a total identification. The Holy Spirit is not restricted to the visible structure of the Roman Catholic Church; He belongs to and manifests Himself in the entire People of God. Curran speaks of a magisterial function residing in the entire People of God which is distinct from, but supplementary to, the hierarchical magisterium. *Humanae Vitae* seemed to ignore the magisterial and prophetic function of the entire People of God; the conclusions of the letter were based primarily on previous statements of the hierarchical magisterium — a reliance which Curran calls "intellectual incest." Christian experience, the values of an inductive methodology, and a historically conscious worldview were subordinated to an *a priori*, physicist, simplistic view of natural law.

Father Curran has clearly shown the inadequacies of a natural law theory which posits negative moral absolutes that condemn an act defined solely in its physical structure. Curran acknowledges the value of natural law theory in providing some basis for objectivity, stability, and general norms. Morality must never become totally subjective, whimsical, and relative. Morality must never ignore the physical act in terms of its structure and consequences. Curran admits that a more historically conscious, *a posteriori* methodology will never carry the degree of certitude and finality that has been claimed by natural law theory with its *a priori* worldview. These are risks that must be taken in moral theology, just as the modern day sciences proceed inductively in the attainment of truth, at no time asserting that absolute certitude and finality have been achieved. If one already possesses all the answers, then progress and development are not possible. Stable frames of reference will always exist for the Christian: the reality of God; Divine Revelation; the person and teachings of Christ; the authority of Sacred Scripture; the authority of the Church's magisterium; and the essential capability of human reason to know truth, natural, dogmatic, and moral.

Regarding the Bible as a stable frame of reference for morality: the problems of hermeneutics and exegesis have always been moot in the history of Christianity. The moral doctrines of the Bible are subject to interpretation. The Bible forbids the taking of interest (cf. Lev. 25:36-37) and the taking of oaths (cf. Matt. 5:34), both of which are found morally acceptable by the Church today. Certain verses seem to approve of slavery (cf. Lev. 25:44); divorce because of adultery (cf. Matt. 19:9); polygamy and concubines; the dominion and superiority of man over woman;

deceit in the attainment of one's goals (cf. the story of Jacob and Esau); an eye for an eye and a tooth for a tooth (cf. Lev. 24:20); arbitrary and unequal justice (cf. Matt. 20:1-16). Leviticus 20:18 forbids intercourse during a woman's menstrual period; cursing one's father or mother is punishable by death (cf. 20:9); homosexual acts are punishable by death (cf. 20:13). Much of the Mosaic code, of course, is considered to be abrogated by the New Law. What is and what is not abrogated (the Ten Commandments, for example) remain a matter of judgment and interpretation. Reasonable men can understandably differ on a given point of moral doctrine contained in the Bible. Some moral doctrines can be understood in a restricted sense, with only a particular, prescriptive application in time and place; others can be understood as having universal application.

The words of Christ on points of morality are to be given the utmost weight. Again, His words are subject to interpretation; Christ sometimes made use of hyperbole in making a point. In the final analysis, the doctrines of Sacred Scripture, both dogmatic and moral, need an authoritative interpreter, a point made elsewhere in this study. The Church established by Christ is that authoritative interpreter. It is not enough to justify a particular moral stance with a simplistic appeal to Sacred Scripture. The positions cited above should be sufficient to show that Biblical moral doctrine is open to a considerable range of interpretation. Biblical moral doctrine, especially the words of Christ, must always weigh heavily in the articulation of Christian ethics; but Biblical teaching must ultimately be seen, not as an *a priori* finality in moral issues, but as an essential part of the total Christian experience developing in time and space. There are sources of ethical wisdom distinct from Sacred Scripture. These sources include human reason, human experience, and the authoritative teaching office of the Church. Together with the ethical thrusts of Scripture, they form a basis for making authentic ethical decisions in living the Christian life.

In conclusion, we regard Charles E. Curran as an articulate, reasonable, and cogent voice in Catholicism today, calling for a renewal in moral theology in coming to grips with the pressing moral issues of our day. One ought not to be justified in rejecting Catholicism because it does not adequately relate to current problems or adequately reflect the practical experience of Christians. Because of the work of the Holy Spirit and the efforts of men such as Father Curran, Catholic moral theology is currently undergoing the renewal and *aggiornamento* that will make it a beacon and a refuge for mankind, as the Pilgrim Church continues its voyage through space and time.

We urge the Church to take a fresh look at "natural law"; the time has come for a reappraisal.

Pleasure. The ethics of pleasure has had an interesting history. (1) Plato (427-347 B.C.) considered spiritual love, devoid of pleasure, to be the ideal. This belief followed from Plato's basic theory that material things are but shadows and poor representations of a world of subsistent spiritual ideas.

(2) Aristotle (384-322 B.C.), in his *Nicomachean Ethics*, analyzed pleasure as a subjective sense experience that accompanies natural functions. Pleasure is not itself an act; but pleasure may be sought for its own sake for a sufficient reason, such as health. Pleasure is *ontologically* good in itself but *morally* neutral. "The pleasure proper to a worthy activity is good and that proper to an unworthy activity bad."

(3) Epicurus (342-270 B.C.) considered pleasure to be the final norm of human behavior. What brings pleasure is good and morally right; what brings pain is bad and morally wrong.[10]

(4) The Stoics rejected pleasure as debasing and beneath the dignity of man. Man ought to be motivated by reason alone, not by feeling or pleasure.

(5) Augustine was in sympathy with Stoicism; along with his Manicheism, he took a dim view of pleasure in terms of having any real human value. Augustine accepted the Platonic doctrine of an accidental union of body and soul; material goods were only incidental to man's well-being.

(6) St. John Chrysostom was the first important theologian to disassociate concupiscence from sexuality; he said that Original Sin and concupiscence had no special connection with sexuality, as was implied by many writers before him.

(7) The medieval Scholastics generally took a dim view of pleasure, justifying it only in the intent to perform the natural act with which the pleasure is associated. Le Maistre is significant because he was one of the first to justify pleasure for any good reason, even to relieve tedium. Rigorists had maintained that to consciously seek pleasure as such was sinful.

(8) Victorians and Puritans held pleasure as suspect.

The pendulum swings. Various ages have regarded pleasure as an unmitigated good or an unmitigated evil. The true answer is obviously in the middle. Pleasure belongs to the psycho-physiological order; as such, it must be governed by moderation and control. Pleasure is subject to satiety, whereas *joy*, which is of the spirit, is not. No one has ever said he was too happy or joyful; but too much pleasure can become pain. Pleasure is conditioned by contrast.

Pleasure has real value in human life. Man is not a disembodied spirit; man is an *unum*, one substance, composed of both a material body and a spiritual soul which are substantially united to make the one person. Plato erred in overemphasizing the spiritual side of man. Man can seek pleasure, which comes from God and was intended to contribute to man's general well-being. As Aristotle noted, with his usual calm penetration, a pleasure is good if the act that produces the pleasure is good. A conscious intent to perform the natural act and achieve its purpose is not absolutely essential.

If the principles of "natural law," applied so rigorously to sexual behavior, were to be applied with equal rigor to other areas of human existence, life would indeed become a grotesque nightmare, "a tale told by an idiot" of which Shakespeare spoke. Imagine the necessity of having "a nutritive intent" for every bite of food taken, not being able to seek food and drink for the pleasure they give. By this criterion every ice cream parlor, every tavern, every candy store would be *per se* immoral, since their primary purpose is to provide for pleasure of the palate.

Imagine the necessity to intend only to clean oneself in taking a bath; to take a bath or shower only for the pleasure it provides, for the relaxation it affords to body and spirit is "to act against the nature of a bath, which is to clean."

Imagine taking a walk *only* to get from one place to another, which is the natural purpose of legs and walking. Who has ever said that walking for the fun of it, for diversion and relaxation is immoral?

Why should sexual pleasure be radically different from other God-given pleasures? In 1951 Pope Pius XII recognized the value of sexual pleasure. We urge the Church to clarify its stance, once and for all, regarding the value and place of pleasure in human life.

III. SEX ESSENTIAL AND SEX EXISTENTIAL

Let it be understood at the outset that we do not espouse existentialism as an adequate philosophy of life. Any worldview that calls the universe "absurd" and espouses a reaction of "nausea," "anguish," "loneliness," and "despair" to the meaninglessness of human existence is not worthy of any man's allegiance. However, there is no system of thought in the history of philosophy and theology that hasn't contributed something of value to a better understanding of man and human existence.

Indeed, some existential concepts have become an integral part of our modern vocabulary. "Doing one's own thing"; personal commitment and responsibility; the authentic life; personalism; person over law; the precedence of subject over object — all have found their way into our mode of thinking. The concepts are not new: the Greek Sophists, who were extreme individualists, and later the subjective idealists had the basic ideas of modern existentialism. Socrates directed much of his attention to showing that the Sophists were wrong.

In the area of human sexuality, existentialism has provided some valid distinctions. We have chosen the terms *sex essential* and *sex existential* to make a distinction that was made very well by Herbert Doms in 1935. *Sex essential* is reproductive. There is no question but that sexuality is essentially ordained to reproducing the human race. The biology of sex is manifestly reproductive in nature. Reproduction can be considered the objective, ontological purpose of sex essential.

This essential view of sex does not exclude its existential nature, which is to fulfill the psychophysiological need of the individual. *Sex existential* exists to satisfy the individual's inherent need for sexual expression; as such, sex existential is not necessarily ordained toward reproduction. Personal satisfaction and fulfillment can be considered the subjective, immanent, psychophysiological purpose of sex existential. Sex essential will be used by most couples less than a half-dozen times, with reproduction taking place. Sex existential will be used any number of times.

We believe the time has come to drop the distinction of "primary" and "secondary" ends of marriage. Genesis states that "it is not good for man to be alone"; no implication is made that this purpose of marriage is in any way inferior or "secondary" to the purpose of procreation, to "increase and multiply." The subjective order is not inferior to the objective order. Each has rights and responsibilities to be acknowledged by the other. Sex existential has no right to exclude sex essential, or the purpose of procreation. Neither does sex essential have the right to exclude sex existential, or the purpose of personal fulfillment apart from procreation.

The historical outline given in Section I of this chapter clearly reveals that the Church had generally not given sufficient recognition to the rights of sex existential. The thrust was mostly toward sex for reproduction; sex for pleasure, mutual love, or personal fulfillment was downgraded. Pope Leo XIII — a man who was always supremely candid and fully committed to the truth, even when it hurt — wrote in 1880: "It is a reproach to some of the ancients that they showed themselves the enemies of marriage in many ways."[11]

Something had to be wrong with a philosophy and theology of sex that would have St. Aloysius Gonzaga interpreting his vow of chastity so strictly that he refused to look any woman in the eye, even his own mother.[12] Aquinas thought it was better never to touch a woman. *Sin* is a three-letter word beginning with *s*, and so is *sex;* not a few writers of the past closely associated the two. Original Sin was thought to be intimately connected with sex. After Adam and Eve sinned, they were ashamed of their nakedness. Many still hold, with Augustine, that Original Sin is transmitted to offspring by means of the act of coitus. Small wonder that sexuality has been held as suspect.

Sex isn't all that bad; the depreciation given to human sexuality and its attendant pleasures was nothing short of an insult to Almighty God, Who created sex and placed it in man and woman in the first place. Christ expressed this truth when He quoted Genesis and attributed the words to God Himself: "Have you not read that the Creator, from the beginning, made them male and female, and said, 'For this cause a man shall leave his father and mother, and cleave to his wife, and the two shall become one flesh'?" (Matt. 19:4-5).

Sex was God's idea, not man's. One need not apologize for his sexuality; on the contrary, everyone has the right to accept comfortably and without guilt this part of his nature. The Canticle of Canticles of the Old Testament certainly takes an appreciative view of human sexuality.

The time has pre-eminently arrived for the Church to state forthrightly the rights and privileges of sex existential as well as sex essential.

IV. THE MORALITY OF CONTRACEPTION

In the broadest sense, *contraception* means any technique or practice intentionally pursued so as to prevent the male sperm from fertilizing the female ovum. In this broad sense, total abstinence and periodic abstinence are contraceptive techniques insofar as they are deliberately pursued to avoid procreation. In a narrower sense, contraception refers to the use of physical or chemical means to prevent conception in coitus. We shall henceforth use the term in this latter sense.

Contraceptives commonly in use today are: condoms and diaphragms, which place a physical barrier between sperm and ovum; spermicidal creams, jellies, and suppositories, which kill the sperm before impregnation can take place; intrauterine devices, placed within the uterus of the woman, which somehow prevent either impregnation or implantation (nidation) in the uterus; "morning-after" pills, which apparently destroy the fertilized ovum; and, finally, anovulants, which duplicate a chemical process occurring naturally during pregnancy which stops ovulation completely.[13]

We rule out the use of intrauterine devices and the "morning-after" pill. At this writing, their function is not fully understood. There is every indication that they act as an abortifacient; i.e., they prevent an already fertilized ovum from achieving nidation and continuing in existence. This amounts to abortion, not contraception, and must be condemned.

In the historical sketch presented in Section I of this chapter, one can clearly discern a consistent condemnation of contraception, based mainly on the premise that sex means reproduction. That contraception repudiates the essential purpose of sex is a logical conclusion *if* one accepts the major premise, which equated sex with reproduction. Even such fair-minded men as St. Albert and Martin Le Maistre and John Major were not ready to approve of contraception. Pius XI, in *Casti Connubii*, made only a passing reference to the lawfulness of coitus even though time or other natural causes rendered conception impossible.

Posterity will surely consider the allocution of Pius XII in 1951, when he explicitly approved of rhythm as a method of contraception that may be deliberately pursued by couples for a good reason, as one of the most significant decisions made on human sexuality in the history of Christianity. The Vicar of Christ had stated unequivocally that sex does not necessarily mean reproduction in every case, that birth regulation is a *posi-*

tive value worthy of all Christian couples. Heretofore, the use of the sterile period was to be recommended only as a remedy for Onanism.

Contraception had always been viewed in a negative sense; contraceptives were frequently referred to as "poisons of sterility." The very word contains a negative combining form, *contra*, meaning *against*. Negative words can denote a positive meaning. Take the word *infinite*, which means not finite or limited. It is the best word we have to describe God, Who is pure act and the most positive being in existence. So also, contraception has a *positive* meaning: to regulate the number of children that a couple can raise responsibly; to space them so as not to impair the mother's health; to promote marital love and affection. These are positive, not negative, values. Contraception is not *against* birth and life; contraception is *for* responsible parenthood.

Granted that responsible parenthood, with every child being a wanted child and not simply an accident, is a positive value and eminently in accord with Christian principles; the problem remains: Is contraception an immoral means to obtaining a good end? No matter how good the end, an immoral means may never be used to achieve that good end.

Contraception is wrong if it can be shown to be against nature and, therefore, opposed to the will of God, Who is nature's Author. We submit that contraception is not opposed to nature. Nature itself provides an imperfect method of contraception in the sequence of fertility and sterility found in a woman's menstrual cycle. We say the method is "imperfect" because the time of ovulation can never be certain. Some women have fairly regular cycles; about 15-20 percent do not. Gynecologists say that it is physiologically *possible* for a woman to ovulate at *any time*, even though an extremely irregular ovulation is rare. The simple fact remains that reliance upon the sterile period is a precarious method of contraception at best.

Can it cogently be said to be intrinsically wrong and against nature to try to improve upon that which nature does imperfectly? It is wrong to use an artificial device to make contraception more certain, to improve upon that which the woman's own cycle does imperfectly? The principle of periodic sterility is written into the nature of the woman's reproductive system. Why cannot the intelligence of man aid nature by making the existence of sterility more certain? Glasses, dentures, etc., aid and supplement nature. Why cannot coitus be aided to ensure responsible parenthood, once the regulation of births and mutual love are seen as positive values resulting from contraception?

The only negative answer that can be given to the above questions is: The act of coition is sacral. It is God's way of communicating life and the occasion for creation of a human soul. As such, it must remain totally intact, wholly itself; its integrity must not be destroyed. Of course, no one can logically disprove an *a priori* assumption which is proposed as self-evident. How do we know that coitus is sacral, unalterable by man? The Bible doesn't say so. Many cogent reasons can be adduced to show why coitus should be subject to man's control and intelligence in providing for a reasonably certain method to regulate conception.

What makes periodic abstinence right but other methods wrong in controlling conception? Rhythm makes use of *time*, which is not considered unnatural. This harkens back to the Platonic-Augustinian belief that time is superior to space and more spiritual, that there is something basically suspect about matter. Man and woman, unlike animals that are in heat, do not ordinarily and naturally express sexual love on a time-scale dictated by the calendar or the thermometer. Sexual love, at best, is spontaneous with human beings. Rhythm, though admittedly grounded in the nature of the woman's cycle of ovulation, involves elements that are decidedly unnatural.

Diaphragms and condoms use *space* to prevent conception; spermicidal preparations use *chemistry;* anovulants use *hormonal chemistry* plus *physiology.* Why are these methods any more immoral than using time? One can grant that these methods involve a greater interference with the act of coitus than does rhythm; but rhythm also involves *some* interference — by time — with reproduction, by means of human calculation. Once one has admitted the principle that conception may be regulated by human intelligence and human calculation, then it is difficult to see why one method is morally less acceptable than another, as long as the method used is medically safe and aesthetically acceptable. If a more certain method of birth regulation is available, why should a couple be morally restricted to a less certain method?

The objection is given that contraceptives encourage premarital and extramarital intercourse. To fault contraceptives for premarital and extramarital intercourse is like faulting an automobile (in safe condition) for fatal traffic accidents. We submit that contraceptives, like an automobile, are morally neutral in themselves; they can be misused. Contraceptives are misused when they are employed exclusively by married couples to avoid all procreation without a sufficient reason, for purely selfish or hedonistic reasons. Contraceptives may not sacrifice sex essential for sex existential. Secondly, contraceptives are misused when used in adultery or fornication, not because the contraceptive *per se* is immoral (the avoidance of procreating an illegitimate child is desirable), but because the context in which the contraceptive is used is immoral. The problem is with *people*, not *things*. Furthermore, the evidence indicates that a high percentage of teenagers fail to take effective contraceptive precautions in premarital coitus.

Our Sunday Visitor published a letter telling of a Canadian woman who suffered postpartum psychosis after her first pregnancy. She gave birth to another child before the first was a year old, again resulting in severe mental depression. Using rhythm, she had a third child a year and a half following the second birth. She was confined in a hospital for three months following her third pregnancy. Her psychiatrist, a Catholic, said under no circumstances should she have another child and recommended taking oral contraceptives.

The woman was told by her pastor, "It is your own soul." She and her husband are now "living celibate lives." The woman's sister wondered if contraception might be permissible in this case. "Try to realize deep in your consciousness what the Pope is after," wrote Msgr. John Sheridan. "He is simply trying to reflect how we can be most human; he is trying to reflect what God wants us to be and do."

What a travesty upon God's will as allegedly reflected in natural law! What a far cry from the sympathetic and loving Christ, Who berated the Pharisees for placing heavy burdens on men's shoulders! This woman might have at least been told the principle of *epikeia*, which states that no law can be considered binding which works upon one an unreasonable hardship.

There is a thesis in criteriology which states that the consensus of mankind cannot err concerning a principle or doctrine that is required for the preservation of the common good.[14] There is good reason to believe that most married couples throughout history have practiced contraception — and not just contraception by total or periodic abstinence. Even among Catholics, a governmental survey in England showed that 47 percent of the Catholic couples interviewed use artificial means to control birth.[15] The Westoff-Ryder study made in the United States revealed that the percentage of Catholic wives using only rhythm to regulate conception fell from 70 percent in 1955 to 47 percent in 1965.[16] Andrew Greeley has reported as high as 83 percent using artificial methods. Medically safe contraception has been approved by virtually all non-Catholic Christian denominations. We submit that all of these people are not in error or in sin. Men like Billy Graham and Norman Vincent Peale and the late Karl Barth, who know, love, and serve the one true Christ, are not in error in approving of contraception.[17]

Given the present socioeconomic condition of the world, the common good as well as the good of the individual family unit require that conception be controlled; and a couple should have the right to use the best means available, apart from total abstinence. We cannot continue on a course that has the world population doubling every thirty to forty years. Along with environmental pollution and the threat of nuclear warfare, an exploding population is the most pressing problem besetting the people of the world today. The Church should facilitate, not hinder, a solution to the problem of a soaring world population. The present position of Catholicism on contraception obviously does not facilitate such a solution, which is but another reason to suspect the rationale which labels contraception as being "against nature."

The time has pre-eminently arrived for the Church to reconsider its position on contraception. We urge the Church to listen to the Holy Spirit speaking through myriad voices dispersed throughout the Mystical Body.

V. PERSONAL SEXUALITY AND MORALITY

When the Creator fashioned human nature, He willed that sexuality would be an integral part of every normal, healthy human being's make-up. The essential purpose for making man a sexual being was to insure the propagation of the human species; however, divine wisdom understood full well that not every man and woman would be able to enter the state of matrimony, and for good reasons. One's health might be such that matrimony, with its serious responsibilities, would make too great a demand upon the individual; one might be psychologically indisposed toward matrimony; uncontrollable circumstances, such as dependent parents, not meeting a suitable partner, etc., might make marriage inadvisable; one might choose a career that is better lived in a celibate state. The all-wise God knew that marriage would not be for everyone.

Is it logical to believe that God would place the psycho-physiological need of sexuality, universally recognized as one of the strongest of human appetites, within every normal human being and not make it possible — physiologically, psychologically, and morally — to satisfy that God-given need? Did He intend that sexual desire would *only* be satisfied in a reproductive function or *only* in an intersubjective relationship? Did God intend the single man and woman, the sexually isolated individual, to live an adult life in which every sexual desire and every sexual pleasure be repressed and denied consent?

If God so intended, one wonders if it would not be advisable for single people to submit to castration, as Origen did. Erasmus once wrote: "In my opinion parents who intend their children for celibate priesthood would be much kinder to castrate them in infancy, rather than to expose them whole against their will to this temptation to lust." A eunuch has no sexual desire and experiences no sexual stimulation; hence, he or she would not be faced with the prospect of consenting to sexual pleasure. Of course, merely to make the foregoing statement is to see its absurdity. Sexuality is not something to be expunged from human nature, something fraught with evil, a snare and delusion. On the contrary, sexuality is a dim reflection of the life of the Holy Trinity as well as a reminder of our own mortality. Furthermore, the Church would object to castration for the above-mentioned purpose as an unjustifiable mutilation of the body. Aquinas specifically opposed castration, even for a spiritual purpose, saying such mutilation is unnecessary because sexual continence can be achieved by the will alone.

Man does not *invent* his own sexuality; sexual gratification is not an ingenious contrivance of man to provide a recreational pastime. Man *discovers* his own sexuality which was placed in him by his Creator. Certainly, God intended man to express his sexuality according to moral norms; but we find it extremely difficult to believe that sexual morality for the single man or woman demands strict, total abstinence. There is simply no parallel with any other psychophysiological human need.

Every normal person experiences hunger for food and thirst for drink; these needs are legitimately satisfied at various times by everyone. Everyone experiences fatigue at one time or another; the need and desire for sleep are satisfied by everyone. Everyone feels the need for defecation of the bowels and voiding of the bladder, and these needs are satisfied by everyone. Every normal person feels the need for cleanliness, and this need is satisfied by bathing. Everyone feels the need for bodily warmth, and this need is satisfied by appropriate clothing and the use of heating devices. In satisfying all of these legitimate, God-given needs, man experiences a sense of pleasure and satisfaction, which are part of living a truly human life.

Are we to draw the line and say that the psychophysiological need for sexual expression, present in every normal adult, may not be deliberately satisfied in the celibate state? Is it really "against nature" and a mortal sin for the unmarried to consent to sexual pleasure, even for one second, as Catholic moral theologians teach?

We do not question in the slightest that heterosexual relations are reserved only to a husband and wife. Fornication and adultery are not morally acceptable forms of sexual expression. We believe this because reason postulates these ethical truths and because fornication and adultery are explicitly forbidden in the Bible, which we believe to be the inspired word of God.

Sexuality expressed between a man and woman must be within the institution of matrimony because such sexual expression ought to involve commitment, mutual love, and a responsible acceptance of the reproductive function of sex — all of which can only take place within a permanent conjugal union. Fornication and adultery are wrong because sex is reduced to a purely physical phenomenon with no social commitment for the well-being of offspring and no psychological commitment to one's partner. That is why Aquinas was careful to say that fornication and adultery do not violate the order of nature, *per se*, but only the order of reason.

Aquinas opposed autosexuality as being intrinsically evil and against nature on the grounds that the male and female generative organs are naturally ordained for copulation. To use them in a solitary context is opposed to the nature of the organs, and is a worse sin than either fornication or adultery. Autosexuality violates both the order of nature and the order of reason.[18]

Once again, we are back to an interpretation of natural law which sees one specific purpose for every natural organ and function; to vary from that inherent purpose and order, even for the welfare of the whole man, is to act against nature and is, therefore, morally wrong.

Scientific studies conducted in the last several decades have shown autosexuality to be a fairly common phenomenon with most men and women. Kinsey's studies placed the figure at more than 90 percent of all men interviewed and about 60 percent of the women. Medical science has thoroughly disproved the thesis that autosexuality can be physically harmful. On the contrary, there is substantial evidence that autosexuality can be positively beneficial, both to the individual and to society.[19]

The nature and function of the male prostate is now better understood. There is evidence that repeated sexual stimulation — to which a man is normally subject in the course of everyday living — without periodic ejaculation (the frequency depending upon individual factors) can result in a bloated, tender, and even painful prostate, with an increased susceptibility to infection. Studies have shown a higher incidence of prostatitis among single men than among married men. The conclusion seems inescapable: orgasm is a normal and healthy function of the human body as God has made it. A fundamental biological principle is "use or lose"; the prostate was made to be used. Involuntary nocturnal emissions are not always sufficient for all men to maintain a healthy prostate. Total sexual abstinence is not considered to be a healthy situation.[20]

Can it be cogently argued that total sexual abstinence is demanded by the order of nature and/or the order of reason? Good morals and good health should go hand in hand. Earlier in this study we noted that there can be no real contradiction between true science and true religion. Apparent contradictions can be resolved by a closer examination of the teachings of both. One cannot help but wonder at a moral theology which brands a form of human behavior as being "intrinsically evil" which the generality of mankind accepts as natural and harmless. How can autosexuality be called "against nature" when this form of behavior is found among animals, which supposedly always follow the nature God has given them? We find no specific condemnation in the Bible.

We urge the Church to take a fresh look at autosexuality and re-examine the reasons for its condemnation.[21]

Human sexuality is a participation in the creative stream of life authored by God Himself. All life is fecund, even the divine life of the Trinity. Sex is both a reminder of human mortality and a mirror of the infinite fecundity of the Life of all living. The mystery of sex is related to reverence for life and life's Creator.

CHAPTER VII

PROPOSALS FOR REFORM

"If I Were Pope. . ."

Blessed are they who hunger and thirst for justice, for they shall be satisfied.

— Matt. 5:6

. . . all the faithful, clerical and lay, possess a lawful freedom of inquiry and of thought, and the freedom to express their minds humbly and courageously about those matters in which they enjoy competence.

— Vatican II, *Gaudium et Spes*, n. 62

Come now, and let us reason together, saith the Lord.

— Isaiah 1:18
(Authorized King James Version)

One who will not reason is a bigot; one who cannot reason is a fool; and one who dares not reason is a slave.

— Anon.

Reform, that you may preserve,

— Lord Macaulay

No army can withstand the strength of an idea whose time has come.

— Victor Hugo

Time does not age the Church but makes it grow, stirs it into life and fullness. The Church can prove itself in still more complete forms, still more beautiful forms and we would even say in still more holy forms, than those which it has shown in the past.

— Pope Paul VI

. . . even the trust in reason is a precarious faith; we are all fragments of darkness groping for the sun.

— Will Durant, *The Reformation*

They are trying to make me into a fixed star. I am an irregular planet.

— Martin Luther

DEMOGRAPHERS estimate that about 100 billion human beings have walked the earth in the last million years. Since 4 billion people are now living, there are about 25 "ghosts" standing behind every living human being; 25 persons whose brief candle once lit the human stage; 25 persons who — for the most part — worked, struggled, and contributed what they could to improve the human condition.

Christianity has existed less than 2000 years. The history of Christianity has been fluid, dynamic, and, like evolution, thrusting forward. Change occurred slowly during some periods, rapidly during other periods. The twentieth century must certainly be reckoned as a time of rapid change. Fulton J. Sheen has observed that the Church undergoes a relatively rapid change about every 500 years.[1] This century began with the 100-foot flight of the Wright brothers at Kitty Hawk. Now unmanned spacecraft soar to Venus and Mars; Pioneer 10, at this writing, has been dispatched on a 620-million-mile voyage to Jupiter, travelling through space in excess of 31,000 miles an hour.

Catholicism today is also on the move.

In his important book *The Remaking of the Church*, Richard P. McBrien points out three ways in which any social institution can respond to the stimulus of environmental change:

(1) The way of *tenacity* can be likened to a rock and its interaction with its environment. A rock resists change as much as possible. It is primarily concerned with maintaining the *status quo*. It gives little and it takes little. Yet over the long run a rock is slowly eroded by wind and water, and is subject to chemical decomposition.

(2) The way of *elasticity* can be likened to kelp, which tends to readily give and take with the ebb and flow of its watery environment. By a great deal of adaptation and accommodation, the kelp manages to preserve itself, but tends to lose its ability for self-determination. The kelp bends with every change of current.

(3) The way of *self-determination* can be likened to a porpoise, which interacts with its watery environment so as to develop and improve the organism's existence within the parameters of its environment. The porpoise is selective, adapting to what is beneficial, rejecting what is deleterious.

Social institutions have a natural proclivity to follow the way of tenacity in the face of environmental change. Change is generally seen as a threat to the institution's integrity. Change may be vigorously resisted; but ultimately the institution must come to grips with change in order to insure its viability. The way of elasticity may require the surrendering of essential components of the institution. The institution may survive, but only at the expense of surrendering its basic integrity. The way of self-determination can be seen to be the best response that a social organization can make to the stimulus of change. The organization is preserved by a selection of those elements of change which will contribute to the growth and integrity of the organization.

Change is a fact of life, and every institution must come to grips with this fact. Not to change can mean death, both for an individual and for a group (like the dinosaurs, that seemed to follow the way of tenacity). "To live is to change," observed Cardinal Newman; "and to be perfect is to have changed often." By following the way of self-determination, an institution insures its survival by growing, developing, and improving within the parameters of its environment. Both tenacity and elasticity may provide for short-term survival; but self-determination alone provides for long-term survival in the context of a changing world. The Constitution of the United States is the viable instrument it is because it is seen as being amendable.

The survival of the Church until the coming of God's Kingdom is guaranteed by divine authority. The Church will eventually blossom forth, along with the entire universe, into the fully realized Kingdom of God, which will be primarily the work of God, not man. But the human side of the Church follows the laws of change written into the nature of the universe. The human Church must take heed of these laws and fulfill its obligation to work for the coming of God's Kingdom.

Are we witnessing the twilight and sunset of the Church? Has the Church been reduced to "bare ruined choirs," as Garry Wills uses Shakespeare to describe Catholicism today? Our opinion is that Catholicism today is opening up to a bright new future. This is a time of sunrise, not sunset; a time of gestation, not death. The late Karl Barth, possibly the most important Protestant theologian since Luther and Calvin, said that a reformation is taking place within the Catholic Church today that will make the Protestant Reformation seem small in comparison. He saw Vatican II as a beginning, not an ending; and he predicted that a future ecumenical council will follow through with the thrusts of Vatican II.

Vatican II taught, in its *Decree on Ecumenism* (n. 18), that "in order to restore communion and unity or preserve them, one must 'impose no burden beyond what is indispensable' (Acts 15:28)." The Council further taught: "Let there be unity in what is necessary, freedom in what is unsettled, and charity in any case" (*Gaudium et Spes*, n. 92). In this spirit we offer the following proposals for reform, not to destroy the Church we love, but to preserve it. "Reform," counseled Macaulay, "that you may preserve." We believe these reforms would follow the way of self-determination, and would avoid the pitfalls inherent in the ways of tenacity and elasticity. These reforms would bring the Church into alignment with the realities of the twentieth century. The last quarter of the twentieth century could very well be Catholicism's finest hour.

I. ELECTION OF THE POPE

Background. Jesus Christ selected Peter to be His vicar on earth, the visible head of the Mystical Body. Peter was given the keys, with the power to bind and to loose; he was given full jurisdiction over Christ's Church with the authority to teach, govern, and sanctify mankind.

The New Testament gives no indication that Christ consulted the apostles, or anyone else, in choosing Peter. After all, Christ was divine and as such He was all-wise and omniscient; there was no need for Him to employ a democratic procedure in selecting His personal representative on earth. Nor does the New Testament indicate that Christ specified the manner in which the successors of Peter should be chosen. This matter of procedure was left to the discretion of His Church, to be developed over the years and centuries.

Men[2] have ascended to the chair of Peter in various ways in the history of the Church. Some of the early popes were undoubtedly named by their predecessors; upon the death of the reigning pope, they assumed the office with at least the tacit knowledge and consent of the clergy and laity. Gradually, a system of election evolved whereby the Roman clergy and people and the neighboring bishops each took part. After Christianity became the state religion, the civil authority took an increasingly stronger role in the selection of the Bishop of Rome. The Roman clergy actually asked the emperor Henry III to give them a pope. The lay investiture of bishops was finally forbidden by Pope Gregory VII (1073-1085).

Pope Nicholas II issued his celebrated bull of April 13, 1059, which determined the electoral procedure for popes. The College of Cardinals exclusively had the right to nominate and elect the pope. The consent of the rest of the clergy and the people was only a formality; the emperor had no rights in naming a pope save those he had received as a concession from the Holy See. The electoral procedure established by Nicholas II remains substantially in force today.

Evaluation and Recommendation. The election of the pope by the *entire* Church, we submit, is "an idea whose time has come." The values of democracy have been learned by mankind over the centuries. We acknowledge that the constitution of the Church is essentially monarchical and secondarily oligarchical; but such a structure does not preclude democratic procedures. The principles of input, of representative government, of government by consent of the governed are firmly ingrained in modern society. We recommend that the Church fully utilize these principles in the selection of a pope. The following is one method that we feel would be effective.

An ecumenical election would be held in which every mature cell, eighteen years of age and older, could vote. Six months prior to the election, the bishops of the world would appoint a nominating committee consisting of one delegate from each national hierarchy, chosen by the bishops, clergy, religious, and laity of that country. The committee would meet to nominate five persons for the office of the papacy. The five nominees would have six months to air their views on current issues.

An ecumenical election would then be held. Everyone who considers himself a Christian, a member of Christ's Mystical Body, and is eighteen years of age, would be encouraged to vote. Surely this election would be one of the most significant occurrences in human history! This ecumenical papal election would be the greatest single common undertaking ever experienced by mankind! The effects of such an election would have to be far-reaching. Such an election, of course, would have been impossible some years ago, but the time has now arrived when communications make such an election not only possible, but eminently desirable.

The election would be in the hands of the nominating committee of bishops; this committee would be the final judge of the outcome of the election. The votes of the bishops would carry a value of one-third; the votes of priests and religious would have a value of one-third; and the votes of the laity would weigh one-third. The pope would be elected for ten years. No pope could succeed himself; he could voluntarily resign at any time, in which case the one who received the secondmost votes would fill out the term. The reigning pope would serve *ex officio* on the nominating committee. The newly elected pope would have the right to establish the Holy See wherever he sees fit. Thus, the Catholic Church would need no longer be the "Roman" Catholic Church.[3]

Some theoretical problems remain. Does the pope inherently, by virtue of his office, possess the right to name his own successor independently of the consent of the whole Church? Is it the consent, implicit or explicit, of the whole Church that supplies the occasion for Christ to bestow the authority to teach, govern, and sanctify upon the pope? Would the pope have the right to veto and render null and void the decision of the whole Church concerning his successor? What procedures can be licitly and validly established to determine the incapability of a reigning pope to continue as pope?[4]

At one time the relatively few people of Rome named the pope. Sometimes one man, the emperor, named the pope. A relatively few men, the College of Cardinals, have been naming the pope since 1059. We feel it is time to do away with the College of Cardinals.[5] It is time to open the selection of the pope to the world.

II. ELECTION OF BISHOPS

Background. The constant teaching of the Church has been that the bishops are the true successors of the apostles and have been invested by Christ to teach, govern, and sanctify in union with the pope. The apostles consecrated bishops and appointed them as successors. Thus, St. Paul consecrated Timothy to succeed to the episcopacy (cf. 2 Tim. 4:5,7). Paul left Titus in Crete, to "ordain priests in every city" (Tit. 1:5).

Appointment and consecration by an existing bishop was a common way of selecting bishops in the early Church. Gradually, the choice of a bishop was determined by an election, with the clergy, religious, laity, and bishops of the province participating. Election of bishops by popular choice gradually gave way to appointment by civil rulers and princes, as the state grew in power. Ultimately, a strengthened papacy was able to outlaw lay investiture, and the right to make episcopal appointments was reserved to the Holy See. The Congregation of the Consistory was established by Pope Sixtus in 1588. This important Congregation appoints bishops and supervises dioceses; it is now known as the Congregation for Bishops.[6]

Evaluation and Recommendation. We submit that the time has arrived to return to the earlier practice of electing bishops. Andrew M. Greeley, in his report to the Ad Hoc Committee on the Implementation of the Priesthood Study, stated:

> The most important task before this commission is the establishment of representative governance in the American Church. . . . Representative governance in the Church, including especially the nomination of the bishops by the dioceses in which they serve, is the absolutely essential requisite for the continued effective governance of the Church. . . . This is the United States of America in 1972; why, in God's name, are we not willing to trust the democratic process? How many times does the same mistake have to be repeated before it is learned that not only can bishops trust their priests but at this point in time they must?
>
> . . . Address yourselves . . . to the profound but essential task of changing the organizational structure and the decision-making mechanism of the Church so that it becomes something of which we Catholics need no longer be ashamed.[7]

John Carroll, the first American bishop, said that the customs and beliefs of America were such that the only appropriate way to select ecclesiastical leadership was by election.

In calling for the people to have a voice in the selection of their ecclesiastical leaders, we make no implication that anyone but the pope and the bishops is authorized by Christ to govern the Church. On the contrary, Catholicism differs from Protestantism on this point. We acknowledge that Christ gave full jurisdiction to Peter and his successors, and that the jurisdiction to govern is passed on to bishops through the pope. Our recommendation is simply to allow priests, religious, and the laity to have a voice in naming their bishop, who alone, under the pope, has the full ecclesiastical authority in his diocese.

The following is offered as a possible method for electing bishops: Everyone in a given diocese who considers himself to be a Christian, a member of Christ's Mystical Body, and is at least eighteen years of age, could vote. Representatives of priests, religious, and the laity would appoint a nominating committee to name three nominees for bishop. The present bishop would be an *ex officio* member of the committee. The nominees would need

the approval of the diocesan priests' senate, the national episcopal conference, and the Holy See. A diocesan election would
then be held. The vote of the priests and religious would carry a
weight of one-half; the vote of the laity would weigh one-half. A
bishop would serve a five-year term and could be re-elected for a
second five-year term. A bishop would have to resign at age
seventy-five (already suggested by Pope Paul VI).

Democracy is eminently in accord with the dignity, value,
and intelligence of the individual. The Church cannot ignore this
fact. Surely priests, religious, and the laity will more readily
follow and obey a leader when they have had something to say
about the appointment of that leader to a position of authority.
Religious communities have long employed democratic principles in naming superiors. The College of Cardinals is itself a form
of democracy, employed a couple of centuries before the Magna
Charta, in selecting a pope. The time has come to extend the
privilege of ecclesiastical nomination and election — now reserved to the College of Cardinals in naming a pope and to the
Congregation for Bishops in naming a bishop — to the entire
Mystical Body. The benefits to the Church and to the world from
such a democratization, we feel certain, will be manifold, benefits
which we cannot presently envision. The Holy Spirit is guiding
the Church in this direction.[8]

III. CLERICAL CELIBACY

Background. We noted in the previous chapter that the Old
Testament generally upheld marriage over celibacy. The New
Testament counsels voluntary virginity as a state higher than
marriage in the economy of Christian perfection. Jesus proposed
celibacy as an example of superior virtue:

Not all can accept this teaching; but those to whom it has been
given. For there are eunuchs who were born so from their mother's
womb; and there are eunuchs who were made so by men; and there are
eunuchs who have made themselves so for the sake of the Kingdom of
Heaven. Let him accept it who can (Matt. 19:11-12).

St. Paul recommended celibacy (cf. 1 Cor. 7:8-10; 32 ff.) but did
not make it a requirement for ordination. The Apostle of the
Gentiles said that a bishop should be married only once (cf. Tit.
1:5 ff.).

Of the twelve apostles whom Christ selected, tradition affirms that St. John was celibate. Peter was certainly married,
since Christ cured his mother-in-law. Paul referred to the apos-

tles being accompanied by their wives (cf. 1 Cor. 9:5). The New Testament in general and the mind of Christ in particular give no indication that celibacy is a requirement, a *conditio sine qua non*, for the priesthood.

Celibacy of the clergy was not obligatory in the early years of Christianity; freedom of choice was the norm. A gradual development toward compulsory celibacy for priests took place in the Western Church. A decretal of Pope Siricius in 386 ordered celibacy for "priests and levites"; Innocent I renewed the decree; and Pope Leo the Great at the beginning of the fifth century demanded celibacy of all priests, deacons, and subdeacons.

Since Pope Leo the Great the ecclesiastical law of clerical celibacy has remained in force for the Western Church, though the law was frequently violated at various times in Church history. It was not until the twelfth century that the First (1123) and Second (1139) Lateran Councils declared the marriages of priests to be invalid; Pope Alexander III in 1180 extended the impediment to deacons and subdeacons. The Council of Trent (1545-1563) retained the earlier laws, including the Lateran decrees; and the Tridentine decrees were incorporated in the *Codex Juris Canonici* of 1917.[9]

Pope Pius XII allowed some former Protestant ministers who converted to Catholicism and were ordained to the priesthood to retain their wives. Pope John XXIII, while privately expressing concern for young priests "who so courageously carry the burden of ecclesiastical celibacy," followed the example of Gregory XVI, Pius IX, and Pius XI in rejecting suggestions that the law of celibacy might be rescinded. Pope Paul VI issued the encyclical *Priestly Celibacy* on June 24, 1967, in which he reaffirmed compulsory celibacy for the Western clergy.

The Eastern Orthodox Churches have generally permitted marriage prior to ordination. Since the seventeenth century, some churches allow subdeacons to marry after ordination; Nestorians and Ethiopians allow priests to marry. Bishops are generally chosen from among the celibate clergy.

Evaluation and Recommendation. The Church ought to preeminently seek out the mind of Christ concerning clerical celibacy. Why does the Church insist upon requiring of its priests what Christ Himself did not require of His chosen apostles? Why does the Church insist upon making a command what Christ made a counsel? That a celibate clergy is a more controllable clergy is undoubtedly a factor; that the line of demarcation between a married clergy and the laity would be more nebulous is also a factor; that a married clergy would make greater financial demands upon the Church is a third factor. None of these factors, we submit, is sufficient to warrant a continuance of the rule of compulsory celibacy for the clergy.

To favor optional clerical celibacy is not to deny the value of consecrated virginity. To voluntarily renounce the right to marry in order to devote oneself fully and unencumbered to God's work is indeed a noble and virtuous undertaking. The call to consecrated virginity, however, is a special charism, not necessarily attached to the priesthood. A layman, as well as a priest, can be called to virginity for the sake of the Kingdom of Heaven.

The right to marry is a fundamental human right. "Where the inalienable right to marriage and procreation is lacking," Pope Paul has written, "human dignity has ceased to exist."[10] One wonders why the full thrust of the Pope's statement is not applied to priests of the Western Church. One must also wonder at a dual standard which allows clergy of the Eastern Rite to marry but forbids marriage for the Western clergy.

The ecclesiastical law of celibacy for priests is a human positive law, not a divine positive law; it is a disciplinary law which could be repealed tomorrow, if the Church so decides. Nor is compulsory celibacy demanded by the natural moral law. Bernard Haring has written: "If there are not enough authentic vocations for the celibate life . . . then the Church has a duty to provide people with good priests by ordaining married men. Priestly worship is commanded by God, but priestly celibacy is not."[11]

Historians estimate that approximately forty popes were legally and validly married. These men evidently saw no intrinsic connection between the priesthood and celibacy; nor did they feel that the office of the papacy could not be discharged effectively by a married man.

Time magazine quoted Martin Luther on celibacy:

My advice is, break the bonds, let each follow his own preference whether to marry or not to marry. The ministry was intended to train a church, with pastors living among the people and keeping house as other people do. Such men should be granted permission to marry, in order to avoid temptation and sin. For, if God has not forbidden them, no man should or may do so. The pope in making such a rule has no more power than if he were to forbid eating, or drinking, or the performance of other natural functions. . . .

Optional celibacy would mean that a secular priest would be free to marry at any time; he would also be free, in the absence of marriage, to take a solemn vow of consecrated virginity at any time. The Church would be bound to pay its married priests a living wage. Religious, by definition, take vows of poverty, chastity, and obedience; there is no question of optional celibacy in their regard.

The literature of the Church is replete with treatises that extol the value of virginity; married saints are few in the Church calendar. We feel it is time to recognize the values of matrimony, even for priests. Some priests will be *better* priests if they are married. We simply cannot accept the statement of Chrysostom, cited in the previous chapter, which questioned the possibility of one making the journey to Heaven "encumbered" by a wife and family. We cannot envision the ultimate results of allowing a married clergy.[12] We believe the results would be mostly good for all concerned. A married priest will surely identify more closely with the married laity and have greater empathy in solving the problems of married people. John A. O'Brien writes: "The love of a helpmate will not diminish his [the priest's] love for his people or his God but will give it a new ardor, a new depth, and a greater intensity."[13]

The fundamental right to marry can no longer be denied to our priests.

IV. CATHOLIC SCHOOLS IN AMERICA

Background.[14] To teach the truth of Christianity is an essential function of the Church, as commanded by Christ Himself. The apostles understood their commission and proceeded to evangelize the world. The manner or structure by which Christianity was to be taught to all nations was not spelled out by Christ. History has seen Christian education take various forms.

For many centuries the Church taught the message of Christ without anything like a school system. In the days of the Roman Empire, Christian children received the available pagan education. Tertullian lamented that Christian children were being fed poison; but he never suggested establishing a separate Christian school. During the reign of Julian the Apostate, who demanded that Christians adhere to pagan doctrines, some Christian schools were established. Julian's persecution was short-lived, and the Christian schools soon disappeared.

How did Christian children learn their Christian Faith during the early centuries of Christianity? Their parents gave them elementary instruction; beyond this, Christian formation took place in the context of community worship and liturgy, and in the active charity and concern for the entire Christian community.

Christian education took a different form in the Middle Ages, as the Church became a dominant force in society. The Second Council of Vaison in 529 commanded "all parish priests to gather some boys around them as lectors, so that they may give them a Christian upbringing."[15] H. I. Marrou believed the origin of the modern public school can be traced to this Council's decree. In the Middle Ages Christian schools developed to provide for the education of priests and religious. Public education became religiously oriented by virtue of the union of Church and state, which were seen as indivisible.

The American phenomenon presented a third stage in the history of Christian education. In the middle 1800s Horace Mann in Massachusetts sought to eliminate sectarian elements from public education. The predominantly Protestant character of American society in general, and public education in particular, made Catholics apprehensive about the establishment of compulsory education for all children. It was deemed desirable, and even necessary, to establish a separate Catholic school system which would ensure a Catholic education for every Catholic child. Catholics would thus be preserved from the baleful influences of a non-Catholic social milieu; Catholic schools would serve to preserve the Catholic Faith of American Catholics and establish solidarity with fellow Catholics. The parochial school became a symbol of both social and religious security for Catholics.

The Third Plenary Council of Baltimore, in 1884, decreed that every pastor was to establish a school within two years. Catholic parents were required to send their children to these schools when possible; it was made clear, however, that the prescription did not bind under pain of sin. Bishop Hughes of New York City felt so strongly about the need for Catholic schools that he reportedly told his pastors, "You must proceed upon the principle that, in this age and this country, the school is before the Church."[16]

It is a mistake to believe that the Catholic schools had the unanimous endorsement of the American hierarchy. Archbishop Williams of Boston, for one, never urged the establishment of a separate Catholic school system; Archbishop John Ireland of St.

Paul remained convinced of the possibility of integrating with the public school system. Under the so-called "Poughkeepsie Plan," parochial school buildings were leased to the local public school system, which maintained the buildings, paid the teachers, and had the right of inspection and control. The plan finally became defunct when a school superintendent objected to the religious habit worn by the teaching sisters. Archbishop Ireland operated a similar plan in St. Paul, except that religious instruction was given outside of regular school hours.

The position of the Catholic school system in twentieth-century American society has become increasingly precarious. The 1950s and 1960s saw the Catholic schools fall into serious financial straits, with attendance steadily declining. Vigorous efforts were made to secure tax support for nonpublic schools. The death knell seemed to be sounded for such efforts when the U.S. Supreme Court declared, in *Lemon v. Kurtzman*, that the "parochiaid" programs of Pennsylvania and Rhode Island were unconstitutional. The programs supplemented teachers' salaries and the cost of textbooks in secular subjects. Proponents of state aid for nonpublic schools had maintained that the "purchase of secular services" by the state from parochial schools was constitutional. *Time* magazine observed: "It [the Supreme Court decision] seemed certain to accelerate the end of the comprehensive parochial school as millions of U. S. Catholics have known it."[17] State programs that subsidized parents who chose to send their children to nonpublic schools were likewise declared to be unconstitutional.

Evaluation and Recommendation. The question is not whether there shall be Catholic education. The Church has always carried out its divine commission to teach all nations. The Church will continue to fulfill its teaching office until the consummation of the world. The question at hand is this: How can the Church in America, in the last quarter of the twentieth century, *best* fulfill its divine commission to teach the truth of Christianity?

The sixteenth-century Protestant Reformation inflicted a serious, but not lethal, wound upon Roman Catholicism. The Council of Trent was convened to rally the forces of Catholicism and to anathematize the errors of the Reformers. The post-Tridentine atmosphere was one of defense, "standing up and being counted." The post-Tridentine "state of siege" (a phrase coined by William George Ward) prevailed in Catholicism until recent times. Vatican II made a significant move away from the siege mentality.

Catholics in America were especially aware of the siege; Catholics were, and are, a religious minority in a predominantly Protestant country. The Catholic school system was one answer and one response to the non-Catholic American milieu. Today, in the last quarter of the twentieth century, the "siege mentality" no longer seems to be an appropriate reaction to American culture. A Catholic President has been elected. Catholics serve in many responsible positions throughout the land. Freedom of religion is guaranteed by the U. S. Constitution. Given the set of conditions prevailing in America today, one can rightfully ask: Is a full-fledged Catholic school system, teaching all of the secular subjects and staffed with a preponderance of lay teachers requiring a family living wage, the *best* way to provide boys and girls with a Catholic education?

The problem of finances is crucial. We oppose seeking public tax monies to support Catholic schools, mainly because such state aid is opposed to the First Amendment of the Constitution, which states: "Congress shall make no law respecting an establishment of religion, or prohibiting the free exercise thereof. . . ." The Amendment is supremely wise and necessary in a pluralistic society; Catholics, as much as anyone, have benefited from a separation of Church and state, with all religions having equal rights before the law.

We understand the First Amendment to forbid the use of tax money to support, directly or indirectly, a denominational religion. What right does the government have to take tax money paid by atheists, agnostics, Protestants, Jews, etc., to support a Catholic educational enterprise? If state aid is once granted to denominational education, what is to prevent anyone (the Ku Klux Klan or Black Panthers, for example) from starting schools and demanding state aid? Congress may not prohibit the free exercise of religion; but government is not obliged, and is constitutionally forbidden, to respect an establishment of religion.

The purchase-of-secular-services concept does not really solve the problem. Any educational system functions as a unit; aid to one area of the system at least indirectly amounts to aid to the whole system. Tax money to purchase secular services in the Catholic schools would serve to perpetuate the Catholic school system as a whole. As such, we must conclude that such aid is unconstitutional in the American system of law.

We found the following statement of Vatican II to be inadequate in coming to grips with the problem of parochial education in a pluralistic society:

> ... public authority, which has the obligation to oversee and defend the liberties of citizens, ought to see to it, out of a concern for distributive justice, that public subsidies are allocated in such a way that, when selecting schools for their children, parents are genuinely free to follow their consciences (*Gravissimum Educationis*, n. 6).

The implication is made that tax support might be given to aid parochial education. Nothing is suggested as to a violation of the principle of separation of Church and state by such "subsidies"; nor is there any proposal as to how Catholics in a pluralistic society might better relate to the public school system.

We submit that the question of Catholic schools in America boils down to this: either Catholics want their own schools *and are willing to pay for them* or not. Each bishop should ask the Catholic people of his diocese: Do you want the Catholic school system to function in this diocese? If the answer is "yes," then the financial requirement for maintaining the schools should be made clear, with each adult Catholic committed to contribute his share. In the absence of the required financial support, new directions for Catholic education should be sought.

We further submit that the demise of the Catholic school system might not be the stark tragedy that some Catholics envision. The Supreme Court has made it clear that the *objective study* of religion in the public school is not forbidden by the Constitution. Education is concerned with truth; the doctrines of the various religions are part of our cultural heritage. Public education cannot, need not, and should not ignore religion. The Founding Fathers did not intend Americans to be ignorant of religious doctrine. There is nothing in the Constitution which states that public education should be atheistic. The Supreme Court has decided that religious devotions and denominational prayer cannot be prescribed in the public school; but the free exercise of religion is guaranteed by the First Amendment.

Why should it not be constitutionally possible for the doctrines of all faiths to be taught in the elementary and secondary public schools? Why cannot Catholic boys and girls learn their Catholic Faith in the public school, with the course being taught by a priest, a sister, or one otherwise competent to teach? Why cannot there be an elective class in religion available to all students in the public school? (In 1973 there were more than a thousand public high schools in America offering elective classes in religion.) Classes in Judaism, Protestantism, Catholicism, Islamism, etc., would be open to all who wished to enroll, held during regular school hours, and taught by competent teachers. Would not such an arrangement satisfy the needs of Catholic education, without maintaining a separate school system which duplicates services already competently provided by the public school system?

We recommend that Catholic authorities direct less effort to securing state aid for Catholic schools and more effort to securing a working relationship with the public school system. The possibility of leasing Catholic school buildings to the public school system should be considered. Catholics work, play, and generally associate with non-Catholics in all other areas of life. Perhaps it would be better if our Catholic children were educated together with their non-Catholic neighbors.

The siege is over. The time has arrived to question the wisdom of diverting two-thirds to three-fourths of a parish's income to maintain a school, money that could be used for paying the salary of a married priest, for supporting a vigorous CCD program for adults as well as children, and for the apostolate. We look forward to an era of cooperation, integration, and solidarity between Catholic education and American public education.[18] We look forward to a greater emphasis on the educative import of divine worship and the liturgy. Mary Perkins Ryan has put it well:

As the Christians of the early centuries could profit from the pagan education of their time, making their own contribution to human learning, communicating with their pagan neighbor — by means of a common vocabulary and common patterns of thought — and thus sharing the light of Christ with them, perhaps Christians could act in the same way today in regard to the secular education and learning of our own age.

. . . we cannot dismiss as a wild fancy the idea that participation in the worship of the Church — understood in a far fuller sense than has been possible in recent centuries — could once more become the central and most important formative force affecting all members of the Christian community, and that around this focus other means of religious formation could be organized to supplement and extend it — without the need for also providing Catholic young people with a general education.[19]

V. PIERRE TEILHARD DE CHARDIN, S.J.

Life. The life and doctrines of Pierre Teilhard de Chardin constitute one of the most fascinating chapters in the story of Catholicism today. The odyssey of Teilhard began on May 1, 1881, at Sarcenat, a tiny mountain village in the province of Auvergne, France. Pierre was the fourth of eleven children, seven of whom died at an early age. The great-great-granduncle of Teilhard's mother was Voltaire.

Rocks held a special fascination for young Pierre. Young Napoleon was said to have been especially fascinated by tin soldiers — a presage of his life to be. And so with Teilhard. Even as a child he wanted to find something in the world that would last forever. Iron was the first substance that seemed to him to satisfy that need. "I believed myself, at seven, rich with a treasure incorruptible, everlasting. When it turned out that what I possessed was just a piece of rusted iron, I threw myself on the ground and shed the bitterest tears of my life."[20]

Pierre's mother walked two miles to Mass every morning. His father was a well-to-do country squire who had an interest in science and historical documents. Pierre was educated by the Jesuits. He won top honors in all subjects but one — religion! At eighteen he entered a Jesuit novitiate and took his first vows in 1901.

Teilhard was assigned to teach physics and chemistry at a Jesuit high school in Cairo. After his Egyptian interlude, he returned to England for his theology and was ordained at Hastings in 1911. He then studied under the famous Marcellin Boule in the paleontological laboratory of the Paris Museum of Natural History.

World War I intervened, and Teilhard was drafted as a stretcher-bearer. Father Teilhard won a reputation for bravery and self-sacrifice. He refused the rank of captain, saying he could do more good among the men as a soldier. It was at this time that Teilhard had a vision of the Heart of Christ expanding into the universe.

After the Armistice Father Teilhard returned to Paris to finish graduate studies; in 1920 he began teaching geology at the *Institut Catholique*. His brilliant mind and personal holiness were acknowledged by a host of his contemporaries. Ideas concerning God, creation, evolution, and the supreme role of Christ in the evolution of the cosmos were seething in Teilhard's mind. Original Sin particularly bothered him. In 1921 he wrote to a friend: "Gradually ... science and dogma will reach an agreement on the question of human origins. In the meantime, let us take care not to reject the least ray of light from any side. Faith has need of all the truth."[21]

He recorded some of his ideas in a short essay, which he circulated among his friends for comments and criticisms. The essay finally fell into the hands of the Holy Office. Teilhard found himself under a cloud of suspicion which remained for the rest of his life. He was ordered to stop teaching and was quietly exiled to China. The latter proved to be a blessing; he took part in excavations which brought about the discovery of "Peking Man" — whom he nicknamed "Nellie" (Peking Man actually being a woman).

From 1926 until his death in 1955, Father Teilhard roamed the world, taking part in scientific expeditions, giving lectures, and enhancing his reputation as a paleontologist and Christian evolutionist. He was refused an *imprimatur* for all of his books. His name was not allowed to be submitted for one of the highest honors in France. He was forbidden to give public lectures in France from 1947 on. In 1954 he was forbidden to travel from New York to attend an international paleontological congress in Paris.

He once appealed personally to the Father General of the Jesuit order, John Janssens, to lift the ban on his writings. Teilhard returned from Rome in tears: "They don't want me to write; they don't want me to think; they want me to disappear."[22] Despite the harassment and lack of sympathy which befell him, Father Teilhard remained loyal and obedient to his superiors. He once wrote:

It is essential I show, by my example, that if my ideas are novel, they make me no less faithful. . . . Rome may have its own reasons for judging that . . . my concept of Christianity may be premature or incomplete. . . . I am resolved to remain a 'child of obedience.'[23]

On a March evening in 1955, while dining with friends, Teilhard expressed the hope that when his final day on earth arrived, it would occur on the Day of the Resurrection. Such an event might be interpreted as a sign of divine approval of his life and work. On April 10, 1955, Easter Sunday, the sky was a limpid blue, the air soft. Teilhard attended a pontifical Mass at St. Patrick's Cathedral. He took a stroll through Central Park before lunch. He attended the New York City Center in the afternoon with old friends, Mrs. Rhoda de Terra and her daughter. After the performance they walked back to Mrs. de Terra's apartment. Teilhard was engaged in lively conversation, commenting on the splendor of that Easter Sunday — the loveliest he had ever known. In midspeech he suddenly fell to the floor. A doctor and priest were summoned; but before either arrived, Teilhard's heart had stopped beating.

The remains of Pierre Teilhard de Chardin lie in a simple gravesite at the Jesuit novitiate located at Saint Andrews-on-the-Hudson, seventy-five miles north of New York City.

Doctrines.[24] Teilhard was influenced by the evolutionary theory of Henri Bergson and the theological doctrines of Léonce de Grandmaison. Teilhard revitalized the ideas propounded by Irenaeus and Duns Scotus about the recapitulation of all things in Christ. St. Paul spoke of all things holding together in Christ (cf. Col. 1:17).

Teilhard attempted to bridge the gap between God and the world, between theology and science, between the divine and the human. This is an ambitious enterprise, indeed; but his undertaking is not without antecedents. Aristotle made metaphysics the center of all knowledge, with other sciences revolving about it like planets around the sun. Thomas Aquinas and the medieval Scholastics made theology the center of all knowledge, and showed the compatibility of philosophy and theology. Francis of Assisi related all creation to the divine.

The Copernican revolution radically changed man's concept of the universe. The earth was no longer the center of the cosmos. Discoveries in geology showed that evolution is a fundamental law of the universe. The time was now ripe for someone to attempt a grand synthesis of all sciences — philosophy, theology, astronomy, anthropology, biology, and physics. Such a man was Pierre Teilhard de Chardin.

In propounding his grand synthesis, Teilhard departed from his predecessors on two important points: (1) Neither philosophy, nor theology, nor astronomy, nor physics is regarded as basic to an understanding of the cosmos; *evolution* is. (2) Sciences are not related to each other as branches or planets revolving about a center; all sciences — from physics, chemistry, biology, psychology, philosophy, up to theology — form a *cone*, or a series of cones, one inside the other.

There is a unity of all beings in the universe. Teilhard departs from the extreme duality of matter and spirit, nonlife and life, unconsciousness and consciousness, introduced into philosophy by Descartes. There is a real, not a metaphorical, continuity between a magnet pointing north, hydrogen uniting with oxygen to form water, an animal seeking food, a male and female copulating, and a scientist seeking truth. Teilhard did not deny the differences between life and nonlife, between spirit and matter; but he preferred the term *prelife* to *nonlife* and attributed a kind of spirituality to everything in the universe.

There have been three fundamental stages of development in the cosmos, said Teilhard: (1) *cosmogenesis*, or the evolution of the material universe; (2) *anthropogenesis*, or the evolution of man; and (3) *Christogenesis*, which is the culmination of man's development with the Incarnation of the God-man, Jesus Christ. Cosmogenesis evolved the *lithosphere* (or the world of minerals and prelife); biogenesis evolved the *biosphere* (or the world of living things); anthropogenesis evolved the *noosphere* (or the world of thought). The noosphere is the work of the whole of nature; the *whole* earth has taken part in its creation. The upward tendency of the universe to produce man and the evolution of the noosphere are processes of *hominization*. The whole world is ascending toward Christ the King. Christogenesis is an integral part of evolution.[25]

All men have a "Center of Convergence" which is to pull them together, and that is the Incarnation of the Son of God. The Incarnation was a truly supernatural intervention; yet the ages preceding the birth of Christ "were not empty of Christ, but were penetrated by His powerful influx." Christogenesis provided for the mystical union of all souls in Christ in the Church. The Church is a "phylum of love," said Teilhard, growing within the human phylum — a spiral in a spiral, a cone above a cone. He called Rome "the Christic pole of earth," the axis for all the love of the universe.

Whence comes the power, the thrust, the guidance, the beginning and the final end of evolution? Teilhard answered, there had to be an "Alpha Point" at the beginning of the evolutionary process; it is the Alpha Point which provides the efficient cause for everything that happens in evolution. It is the Alpha Point which evolved matter, life, consciousness, and intellect. There is nothing in evolution that hasn't always existed, at least latently and inchoately, from the beginning. All matter possesses a kind of protoconsciousness, which belongs to the "inside of things."

Evolution has not only a starting point, called the Alpha Point; evolution has also an "Omega Point," a final goal or target. Omega Point is not the end *product* of evolution, because the Omega Point already exists, making "this cosmic coiling irreversible." Omega Point is both the axis of development and the goal. Noogenesis mounts irreversibly toward Omega Point.

While being the last term of its series, it is also *outside all series*. Not only does it crown, but it closes. . . . If by its very nature it did not escape from the time and space which it gathers together, it would not be Omega. Autonomy, actuality, irreversibility, and thus finally transcendence are the four attributes of Omega.[26]

Teilhard identified Alpha-Omega with Love, the "Center of Centers," which is in all things. And so we are back to St. John, who said nearly two thousand years ago, "God is Love" (1 John 4:8). And finally, Teilhard identified Alpha-Omega with God and Christ; "in Him we live and move and have our being" (Acts 17:28). "I am Alpha and Omega, the beginning and the end, saith the Lord God, Who is, and Who was, and Who is to come, the Almighty" (Apoc. 1:8).

Evaluation and Recommendation. Teilhard has been variously accused of being a monist, a materialist, a pantheist, a naturalist, a positivist, a rationalist, a fatalist, a panpsychist, a communist, "the Trojan Horse of Catholicism," a man with dangerous theories in which "maximum seduction coincides with maximum aberration," the Pelagius of the twentieth century, and even an atheist.

The Holy Office in 1957 banned Teilhard's works from Catholic bookstores. In 1962 the Holy Office issued a *monitum* (a formal warning) about "ambiguities" in his thought. Pope John approved of the *monitum*, probably as a concession to the archconservative Alfredo Cardinal Ottaviani, who headed the Holy Office. Later, Pope John called the *monitum* "regrettable"; "I am here to bless, not condemn," he remarked. The Pope had no wish to foment another Galileo case. The Pontiff complained, "Why did he have to write such difficult things?" Teilhard presents the unique case of a major scholar never seeing one of his major works in print.[27]

Pope Paul VI has said of him: "Father Teilhard is an indispensable man for our times: his expression of the Faith is necessary for us."[28]

Teilhard generally eschewed Aristotelian-Scholastic terminology. Like Aristotle and Kant, Teilhard felt the need to originate his own terminology. The reader of Teilhard is thus faced with such neologisms as *noosphere, Christogenesis, hominization, radial* and *tangential energy.* Novelty is generally held as suspect by orthodox theology. Novelty in theology and philosophy is not necessarily wrong; innovation must stand or fall on its own intrinsic worth. Although Teilhard avoids Aristotelian-Scholastic terminology, we still detect a familiar ring to many of his ideas. Panpsychism, for example, is certainly nothing new in philosophy. Some ancient Greeks proposed the thesis that all nature is endowed with at least a primitive form of consciousness. Evolution as a theory goes back at least to Anaximander (611-547 B.C.). Teilhard prefers to speak of the "inside" and "outside" of things, of a thing's "radial" (inside) and "tangential" (outside) energy. Though Teilhard would certainly deny it, we see these concepts closely related to, if not identified with, the Aristotelian hylomorphic theory of matter and form and the distinction between substance and accident. "Is there really anything new under the sun?"

Many theologians are apprehensive about Teilhardism. By what prerogative, they ask, does evolution become the central theme, the leitmotiv, of the cosmos — a theme to which all philosophy and all theology and all science must march in step? *Complete cosmological evolution* remains a *theory*, and is by no means a confirmed, proven fact. Again, why must the Incarnation of the Son of God be subject to the laws of evolution? What place does Grace, as a free gift elevating man to a supernatural life, have in Teilhardism? What about Divine Revelation? Doesn't Teilhardism minimize the importance of the Redemption? What happens to the doctrine of the Trinity in Teilhardism? Does Teilhardism adequately treat the existence of evil, suffering, sin, and the possibility of Hell? What place does Original Sin hold in Teilhardism?

Scholastic philosophers are concerned about the Teilhardian concept of Alpha Point and Omega Point. Teilhard makes it clear that Alpha-Omega is outside of all series; yet he also speaks of Omega *escaping* from time and space and *finally* becoming transcendent. In listing the attributes of Omega, Teilhard makes no mention of intelligence, omniscience, or omnipotence. Can one pray to Alpha-Omega? Can one's prayers be heard and answered? What place does the possibility of miracles hold in Teilhardism? What about creation? Leslie Dewart, whose theories we find to be closely aligned with Teilhard's, considers Teilhardism to be philosophically weak.

These are all moot questions. We do not intend to condemn Teilhardism by asking them. We simply feel that *The Phenomenon of Man*, Teilhard's *magnum opus*, gives all of the above-mentioned questions a subordinate place in his cosmology. There is no doubt that Teilhard believed in prayer, in the miracles of Christ, in divine and human freedom. His views on these topics are stated more clearly in some of his minor works.

Let it be recognized, as did Pope John, that Teilhard grappled with some of the most difficult and abstruse problems that have always confronted philosophy and theology. Some theologians complain, for example, that Teilhard makes Christogenesis a *necessary* part of evolution. One must remember that everything God does He does necessarily; for God must be what He is. But everything God does He also does with perfect freedom. Freedom and necessity are one in God. Teilhard could not resolve this seeming contradiction; nor has anyone else been able to solve the difficulty.

The mysteries of creation, Original Sin, the Incarnation and Redemption, the infinite nature of God — no one has a complete understanding of their full import. Teilhard, so far as we can ascertain, did not deny these doctrines; he did place them in an evolutionary perspective and seemed to have submerged Divine Revelation in the total context of the evolutionary process. There is an insidious danger, we submit, in confusing *description* with *explanation;* evolution describes, but it does not explain.

Our recommendation is that the Church refrain from condemning Teilhardism, in the absence of any concrete, specific heretical doctrine. Much of Teilhard's thought is colored by a scientific outlook and background. There are scientists who disagree with some of Teilhard's scientific conclusions. The Church will do well, we submit, to wait until all of the facts are in before making a categorical decision concerning Teilhardism. The case of Galileo makes it crystal clear that the Church should never precipitously condemn a scholar before all of the facts are in. As we noted, all of the facts may never be in regarding Teilhardism, since he wrote on the most profound and recondite questions of the universe. The Church should encourage the study of Teilhardism, and encourage scholarship in general, with the purpose of shedding as much light as possible upon the profound problems of human origins and human existence.

Fulton J. Sheen may have been right when he wrote:

It is very likely that within fifty years when all the trivial, verbal disputes about the meaning of Teilhard's 'unfortunate' vocabulary will have died away or have taken a secondary place, Teilhard will appear like John of the Cross and St. Teresa of Avila, as the spiritual genius of the twentieth century.[29]

Unable to read Mass while on an expedition in Inner Mongolia in 1923-24, Father Teilhard composed one of the most sublime utterances in all Christian literature, his "Mass upon the

Altar of the World." With no bread, no wine, no altar, he offered "upon the altar of the entire earth, the labor and suffering of the world" — the bread of human effort and the wine of human anguish. In the depths of this inchoate mass is the divine impulse placed in each one of us to cry out: "O Lord, make us one!"[30]

Here undoubtedly was one of the most profound spirits in the history of Christianity!

VI. ADAM AND EVE

Background. Like the Ten Commandments the story of Adam and Eve has been around for a long time. Old Testament scholars now seem agreed that the first chapter of Genesis which tells of creation, was written at or near the end of the Babylonian Captivity, about 500 B.C. Chapters 2 and 3, which tell of Adam and Eve and the Fall, were written about three or four centuries earlier. Genesis, as we now have it, is the work of several authors who remain nameless, writing independently; the book was probably compiled around 500 B.C. Although Moses probably wrote parts of the Book of Genesis, his authorship of the first three chapters is now generally discredited.

We speak of the "story" of Adam and Eve. A story can be a *true* story inasmuch as it tells of real people, real places, and real events. A story can be *partly true* and *partly fictional*, such as a historical novel. A story can be *allegorical* inasmuch as a fictional episode is used to illustrate or inculcate a moral principle or a spiritual truth. Christ's parables fall into this category. And lastly, a story can be *purely fictional*, such as *Alice in Wonderland*.

The first chapter of Genesis tells of all things being created in six days. With the advent of a more scientific understanding of the universe, it became apparent that the word *day* should not be understood as a twenty-four-hour day. St. Augustine warned against a too literal rendering of the six days of creation.

Genesis goes on to tell of the creation of man: "God formed man out of the dust of the ground and breathed into his nostrils the breath of life, and man became a living being" (2:7). A rib was taken from man's side to form woman. Adam and Eve were placed in the Garden of Paradise, located in Eden; the Garden was beautiful "as only God knows how to make a garden beautiful." Adam and Eve were preserved from suffering and death. Their pristine happiness would continue as long as they ate not the fruit of the Tree of Knowledge of Good and Evil.

Lucifer, the most intelligent angel, had already rebelled against God and was condemned to Hell. As Satan he took the form of a serpent and tempted Eve to eat of the forbidden fruit. When Adam also ate the fruit, the two were expelled from Paradise. They were now subject to suffering and death, to work "by the sweat of thy brow." So goes the story of our first parents, of their gifts and their Fall.

Is the story of Adam and Eve a true story? For many centuries both Jews and Christians did not seriously question the literal meaning of "Adam" as one man and "Eve" as one woman, from whom the entire human race has been propagated. There was no serious reason to question that there was originally a single pair of progenitors, as far as scientific evidence was concerned. There is no doubt that St. Paul accepted the literal meaning of Adam and Eve as recorded in Genesis: ". . . through one man sin entered into the world and through sin death. . ." (Rom. 5:12). Again, preaching to the Athenians, Paul said: "From one man He has created the whole human race and made them live all over the face of the earth. . ." (Acts 17:26). Wisdom 10:1 seems to support monogenism.

Patristic and medieval religious literature is replete with references to "our first parents, Adam and Eve." Original Sin was spoken of in terms of a single act committed by a single pair in a specific historical setting. Church councils adopted the terminology of Genesis. The Second Council of Orange said that the human race "had received salvation in Adam." The Council of Trent declared that Adam "lost the sanctity and justice received, not only for himself, but also for us." There can be no doubt that both Scripture and tradition have thought of Adam and Eve as a literal, historical couple from whom the entire human race has descended.

In Catholicism today a fair number of theologians are not so sure that monogenism must be regarded as a defined and essential doctrine of Christian theology. We mentioned in Chapter II that Karl Rahner does not believe that any ecumenical council intended to define monogenism as an article of faith. There is even some basis to question whether the authors of Genesis itself intended *Adam* to be understood necessarily as one man. In Hebrew the word for *man*, a common noun, is *adam*, which is taken from the word for *ground*, which is *adamah*. *Eve* is related to the Hebrew verb *to live*. Eve was "the mother of all the living" (Gen. 3:20).

The development of the sciences of historical geology, paleontology, anthropology, comparative anatomy, and embryology has stimulated interest concerning man's natural origins. Science has shown the earth to be at least 4.6 billion years old. Real human beings capable of using fire and tools inhabited the earth a million years ago. Genera, species, and phyla are observed by science in terms of *groups* of individuals. Monogenism is simply not observed, and probably not *observable*, by science. Most scientists are inclined to believe, on the basis of evolutionary principles, that *polygenism*, not *monogenism*, is the method by which genera and species are evolved.

Teilhard de Chardin has observed:

... the problem of monogenism in the strict sense of the word ... seems to *elude* science as such by its very nature. At those depths of time when hominisation took place, the presence and the movements of a unique couple are positively ungraspable, unrevealable to our eyes at no matter what magnification. Accordingly one can say that there is room *in this interval* for anything that a transexperimental source of knowledge might demand.[31]

It was Teilhard's personal conviction that mankind is the product of total evolution, that the human soul was being produced from the first moment of evolution. He did not rule out the possibility of a special creative act by God; but Teilhard's whole protology does not support the theory of the direct and immediate creation of the human soul and all subsequent human souls by God. *The Phenomenon of Man* generally prescinds from the doctrine of Original Sin; but Teilhard speaks of Original Sin a number of times in *The Divine Milieu*. One should note that Teilhard was decidedly against *polyphyletism*, i.e., the theory that mankind descended from more than one phylum: "... if the science of man can say nothing directly for or against monogenism (a single initial couple), it can on the other hand come out decisively, it seems, in favor of monophyletism (a single phylum)."[32]

Evaluation and Recommendation. Again we ask the question, Is the story of Adam and Eve a true story? The answer must involve several elements.

As we have pointed out, science has not been able to show that monogenism could not have taken place; nor has science proved that polygenism accounted for the origin of the human race. In the absence of conclusive proof, either scientific or theological, either for or against monogenism, prudence demands that the question of human origin in the natural order of things be left an open question.

We do not believe that either Scripture or tradition has fully committed itself to monogenism as a revealed doctrine of the Christian Faith. Human origins in the natural order, after all, is a valid area of investigation for the sciences. Theology should welcome any light that science can provide. As we mentioned in other places, the Bible should not be used as a textbook of natural science; the sacred writers used the scientific terminology that was available to them at the time they wrote. The Church came fairly close to condemning evolution as being anti-Biblical; but, happily, no formal condemnation was ever made. The Church had learned a lesson from the Galileo case. Evolution had remained suspect for many years; not until Pius XII did a pontiff speak approvingly of evolution as a possible theory for the origin of man's body.

Pope Pius XII's encyclical *Humani Generis*, issued in 1950, in addition to permitting Catholic scholars to investigate evolution, warned against theories which deny the special creation of man's soul. Concerning polygenism the encyclical stated:

... it is in no way apparent how such an opinion can be reconciled with what the sources of revealed truth and the documents of the teaching authority of the Church propose with regard to Original Sin, which proceeds from a sin actually committed by an individual Adam and which through generation is passed on to all and is in everyone as his own.

The key words are, "no way apparent." F. J. Sheed says that the first version of the encyclical stated, "it is clear that it cannot be reconciled...," but was later changed to allow for a possible option.[33]

St. Paul had no reason to question the literal truth of Genesis regarding Adam and Eve as a single pair of progenitors; thus he spoke in those terms. But did Paul believe he was uttering a revealed truth of the Christian Faith? The councils spoke in terms of Adam and Eve. But were they defining an anthropological fact or condemning the errors of Pelagius, who denied Original Sin?

Many theologians are reluctant to accept the possibility of polygenism because they share the feeling of Pius XII that Original Sin cannot be reconciled with polygenism. F. J. Sheed admits that he once felt that the doctrine of Original Sin would collapse without monogenism.[34] More theologians are now coming to see that Original Sin does not rise or fall on the doctrines of monogenism or polygenism. What is crucial and basic is the *solidarity* and *essential unity* of the human race, whether it began with two, a hundred and two, or a million and two. Polyphyletism — which attempts to explain the Negroid, Caucasian, and Mongoloid races of man as stemming from separate phyla — is not only unacceptable to many scientists, but seems to be unacceptable to Christian theology. *All* have fallen in Original Sin; *all* have been redeemed by the blood of Christ.

What is Original Sin? We use the term glibly; yet the term is shrouded in mystery. There are some who would simply equate Original Sin with the human condition, with man's finite nature, his inborn weakness, his need for divine help and redemption, his need to be "born again." All of this seems to be close to, if not identified with, Pelagianism, which the Church has condemned. The Church insists that the Fall was a real fall, that men are not what God had planned for them to be. Original Sin remains a mystery even if one accepts the doctrine as a specific act committed by a specific couple in a specific time and place. How could one act so profoundly affect and infect all mankind? The Gospels do not have Christ ever once referring to "Adam" or to "Eve" or to our "first parents." In fact, Christ never referred to a specific "original" sin of the human race. But He did make it clear that He was the Redeemer and Savior of mankind.

The story of Adam and Eve as recorded in Genesis *could* be literally true. So far science has not conclusively proven otherwise. Perhaps man was specially formed by God, apart from the evolutionary process. Perhaps the human soul is directly created by God and was originally infused in one man and one woman, from whom all mankind has descended. Perhaps Original Sin consisted in the act of disobedience, the eating of forbidden fruit, committed by the first couple, as recorded in Genesis. We really don't know for sure; at this point in time, no one knows for sure. We do not believe that the account of Genesis binds the Christian to a literal acceptance of the above-mentioned doctrines.

In *A Theology of the Old Testament*, Scripture scholar John L. McKenzie speaks of the "creation myths" contained in the Book of Genesis. *Myth* does not necessarily mean *fiction* or *falsehood;* but it does mean information presented from a source other than science, philosophy, or theology. The best Scriptural scholarship today tends to regard everything in Genesis prior to

Abraham — including the story of the flood and the story of Sodom and Gomorrah — as mythological and ahistorical. It is an abuse of Genesis to make it into a detailed scientific anthropology.

We submit that Genesis teaches the following essential religious truths, sometimes in a literal and sometimes in an allegorical manner: (1) God exists. He transcends the universe and is the Creator, in the literal sense of the word, of the universe and all that is in it. Hence, atheism, materialism, pantheism, and atheistic evolution are erroneous. (2) The world and the universe had a beginning. Matter is not coeternal with God. (3) God bestowed special gifts upon His prize creation, man. God and man shared an extraordinary intimacy. Man was not subject to bodily death. (4) Retention of the special gifts given to man by God was conditioned by the observance of a commandment of God. (5) Man, influenced by the Devil, lost his special gifts by disobeying God, by a sin of pride. (6) A Redeemer was promised to satisfy for man's transgression and to restore the lost friendship between God and man.

These truths of Genesis, we submit, a Christian is bound to believe. We are personally inclined to believe that Adam and Eve as one man and one woman, committing a specific act known as Original Sin, is taught by Genesis only in an allegorical sense through the literary medium of mythology. Whether or not the inspired writer intended a literal meaning is a moot question. We simply feel that he was limited by the scientific knowledge available to him at the time he wrote. At any rate, the writers of Genesis must certainly be reckoned as having the most profound spiritual insights concerning God, man, and the universe of any writers in history — even apart from the fact of divine inspiration.

The Church may some day decide to solemnly define the literal meaning of the story of Adam and Eve. Until such time, an open mind concerning the specific, historical circumstances of man's beginnings is highly desirable. Perhaps science will some day uncover some significant evidence that will dissipate much of the mist that envelopes the natural origin of man. In any event, sin and Redemption are realities no Christian may ignore. "You did not come from the dogs," writes Fulton J. Sheen, "but you can go to the dogs. . . . You are less a risen monkey than you are a fallen angel. . . . You are more a disinherited king than you are an enthroned beast."[35] Such is the Christian view of man.

Christogenesis has crowned the cosmos!

VII. THE MORALITY OF HOMOSEXUALITY AND
THE MORALITY OF DIVORCE

In Chapter VI we considered the morality of premarital and extramarital sex, the morality of contraception, and the morality of masturbation. In this section we shall consider the morality of homosexuality and the morality of divorce — two moral problems of utmost concern in Catholicism today. An *a priori* legalism will no longer suffice in solving these complex and nuanced moral problems. Morality is for persons, Bernard Haring tells us; and only by taking adequate account of all elements of a moral situation will the truth be found. The most recent statements of the ordinary magisterium remain adamant in their condemnation of all homosexual acts; and the indissolubility of a valid, sacramental, consummated marriage is irrefragably reasserted. It is not our purpose to add fuel to the polemical fires; our sole aim is to get at the truth, which alone can make man free (cf. John 8:32).

Homosexuality and Morality. After nearly two thousand years of regarding all homosexual behavior as immoral, Catholic moral theologians today are taking a fresh look at the issues involved. Some notable homosexuals of history would include Plato, Alexander the Great, Julius Caesar, Leonardo da Vinci, Michelangelo, Francis Bacon, Oscar Wilde, Peter Tchaikovsky, and Somerset Maugham.

Charles E. Curran has taken the position that homosexual acts might not be sinful for the "irreversible homosexual." Homosexual behavior is never to be regarded as an acceptable general norm or ideal for all mankind, on a par with heterosexuality as an "alternative life-style." But the irreversible homosexual presents a special problem. An *irreversible homosexual* is one who has made a genuine effort to change his or her sexual orientation, but finds such a change to be a practical impossibility. The irreversible homosexual has further discovered that a life of celibacy is a moral impossibility in his or her own circumstances. In such a restricted case, a theology of compromise would dictate that a homosexual relationship, though less than ideal and not generally acceptable, might be the best option for this individual and contribute the most to personal fulfillment. Such a relationship, according to Father Curran, would not necessarily involve a fundamental option opposed to

God's purposes. Such a person would be free of mortal sin and should be allowed full participation in the Holy Eucharist.

We favor Curran's position because it comes to grips with all significant aspects of a many-faceted question. Curran is careful not to approve of homosexuality *per se*; nor does he place homosexuality on a par with heterosexuality. We believe that homosexuality is a dysfunction of one's psychosexual orientation which the homosexual has an obligation to try to correct. We further believe that the homosexual has a moral obligation to make a sincere effort at living a celibate life. But we also recognize that in some restricted cases both of these options may be psychologically or morally impossible to fulfill. We must conclude with Father Curran that in the case of the irreversible homosexual, as defined above, homosexual behavior need not always involve mortal sin. How could God be seriously offended by conduct which represents the best option that one can exercise in the context of circumstances that are less than ideal and not of one's own free choice?

One might argue that celibacy is impossible for no one, or that homosexual acts are intrinsically evil. These would be simplistic solutions to a complex problem, and the difficulties would remain. Christ Himself suggested that celibacy is not an option for everyone: "Let him take it *who can*." As to regarding homosexual acts as "intrinsically evil," we deny that any human act can be correctly defined as intrinsically evil and always morally wrong when the act is described only in its physical or mechanical aspects. The Biblical proscription of homosexual conduct can correctly be applied to homosexuality as a freely chosen life-style or as a perversion committed by heterosexuals.

The homosexual, of course, must reckon with himself or herself as to how genuine an effort has been made to correct one's condition and to live a life of celibacy. We are now in a tenuous area known only to God and the individual conscience. We do not feel that every homosexual can justify homosexual behavior simply on the grounds that "God made me that way." Nor do we believe that every homosexual has a "right" to freely choose a homosexual life-style. We do assert that every homosexual has a right to follow his or her own sincere conscience, and to do so with impunity from either the Church or the state.

Both gays and straights always need to ask these questions: Am I at peace with my God? Is my conduct in accord with His purposes? An informed conscience will supply the answers. Catholicism today is initiating efforts to provide a truly Christian response to homosexuals so that they may be brought into full participation in the Christian community and the life of the Church. Fortified by a good self-concept, a conscience at peace, and the pastoral concern of the Church, the homosexual can say with David: "My Shepherd is the Lord; nothing indeed shall I want."[36]

Divorce and Morality. In Luke 16:18, Christ states: "Everyone who divorces his wife and marries another commits adultery. The man who marries a woman divorced from her husband likewise commits adultery." In 1 Cor. 7:10-11, St. Paul writes: "To those who are married, not I, but the Lord commands that a wife is not to depart from her husband, and if she departs, that she is to remain unmarried or be reconciled to her husband. And let not a husband put away his wife."

Christ's disciples, like many today, found His teaching on divorce hard to accept. They cited the example of Moses, who permitted a written notice of dismissal. Christ answered that it was not so from the beginning, that Moses permitted divorce "by reason of the hardness of your heart." The disciples then opined that if divorce is never permitted, it is better never to marry. Christ replied that "not all can accept this teaching" and He proceeded to recommend celibacy as an acceptable alternative (cf. Matt. 19:3-12).

In forbidding divorce, was Christ upholding an ideal or expressing a command binding in all circumstances? In a sincere effort to reconcile the teaching of Christ with the exigencies of many desperate Catholic couples, there are theologians today who feel that Christ's teaching ought to be interpreted as the goal and the ideal of every Christian marriage, but not an absolute roadblock to divorce and remarriage.

Some feel it is within the competence of the Church to allow divorce. They point out that no *man* may put asunder what God has joined together; but the Church in allowing divorce would act with *divine* authority, as given in the power to bind and to loose.

The *absolute* indissolubility of the marriage bond is not a defined article of faith. The Pauline privilege allows marriage between non-Christians to be dissolved in favor of one who converts to Christianity and cannot live peaceably with the non-

Christian party. A nonconsummated marriage (one where coitus has not taken place) is sometimes dissolved, e.g., to allow one or both partners to take solemn vows in a religious order.

The Church continues to understand the "consummation" of a marriage in a physical sense, in the performance of sexual intercourse. One wonders if the consummation of a marriage would not be better understood in a larger psychological and personal sense: the total self-giving and lifelong commitment to one's partner. Where such a "spiritual consummation" is lacking, might it not be possible to invoke the "Petrine privilege" to dissolve a marriage, now reserved to the pope for certain cases involving nonconsummated marriages in the physical sense? Again, an exaggerated physicism predominates a Church doctrine and seems to distort the true personal realities of a moral situation.

Most Protestant churches tolerate divorce as the lesser of two evils, preferable to the continuance of a loveless marriage and/or preferable in some cases to enforced celibacy. Paulist Father James J. Young has pointed out that Eastern Orthodoxy has permitted divorce and remarriage since apostolic times. Orthodox theology interprets Christ's words as moral counsel rather than divine law.

In California, the most populous state, nearly one out of two marriages ends in divorce. *Time* magazine reported 357 divorces for every 1000 marriages in America. Father Young estimates that 6 to 7 million of America's 48 million Catholics (1974) are divorced, and some 3 million have remarried.

Christ made no mention of impediments to a valid marriage; this He left to His Church. We believe that the Church ought to widen the circumstances that could render a marriage null and void. Presently, the Church recognizes the following diriment impediments, rendering a marriage invalid: nonage; impotency; an existing marriage bond; disparity of cult; major orders (C. 1072); solemn vows; abduction; crime; consanguinity; affinity; public decency; spiritual relationship; legal relationship.[37] The Church further recognizes that ignorance and error concerning the identity and *quality* of one's partner can invalidate a marriage; likewise, violence and fear can void a marriage.[38] We believe these latter categories especially need to be more fully explored by the Church as an acceptable alternative to divorce.

In 1972 there were eight American dioceses which established "good-conscience procedures" whereby divorced Catholics who had remarried might be allowed to receive the Sacraments provided (1) the present marriage is deemed stable and binding; (2) the former marriage is regarded as invalid, though it cannot be proven so by present Church law; and (3) the risk of scandal is minimal. In Aug., 1972, John Cardinal Krol, President of the National Conference of Catholic Bishops, relegated the good-conscience cause to limbo, pending the results of a study currently under way in Rome.

Addressing the Canon Law Society of America in Oct., 1974, Father Charles E. Curran, professor of moral theology at the Catholic University of America, called for a change in the Catholic Church's teaching on divorce and remarriage. He advanced the following arguments, which we here paraphrase:

(1) There is an inconsistency in championing indissolubility in theory while at the same time favoring, as increasing numbers are now favoring, the pastoral practice of allowing divorced and remarried Catholics to participate in the sacramental life of the Church under certain conditions, as noted above. Theory and practice ought to be compatible. Fewer couples are being asked to live as "brother-sister." "Once you acknowledge the pastoral practice," said Curran, "you cannot seriously maintain an opposing theory."

(2) The Scriptures cannot be used as "proof-texts" absolutely proscribing divorce and remarriage. Christ's words have always been subject to interpretation by the Church. For example, His teaching on the necessity of Baptism of water has been interpreted and widened to include Baptism of blood and desire; the necessity of receiving the Eucharist is relaxed for the invincibly ignorant. Christ's words on divorce can well be interpreted by the Church as expressing an ideal and a goal toward which every marriage should strive, but which not all marriages will be able to achieve. Christ sometimes spoke in hyperbole; and He was strongly opposed to the facile dismissal of a wife which was possible under the Mosaic law.

(3) A change in the Church's teaching on divorce — like its teaching on religious liberty, for example — is possible if one proceeds from a historical, *a posteriori* methodology which recognizes through Christian experience that many well-meaning, conscientious Christian couples have been unable to achieve a permanent conjugal union, *and often with no personal sin involved.* Marriage is now seen less as an "institution" and a "contract" with the mark of indissolubility, and more as a "covenant of love" which regrettably may fall short of lifetime permanence.

(4) Personalism in moral theology recognizes that "you can't make nature the criterion any more." Thus, personalism does not see contraception or abortion to save the life of the mother as being "intrinsically evil." Similarly, divorce should no longer be seen as being intrinsically evil and thus always forbidden; rather, divorce might be the lesser of two evils in a conflict situation. A theology of compromise could permit divorce and remarriage to achieve a higher goal and value. The Pauline privilege seems to be based on such a compromise. "Spiritual death" as well as "physical death" should be seen as dissolving a marriage. Many cases can be documented where remarriage after divorce has resulted in stability, happiness, and fulfillment for the divorced person.

(5) No human decision should be considered infallible, unchangeable, absolute, permanent, and not subject to amendment. Even the solemn vows of religious can be dissolved for a sufficient reason. Marriage involves human decisions which may or may not be well grounded and capable of fulfillment.

(6) As Msgr. Stephen J. Kelleher, former presiding judge of the New York tribunal, has pointed out, the present tribunal system of the Church is grossly inadequate. Personalism and *epikeia* are smothered in legalism.

Something has to be wrong with a legalism which permits a Catholic who may have contracted any number of "invalid" marriages outside of the Church to leave his or her spouse and marry "validly" in the Church; yet a Catholic whose valid marriage in the Church fails is allowed no right to remarry. Or, to cite a *reductio ad absurdum*, one could murder his spouse, confess the sin, and be free to marry — so far as canon law is concerned. The tribunal system would seem to be rewarding invalid marriages and punishing valid marriages.

Most of the tribunal's efforts are spent in finding grounds for annulment. If the efforts are successful, the tribunal tells the couple — possibly "married" for many years — that they have not *really* been married all these years and the offspring of their union are, in effect, bastards. A better, more humane approach seems to be to prescind from the origin and validity of a marriage, and simply recognize the existential fact that a marriage has ceased to exist.

Curran's arguments are persuasive and convincing from the standpoint of moral philosophy. Catholic moral theologians of the past have tended to base their case against divorce mainly on

Christ's words, and only secondarily on the demands of natural law. Church legislation already recognizes circumstances that could dissolve a marriage bond, in the cases of the Pauline and Petrine privileges. St. Paul acknowledged the doctrine of no divorce as being commanded by the Lord; yet he was very quick to make an exception to this apparent moral absolute.

We personally have difficulties regardless of which side we take. In siding with the traditional teaching of the Church (which takes Christ's words on divorce quite literally), we have to nullify the convincing arguments from personalist ethics cited above. In siding with personalist ethics, we must take much of the force out of the Gospel teaching. Christ at times did speak of moral absolutes: for example, His categorical condemnations of adultery, murder, blasphemy, hypocrisy. Yet we know that the God of philosophy and the God of theology are one.

The ultimate decision, of course, must come from the magisterium. Should the Church someday revise its teaching and see Christ's words as expressive of an ideal and goal inherent in the conjugal union, we would applaud that revision. But the change must come from the magisterium, the infallible teaching office of Christ's Church which alone has the power to bind and loose. Theologians can propose; but only the magisterium can dispose. Would the Church be opening a Pandora's box? Not necessarily. The Church would grant divorces parsimoniously. Grave reasons would be required to obtain a divorce, such as habitual cruelty, habitual infidelity, chronic incompatibility, spiritual harm, etc. The "seven year itch" would not be good enough. Couples would still need to work hard to make their marriage work. It seems to be a sound Christian principle of justice that an innocent party in a broken marriage should be allowed the freedom to find happiness and fulfillment in another marriage blessed by the Church.

VIII. THE ROLE OF WOMEN IN THE CHURCH

Background. Ever since Eve ate the forbidden fruit and passed it on to Adam, women have been relegated to a secondary role as far as decision-making is concerned — Cleopatra, Queen Elizabeth, Queen Isabella, Queen Maria Theresa, and Queen Victoria notwithstanding. To Eve's credit Rabbi Seymour Siegel has noted that it was she who had to be tempted; Adam fell without a struggle. Adam seemed to be carping when he said to God, "The woman You placed at my side gave me fruit from the tree..." (Gen. 3:12).

In the Old Testament divorce was easy for a man, but not for a woman. Wives were guilty of adultery if they had relations with any other man; husbands, only if they had relations with another married woman. Women were often classed as slaves before the law.

In the New Testament Christ prohibited divorce; He condemned adultery without reservation. He first manifested His divinity to a woman, who came to draw water from a well. Christ worked His first public miracle at the request of His mother, when the waters of Cana blushed to see their Creator. After His Resurrection Christ first appeared to Mary Magdalene, who had come to anoint His body. And above all, Almighty God chose a simple Jewish maiden to be "the flesh-girt Paradise" for His divine Son, to provide the body and blood for Christ's soul and divinity, by which the world would be redeemed. It was Mary alone who could look up at the Cross on that first Good Friday and truly say, "This is my body; this is my blood!"

During the greatest crisis the world has ever known, the drama of Calvary, women did not fail Our Lord, *but men did*. Judas sold Our Lord for thirty pieces of silver. Pilate, though personally convinced of Christ's innocence, let the politician in him prevail and sentenced the Galilean to death. Annas and Caiphas subjected Our Lord to mockery and a sham trial. Peter denied Jesus three times. A man had to be *forced* to help Jesus carry His cross. Only one of the twelve, John, was present at the Crucifixion.

Women did not fail Our Lord. At His trial a woman's voice is raised in His defense; Pilate's wife bids her husband not to condemn this "just man." The pious women of Jerusalem consoled and wept over Jesus on His way to Calvary. Veronica wiped His divine face, and tradition says that Christ's image was left on the towel. Three women were at the foot of the Cross: Mary Magdalene; Mary of Cleophas, the mother of James and John; and Mary, Christ's mother.

St. Paul took a somewhat ambiguous stance concerning women. On the one hand, he encouraged women to prophesy, according to Jewish tradition. One of his close colleagues was a woman, Priscilla. He noted that there is neither male nor female in Christ (cf. Gal. 3:28). But to the Corinthians he admonished women to wear veils and be silent in church — a text often cited to exclude women from the priesthood. Paul said it was better to marry than to "burn." It is no sin to marry, but celibacy is preferable.

Subsequent tradition has viewed women in various ways. Tertullian, in the third century, thought that women were "the Devil's gateway." There were medieval Scholastics who debated whether or not women possessed a human soul. Thomas Aquinas followed the Aristotelian supposition that nature, "like a medieval patriarch," tries to produce a male, and that woman is something defective and accidental (*deficiens et occasionatum*). A female is a male gone awry (*mas occasionatum*); she may be the result of some weakness in the father's generative faculty, or of some external factor, like a damp south wind.[39]

Relying on Aristotelian biology, Thomas believed that woman contributes only passive matter to offspring, while the man provides the active form. A female is the triumph of matter over form; consequently, she is weaker in body and mind and will. She is to man as the senses are to reason. Both man and woman are made in God's image, but man more especially so. Woman is unfit to fill any vital position in the Church or state. Woman should look upon man as her natural master; she is a part of man, literally a rib.[40] It was suitable that woman was taken from man's side, indicating social equality and companionship; she was not taken from man's head to rule him, nor from his feet to be his slave.[41]

In the course of time, the lot of womankind has steadily improved. It took a constitutional amendment to allow women to vote in the United States. Equal pay for equal work has become an established principle. Sex discrimination is being recognized as untenable in the twentieth century. So far there has been no female President of the United States; nor has a woman ever sat on the Supreme Court of the land. "With respect to the fundamental rights of the person," declared Vatican II, "every type of discrimination, whether social or cultural, whether based on sex, race, color, social condition, language or religion, is to be overcome and eradicated as contrary to God's intent" (*Gaudium et Spes*, n. 29).

Evaluation and Recommendation. Let us state forthrightly that there is no sound philosophical, theological, or scientific basis for the thesis that woman is essentially and ontologically inferior or in any way subordinate to man. Aristotle, St. Paul, Tertullian, Jerome, Aquinas, Schopenhauer, Nietzsche, Shaw, *et al.*, of course, were entitled to their opinions concerning women. In his *Essay on Women*, Schopenhauer could say: "When the laws gave women equal rights with men, they ought also to have endowed them with masculine intellects." Nietzsche could say: "Man shall be educated for war, and woman for the recreation of the warrior.... Everything in woman is a riddle, and everything in woman hath one answer: its name is childbearing." Woman was God's second mistake, thought Nietzsche.

The fact remains that women are fully human, with all of the rights and privileges that attend that fact. Modern biology has shown the Aristotelian view that woman supplies only "passive matter" in generation to be completely false. Half of the zygote's chromosomes are supplied by the ovum; half, by the sperm. When the ovum is fertilized by a sperm which possesses the X chromosome, the zygote develops as a female. The development of a female is in no way attributable to a "defect" in fertilization; and least of all is a female the result of a "damp south wind."

To state the equality of women with men so far as essence and fundamental rights are concerned is not to deny that differences do exist between the sexes. There are natural differences of anatomy, physiology, psychology, temperament, emotion, physical strength, propensities, etc., which distinguish the sexes; man has neither the right nor the power to erase these differences. None of these natural differences, however, suggest that a woman be denied the elementary rights that belong to human beings in general. One sex is meant to complement and fulfill the other, not to exclude or deny basic human rights belonging to the other.

Fulton J. Sheen has said that man favors reason, whereas a woman favors intuition; a man tends to govern, whereas a woman reigns; a man tends toward the material, whereas a woman is more idealistic; man is generally the giver, woman the gift.

May not this be the key to the crisis of our hour? Men have been ruling the world, and the world is still collapsing. Those very qualities in which man, apparently, shone are the ones that today seem to be evaporating. The first of his peculiar powers, *reason*, is gradually being abdicated, as philosophy rejects first principles.... The second of his powers, *governing*, is gradually vanishing, as democracy becomes arithmocracy.... The third of his powers, *dedication to the temporal and the material*, has become so perverted that the material, in the shape of an atom, is used to annihilate the human.... His fourth attribute, that of being the *giver*, has in its forgetfulness of God made him the taker.... In this time of trouble, there must be a hearkening back to a woman.[42]

We simply fail to understand the mentality that has kept women in an inferior, subordinate, and often nonexistent role in the Mystical Body — other than bearing children. Of course, civilization in general has been slow to give women their rightful place in human affairs; and the Church tends to reflect to some degree the culture in which it exists. There is absolutely no justification, we submit, in forbidding women to be ordained as priests. What is there in the nature of woman that prohibits her from being a priestess? Even some primitive cultures had their priestesses.

Not a few textbooks of dogmatic theology have implied that a male priesthood is of divine faith. Canon 968 states: "Only males receive sacred ordination validly." The noted French theologian Yves Congar, O.P., has said: "It is not certain that the exclusion of women from the priesthood is a matter of divine law. But I add this: what permits us to say that the reason for this restriction is uniquely socio-cultural? I deny that one can make such an assertion with full certitude." There is no certain evidence that the deaconesses of the early Church were the equivalent of male deacons admitted to the hierarchy of orders.

More voices in the Church are being heard which favor the ordination of women. Bernard Haring, for example, has said: "I expect that we will have women priests within the generation of the young people today. There is no difference between a man and a woman before God." U.S. Presbyterians began ordaining women in 1956. American Lutherans decided to accept women pastors in 1970. Reform Judaism ordained its first woman rabbi, Sally Priesand.

The time has come for a change in the Church's treatment of women. The *National Catholic Reporter*, commenting on a statement by thirty-four theologians encouraging reform, stated forthrightly:

There is no mention of one of the gravest violations of justice in the Church today: the continuance of prejudicial attitudes toward women among Church officials, and the institutional constructs perpetuating discrimination against women at all levels of Church life.... Male chauvinism seems to be a sad state of mind afflicting Churchmen both left and right.[43]

Let us frankly acknowledge that the Church's teaching on contraception serves to hurt women most of all.

In December, 1972, the U.S. Bishops issued a report entitled *Theological Reflections on the Ordination of Women*. The study, funded at $500,000, concluded that there is no absolute theological impediment proscribing the ordination of women; but the report offered seven "justifications" for not ordaining women. The Joint Committee of Organizations Concerned with the Status of Women in the Church issued a response to the Bishops' report. We summarize the response as follows:

(1) *The Old Testament:* the claim that the total exclusion of women from the priesthood of the Old Testament was an indication of God's will is rejected. Unjust discrimination can never be imputed to God; such an imputation would be blasphemous. The Pontifical Biblical Commission decreed in 1976 that women priests are not forbidden by the Bible.

(2) *Women deacons:* whether or not real women deacons were ordained in the early Church is neither central nor crucial to the question at hand.

(3) *Pauline authority:* the study recognized that St. Paul's direction that women hold a subordinate position in the Church is of Pauline authority alone and not necessarily binding upon the universal Church at all times.

(4) *Doctrine on headship:* the teachings of Genesis prescribe no *a priori* mandate that man is to rule over woman or that woman is essentially inferior to man. Both were made in the image and likeness of God.

(5) *Male incarnation:* it was Christ's humanity, and not specifically His maleness, which is to be identified with the Incarnation and Redemption. It is "sheer arrogance" to claim that males have an identification with the Deity which is denied to females.

(6) *Divine choice:* that Christ apparently had no women apostles offers no valid argument against the ordination of women. Some Biblical scholars believe that women were present at the Last Supper and that some of the seventy-two disciples were women. Furthermore, if the sex of those at the Last Supper was to be a deciding factor for ordination, why not also religion, race, or nationality? The Gospels cite numerous instances where Our Lord favored women.

(7) *Tradition:* while it has been a "venerable" tradition of the Church to exclude women from Holy Orders, the argument from tradition must be rejected. An error once committed and repeated should not be perpetuated. Injustice should not be sanctified by tradition.

IX. FREEDOM IN THE CHURCH

Background. Heresy has always presented a problem to the Church, as well as to the heretic. The Church has responded to heresy and insubordination to authority in various ways throughout the centuries. When the people of a city in Samaria refused to receive Christ and His disciples, James and John thought that fire should be sent from Heaven to consume the refractory city. Christ rebuked them, saying: "You do not know of what manner of spirit you are; for the Son of Man did not come to destroy men's lives, but to save them" (Luke 9:55-56). On another occasion, the Divine Master said, "Love your enemies; do good to those who hate you" (Matt. 5:44).

During the first three centuries of Christianity, the penalties against heresy were exclusively spiritual, usually excommunication. Gradually, as Christianity became more closely identified with the state, heretics came to be regarded as enemies of the state. Confiscation of property, exile, and even the death penalty were finally employed against heresy. Bishop Priscillian has the dubious honor of being the first heretic to receive capital punishment, in 385. Augustine at first opposed the use of temporal punishment for heresy, but he later favored moderate severity.

Eventually the Inquisition came into existence. One need but mention the word and up crops images of cowled monks watching complacently as torture — such as the rack, the *strappado*, and the water torture — is administered to a hapless victim. Bernard of Clairvaux had stated the traditional position: "*Fides suadenda, non imponenda*" (faith must result from conviction, not from force). The position was gradually abandoned as the doctrines of the Cathars and the Waldenses, teaching the evil of matter and procreation, threatened the social order.

Pope Gregory IX instituted the papal Inquisition in February, 1231. Life imprisonment was decreed as a "salutary" punishment for repentant heretics and capital punishment for obstinate heretics who were turned over to the secular arm. The ecclesiastical Inquisitors generally emphasized the fact that the Church itself did not shed blood; yet, in turning the unrepentant heretic over to the secular arm, it was understood that burning at the stake would be the penalty administered.

The Church simply cannot wash its hands of the guilt involved in putting to death the unrepentant heretic. The practice of persecuting, torturing, and burning to obtain confessions was recommended and doctrinally justified by Pope Innocent IV in his bull *Ad Extirpanda*, issued in 1252. Due process of law, the right to confront one's accusers, to have counsel and present witnesses in one's own defense — all of these elementary requirements of justice were commonly denied. John A. O'Brien writes:

For six centuries, from the twelfth to the eighteenth, the Church displayed a wanton disregard for elementary human rights and for the dignity of the person, and an implacable savagery toward all who disagreed with its teachings, that blacken its name with an infamy which a thousand centuries will be unable to erase.[44]

A number of memorable names are related to the Inquisition. St. Peter Martyr was appointed Inquisitor by Gregory IX in 1234. Peter was known primarily for his efforts to convert heretics; he was canonized the year following his assassination. St. Joan of Arc was a victim of the medieval Inquisition. The Maid of Orleans declared that she must follow her "voices" in preference to the pope, that she would rather forego Paschal Communion and a Christian burial than to act against her conscience. By canonizing her, the Church has acknowledged the essential validity of her position.

John Huss of Bohemia was burned at the stake in 1415. Jerome Savonarola dared to attack Pope Alexander VI, who, among other things, kept a seventeen-year-old mistress. Savonarola was imprisoned, forced to make an ambiguous confession, and finally burned at the stake in 1499.

As the Prior of St. Mark's in Florence was about to be hanged and his body burned in ignominy, the Bishop of Vasona confronted the Dominican, saying: "I separate thee from the Church Militant and from the Church Triumphant!" Savonarola answered: "Not from the Church Triumphant; that is beyond thy power." One wonders if Savonarola's efforts for reform — so badly needed in the Church of his day — had succeeded, the impending sixteenth-century Reformation might have been obviated.

Thomás de Torquemada (1420-1498) was the first grand Inquisitor in Spain. He has become the symbol of inquisitorial terror. The Dominican was responsible for an estimated two thousand burnings at the stake. St. Ignatius Loyola, founder of the Society of Jesus (the largest religious order in the Church today), was twice arrested by the Inquisition on suspicion of heresy.

It was not until 1834 that the Spanish Inquisition was finally suppressed. The name of the Holy Roman Inquisition was changed to the Sacred Congregation of Roman and Universal Inquisition by Pope Paul III in 1542, and in 1908 by Pope St. Pius X to the Congregation of the Holy Office. On Dec. 7, 1965, Pope Paul VI established new procedures and changed the name to the Sacred Congregation for the Doctrine of the Faith. The Congregation decreed in 1971 that one who holds "doctrinal error" will no longer be called a "heretic" or be excommunicated. "The electric chair is no more," said Msgr. Joseph Tomko of the Congregation. The severest punishment an unrepentant theologian can undergo is being blacklisted as an author in error and expelled from his teaching post.

Though a long time in coming, and certainly a far cry from the spirit that permeated the *Syllabus of Errors* of Pope Pius IX, Vatican Council II stated in its *Declaration on Religious Freedom* (nn. 10 ff.):

It is one of the major tenets of Catholic doctrine that man's response to God in faith must be free. Therefore no one is to be forced to embrace the Christian Faith against his own will. . . . It is therefore completely in accord with the nature of faith that in matters religious every manner of coercion on the part of men should be excluded. . . .

In the life of the People of God as it has made its pilgrim way through the vicissitudes of human history, there have at times appeared ways of acting which were less in accord with the spirit of the Gospel and even opposed to it. Nevertheless, the doctrine of the Church that no one is to be coerced into faith has always stood firm.

Thus far has the Church progressed from the infamous days of the Inquisition.

Evaluation and Recommendation. "The first law of history," wrote Pope Leo XIII, "is to assert nothing false and to have no fear of telling the truth."[45] Thus did Vatican II acknowledge, though briefly, "ways of acting which were less in accord with the spirit of the Gospel." Many efforts have been made by apologists to whitewash the scandalous practices of the Inquisition. Most of these efforts have proved futile. Equally unjustified are efforts to blacken the facts and denigrate the intentions of the Church concerning the Inquisition. We shall not consciously add to either list.

There are five cardinal points to be considered in making a valid appraisal of the Inquisition.[46] (1) The Church, like the state, is a "perfect society," in the sense that it possesses the right and the power to perpetuate itself, to protect itself, and to provide for the common good by the use of executive, legislative, and judicial powers. (2) The people of the Middle Ages held their Christian Faith in the highest esteem, comparable to no earthly possession, even life itself. Orthodoxy was paramount. (3) In the Middle Ages there existed a union of Church and state; each was but one facet of a closely knit polity. There was one Christian Church, the Roman Catholic Church. The modern concept of a separation of Church and state would have shocked the medieval mind. (4) The penal code of the Middle Ages was unusually severe, by modern standards. Counterfeiters, for example, were burned alive. During the reigns of Henry VIII and Elizabeth, convicts were drawn, disemboweled, and quartered. John Calvin had no scruples in having Michael Servetus burned to death. (5) Due process of law; trial by jury; the right to have counsel and present witnesses in one's own defense; freedom of conscience and religion — none of these were well-established principles in the Middle Ages. We in twentieth-century America tend to take these constitutional guarantees for granted, not realizing how relatively recent has been their firm establishment in the fabric of democratic civilization.

With the above-mentioned principles in mind, one can better assess the Inquisition in terms of historical perspective. Let it be said, and it has been said by almost every present-day Catholic theologian, that no one of the above points can vindicate the wanton cruelty and lack of respect for the dignity of the human person and personal conscience that was perpetrated by the medieval Church, acting in union with the state. Nor can the popes and the Church be completely vindicated of wrongdoing by the theoretical declaration that the Church never sheds blood. A number of the popes threatened with excommunication any civil ruler who refused to inflict the death penalty upon an obdurate heretic, once turned over to the secular arm by the Inquisition. Such a ruler would then himself be subject to the machinations of the Inquisition and might be faced with a possible death penalty.

One wonders why the medieval Church failed to distinguish between "good faith" and "bad faith" on the part of the heretic. A heretic in good faith was blameless in the eyes of God. Why should one who held a purely speculative disagreement with official Church doctrine have been subjected to such cruel and inhumane treatment by the Church? One must wonder at a King St. Louis IX of France, who manifested a high degree of personal holiness and benevolence to his subjects, but conformed to the prevalent manner of the day in treating heretics. One must also wonder at a St. Thomas Aquinas, keen of intellect and spotless in character, who saw no inconsistency in defending the right of the Church to put recalcitrant heretics to death.

On the positive side, it should be said that some popes urged moderation in meting out punishment for heresy, and even deposed some Inquisitors who exhibited inordinate cruelty and severity. It is an error to say that most of the Inquisitors were hard-headed, stupid religious fanatics. On the contrary, most of them, taken from the Dominican order, were men of unblemished character and keen intellect; not a few are listed among the saints of the Church. In one sense the Inquisition marked a step *forward* from mob rule and lynching, which were often previously employed to punish heresy.

One must further recognize that the doctrines of the Cathars had significant antisocial implications. Besides denying that Christ had a real material body, that the Old Testament was inspired, that the Sacraments have power to effect Grace, Catharists rejected as evil everything connected with matter (a revival of the Manichean belief). Thus, marriage, procreation, private property, even the eating of meat were considered sinful. Suicide, in the form of the *endura* (death by either suffocation or fasting), was recommended for the critically ill. One can appreciate the concern of the Church as well as the state in suppressing such a bizarre and deleterious social philosophy.

The *Encyclopaedia Britannica* states forthrightly:

The medieval Inquisition was concerned with the heretics of the time ... most of whom, because of their antisocial tenets, would be treated harshly even by many modern governments. ... The principles and practices of the Inquisition were no crueler than those of the contemporary civil courts; if it is condemned on such grounds, the Middle Ages and the Renaissance must also be condemned. Not only Catholics but the early Protestants ... used force to impose religious unity.[47]

In the final analysis, the medieval Churchmen must be seen as children of their age. A pluralistic religious society and a religiously neutral government were ideas whose time had not yet come. It is a rare genius indeed who is able to rise above the contemporary milieu and presage an idea. Such geniuses have been exceedingly rare in the history of civilization. Religious pluralism, of course, is not necessarily an unmitigated blessing; but the place of freedom in religion is now firmly established. The methods of the Inquisition would simply not be tolerated in any modern democratic state.

The theoretical right of the Church to impose capital punishment for heresy remains a moot question. We can still hear our seminary professor staunchly defending the Church's right to inflict capital punishment upon refractory heretics. His argument went something like this: If the state possesses the right to defend itself from pertinacious criminals by the imposition of the death penalty for the severest crimes, then, *a fortiori*, the Church possesses the right to defend itself and protect the spiritual welfare of the People of God by the imposition of capital punishment upon unrepentant and pertinacious heretics. The good professor, while ascribing this theoretical right to the Church as a perfect society, went on to say that *in practice* the Church probably should never exercise this right.

The Bible says, "Thou shalt not kill"; the Bible also says that one who kills his brother should himself be put to death. Until very recent times, most states have exercised the right to punish the most severe crimes with capital punishment. Most moralists throughout history, as we noted in Chapter III, have conceded this right to the state. An increasing number of states today are abolishing the death penalty. In 1972 the Supreme Court of the State of California decided that capital punishment constitutes "cruel and unusual" punishment, forbidden by the Constitution. It is our opinion that capital punishment ought to be never imposed, by either the Church or the state. Christ never did so. He refused to condemn the woman caught in adultery, and He prevented her from being stoned to death.

We have dwelt at some length on the Inquisition because we believe an understanding of the causes, principles, and consequences of that dreadful medieval institution is paramount to an understanding of Catholicism today. "The present is the past rolled up for action," writes Will Durant, "and the past is the present unrolled for our understanding."[48] Never again must the Church even faintly suggest that faith can be imposed by the use of force or that heresy can be extirpated by inflicting excruciating torture. Never again may the Church suggest that power makes right, that uniformity of thought is superior to personal freedom and human dignity. Never again may the Church ignore such elementary human rights as freedom of speech, due process of law, the right to a speedy and fair trial. Never again may the Church sanction the taking of a human life, which belongs to God alone and is precious in His eyes. Never again may the Church suppress true scholarship and true science, as was done with the Copernican system and with Galileo by the Roman Inquisition in 1616 and 1632, respectively.

Let us recognize that vestiges of the Inquisition remain in Catholicism today. The writings of John Courtney Murray of the United States on pluralism, religious freedom, and the separation of Church and state were suppressed by his Jesuit superiors prior to Vatican II. Murray became the prime architect of Vatican II's *Declaration on Religious Freedom*. In 1953 Cardinal Ottaviani of the Holy Office upheld the right of Catholic states to grant special privileges to the Catholic Church and to restrict the religious activities of non-Catholic groups. He decried the idea of a religiously neutral civil government, as advocated by certain "liberal" Catholics in the United States. "It is not easy for the leopard to change its spots," writes Father O'Brien. "Neither is it easy for an organization of Inquisitors, long accustomed to repression and persecution, to change its spirit or its tactics."[49]

The "bottom line" on any discussion of freedom in the Church was stated most aptly by Vatican II: ". . . all the faithful, clerical and lay, possess a lawful freedom of inquiry and of thought, and the freedom to express their minds humbly and courageously about those matters in which they enjoy competence" (*Gaudium et Spes*, n. 62).

X. HOLY MASS

Background. Sacrifice has been an integral part of religion from time immemorial. By *sacrifice*, in the religious sense, is meant any visible gift that is offered to God and is either wholly or partially destroyed in His honor and adoration. Christ offered Himself to His Heavenly Father as a bloody sacrifice on the Cross (cf. Heb. 9:14). The constant tradition of the Church has taught that the Mass is a true sacrifice — the unbloody renewal of that first Good Friday.

The sixteenth-century Reformers rejected the sacrifice of the Mass, maintaining that Christ is only present at the moment of Communion or is only present symbolically in the bread and wine. Catholic teaching maintains that Jesus Christ is "truly, really, and substantially" present in the Eucharist. After the priest pronounces the words of consecration, the substance of the bread and wine is miraculously changed to the substance of Christ — His body, blood, soul, and divinity; only the accidents — the appearance, taste, smell, etc. — of the bread and wine remain. Such is the Catholic doctrine of transubstantiation.

Christ promised the Eucharist: "Except you eat the flesh of the Son of Man and drink His blood, you shall not have life in you. He who eats My flesh and drinks My blood has life everlasting. . ." (John 6:54-55). Christ called Himself the living bread Who had come down from Heaven, just as manna had fed the ancient Israelites. St. Paul said that anyone who partakes unworthily of the Eucharist is "guilty of the body and the blood of the Lord" (1 Cor. 11:27). The evidence from both Scripture and tradition is too overwhelming, says the Church, to accept any interpretation other than the literal of Christ's words at the Last Supper.

The duty to worship God is contained in the natural moral law, the divine positive law, and ecclesiastical law. Mankind has universally felt the need to worship the Supreme Being behind the universe. Divine worship has taken various forms throughout the ages of man. For the Christian the perfect act of divine worship is the Holy Sacrifice of the Mass. At the Last Supper Christ commanded, "Do this in remembrance of Me" (Luke 22:19).

Canon 1247 requires attendance at the Holy Sacrifice of the Mass on all Sundays and the Feasts of Christmas; Solemnity of Mary, the Mother of God; Ascension; Assumption of the Blessed Virgin Mary; All Saints; and the Immaculate Conception. The obligation to hear Mass on Sundays and Holy Days is *grave*, binding under pain of mortal sin. One is excused from the obligation for any "moderately" grave reason, such as considerable hardship or corporal or spiritual harm either to oneself or another. The Fourth Lateran Council (1215), by the decree *Omnis Utriusque Sexus*, required yearly confession (for one in mortal sin) and paschal Communion, binding gravely. Pope St. Pius X (1835-1914) recommended frequent, even daily, reception of Holy Communion.

Evaluation and Recommendation. Our position is that every ecclesiastical law should be judged according to the mind of Christ. How faithfully and accurately does a given Church law reflect the mind of Christ? To the point, how accurately does the ecclesiastical law requiring attendance at Mass on Sundays and Holy Days, binding under penalty of mortal sin, reflect the mind of Christ at the Last Supper?

We submit that Christ had no intention to bind Christians to a weekly observance of the Sacred Mysteries under pain of sin.

We recommend that the Church remove this penalty. To make this recommendation is not to minimize the importance and the necessity of the Mass for a believing Christian. The Mass would remain as the one perfect form of divine worship and the best way of keeping Sunday holy. But such a relaxation of Church law would recognize that at certain times and in certain circumstances, one might also keep Sunday holy in other ways besides attendance at Mass—such as visiting the sick and lonely, calling on a fallen-away Catholic, etc.

We question the ultralegalism which attaches a penalty of mortal sin (which means damnation if unrepented) for non-attendance at Mass on Sundays and Holy Days. Surely the mind of Christ saw, and sees, the Mass as a supreme act of *love*. One who truly loves the Mass and realizes what it is will want to share in it at least every Sunday and more often when possible. The penalty of sin should be far removed from attendance at Mass; faith and love should and must be the motivation for participating in the Holy Sacrifice.

Of course, we are face-to-face here with a more fundamental question being considered by many theologians in Catholicism today: should any ecclesiastical law be binding under pain of mortal sin? Many theologians today are coming to agree with the statement of Father Charles E. Curran: "The Church has no right to use the penalty of sin for its own laws."[50] The Church should not place unnecessary burdens on men's shoulders (cf. Matt. 23:4), burdens which do not appear to be required by either the natural moral law or the divine positive law. The relaxation of Church laws regarding fast and abstinence has already been noted.

The essence of the Mass, we submit, does not demand a weekly observance under pain of sin. To deliberately and negligently avoid attending Mass over a considerable period of time would, in our judgment, be a grave matter. But to specify a time, weekly or otherwise, for Mass attendance misses the whole essence and spirit of the Mass. Man is bound to keep one day of the week holy, as required by the Third Commandment. A believing Christian is bound to participate in the Holy Sacrifice from time to time. But the question of mortal sin in observing these divine laws should be a personal matter between the individual conscience and God.[51]

In like manner, man is bound by divine command to do penance; but the Church has wisely recognized that the *form* of penance to be done, and the *time* and *place* that it is to be done, should be freely undertaken apart from the penalty of mortal sin. Eating meat on Friday violated no natural or divine positive law; only an ecclesiastical law was violated, involving a rejection of Church authority.

The Fourth Lateran Council required reception of the Holy Eucharist at least once a year, during Eastertime. Again, we question the wisdom of placing a time requirement in the performance of a spiritual obligation. If one is to understand the duty to attend Holy Mass and receive Holy Communion in a time-context, in the strict sense one should have a *daily* obligation to do both. Knowing what the Mass truly is, one could perform no more important act for that day. Of course, Christ did not intend to bind a Christian to a daily attendance at Mass, and neither has the Church. We simply feel that it is unwise to attach any specific time requirement — other than a "prolonged period" — to attendance at Mass and reception of the Holy Eucharist.

The late Thomas Merton, who had many profound spiritual insights, once said that it is better to fail well than to succeed poorly. Our Lord "failed well" on Good Friday. Perhaps some of the recommendations we have made would "succeed poorly"; in that event, we would rather have them "fail well." The seeds for reform have been planted in Catholicism today. In time, we feel certain, after a period of gestation, these seeds will bear much good fruit. "Something is afoot in the universe," said Teilhard, "something that looks like gestation."

Christianity today, as always, is the newest thing in the universe.

PART IV

CATHOLICISM AND AUTHORITY

Whoever wishes to become great among you shall be your servant; and whoever wishes to be first among you shall be your slave; even as the Son of Man has not come to be served but to serve....

— Matt. 20:26-28

CHAPTER VIII

STRUCTURE AND AUTHORITY IN THE CATHOLIC CHURCH

He said to them, 'But who do you say that I am?' Simon Peter answered and said, 'You are the Christ, the Son of the living God.' Then Jesus answered and said, 'Blessed are you, Simon, son of Jona, for flesh and blood has not revealed this to you, but My Father in Heaven. And I say to you, you are Peter, and upon this rock I will build My Church, and the gates of Hell shall not prevail against it. And I will give you the keys of the Kingdom of Heaven; and whatever you shall bind on earth shall be bound in Heaven, and whatever you shall loose on earth shall be loosed in Heaven.'

— Matt. 16:15-19

Simon, Simon, behold, Satan has desired to have you, that he may sift you as wheat. But I have prayed for you, that your faith may not fail; and do you, when once you have turned again, strengthen your brethren.

— Luke 22:31-32

Feed My lambs . . . ; feed My sheep.

— John 21:15, 17

The Church, instructed by the teaching of humility, does not command as though by authority, but persuades by reason.

— Pope Gregory the Great

We declare, say, define and pronounce that it is absolutely necessary for the salvation of every human creature to be subject to the Roman pontiff.

— Pope Boniface VIII, *Unam Sanctam*

No congregation whatsoever, separated from the eternal visible communion and obedience to the Roman pontiff, can be the Church of Christ or in any way whatsoever belong to the Church of Christ.

— Pope Pius IX

I am here to bless, not condemn.

— Pope John XXIII

If Christ had not entrusted all power to one man, the Church would not have been perfect because there would have been no order, and each one would have been able to say he was led by the Holy Spirit. . . . Christ

213

wills that His power be exercised by one man. . . . He has made this power so strong that He permits all the forces of Hell to be let loose against it without injury.

> — Martin Luther, from a sermon preached in 1516

You [the pope] are a servant of servants, and more than all other men you are in a most miserable and dangerous position. Be not deceived by those who pretend that you are lord of the world. They err who exalt you above a council and the Church Universal.

> — Martin Luther

I have sworn upon the altar of God eternal hostility against every form of tyranny over the mind of man.

> — Thomas Jefferson

Democracy is the worst form of government, except for every other form of government.

> — Winston Churchill

Power tends to corrupt; absolute power corrupts absolutely.

> — Lord Acton

Kings will be tyrants from policy, when subjects are rebels from principle.

> — Edmund Burke

Those who make peaceful revolution impossible make violent revolution inevitable.

> — President John F. Kennedy

. . . man, proud man
Dressed in a little brief authority . . .
Plays such fantastic tricks before high Heaven
As make the angels weep.

> — William Shakespeare, *Measure for Measure*

I. THE ELEMENTS OF RELIGION

WE noted earlier that religion is a well-nigh universal phenomenon whereby man pays homage and adoration to his Maker and acknowledges dependence upon a Supreme Being. Religion has taken myriad forms over the centuries; but central to all religious systems is the elementary recognition of the existence of an extramundane and a supramundane Reality to which man must relate. The universe does not explain itself; effects do not always point self-evidently to their respective causes. There must be a Supreme Cause, a First Cause of all causes, which most men have called God.

There are three elements to be found in varying degrees in all religious systems: (1) the traditional, historic, visible, structural, organizational, hierarchical, authoritarian element which can be called the *Petrine* element (in the spirit of St. Peter); (2) the speculative, reasoning, philosophical-theological element which can be called the *Pauline* element (in the spirit of St. Paul); and (3) the experimental, mystical-internal, existential element which may be called the *Johanine* (in the spirit of St. John).[1] All three elements have been present in varying proportions in every religious system known to history.

First, every system of religion has had a structure, some form of organization, government, and cohesion. No society, religious or otherwise, can exist without some form of authority and structure. These may be extremely nebulous and inchoate, taking secondary importance to the speculative and/or the mystical. Gnosticism and theosophy, for example, stress the mystical over the organizational. Protestantism generally de-emphasizes authority and structure in favor of the personal and existential element in religion. Catholicism has laid more stress on authority and structure, along with a highly developed Scholastic philosophy and theology.

Secondly, a system of religion must have some kind of a rationale, a body of doctrine, a point of view concerning the meaning of human existence. Again, this element may dominate or take a secondary place in relation to the other elements. In fact, a given religious system may renounce all "dogmas"; but that, of course, is itself a dogma and a rationale. Scholastic philosophy and theology represent a highly sophisticated and developed system of speculative thought, associated with Catholicism. Protestantism has stressed the Bible as the prime source of Christian doctrine.

And, lastly, every religion contains an element of mysticism — an undefinable, personal, experiential relationship between God and man. Hinduism and other Oriental religions give primary emphasis to the mystical. Catholicism has had great mystics — St. Teresa of Avila and St. John of the Cross, to name only two. The Pentecostal movement in Catholicism today leans toward the mystical. Certain Protestant sects emphasize the mystical over the structural and the theological.

All three elements have their rightful place in the true religion. Religion must have structure, for man has a body as well as a soul; religion must have theology, for man has a mind and is a rational animal; and religion must have mysticism, because the ultimate relationship between God and a human soul is undefinable. The crux of the matter is: what form and proportion should each element receive? For one who believes that God has given man a special Divine Revelation and has established His own Church on earth, the question is not to be resolved by human wisdom alone. How these elements are to exist in Christianity must, in the final analysis, depend on the true answer to the question: what is the mind of Christ? The place of authority, structure, doctrine, and personalism must have as its ultimate criterion, what did Christ intend?

II. THE PAPACY

Papal Primacy. Catholics believe they read the mind of Christ correctly when they understand Christ to have appointed Peter and his successors to head the Church on earth, with the authority to bind and loose. The principal Scriptural justification for this belief is Matthew 16:18-19. Peter is given the *keys*, used elsewhere in Scripture (cf. Is. 22:22; Apoc. 1:18; Apoc. 3:7) as a symbol of power and authority. Peter is charged to feed the entire flock (cf. John 21:15-17). To feed the flock of Christ means to rule them, to supply their religious needs. To Peter alone Christ gave a name (rock) bearing upon the constitution of the Church. To Peter alone Christ promised he would be a fisher of men (cf. Luke 5:10). Christ washed Peter's feet first at the Last Supper (cf. John 13:6).

After His Resurrection Our Lord made a special appearance to Peter (cf. Luke 24:34). Christ predicted that Peter would die a martyr's death (cf. John 21:19). After Christ's Ascension Peter acted as head of the Church (cf. Acts 1:15; Acts 2, 10, 11). St. Paul remained with Peter in Jerusalem for fifteen days (cf. Gal. 1:18). Peter is mentioned 195 times in the Gospels, while all of the other apostles together are mentioned 130 times.[2] Peter is always mentioned first in any listing of the apostles by the evangelists; but he was not the first called, nor the oldest, nor the most dear to Our Lord. Moreover, Peter is expressly called "the first" (cf. Matt. 10:2). Catholic tradition has steadfastly maintained the primacy of Peter and his successors in the papacy, a belief explicitly defined by Vatican Council I.

In his epistles St. Paul never explicitly acknowledged Peter, or anyone else, as Christ's vicar and visible head of the Church.

Paul said he "withstood Cephas to the face" (Gal. 2:11 f.). However, the implication here is that Peter did possess authority and even primacy; otherwise Paul would have felt no need to assert himself to Peter. In 1 Cor. 1:10-13 Paul laments the divisions which had arisen: ". . . each of you says, I am of Paul, or I am of Apollos, or I am of Cephas, or I am of Christ. Has Christ been divided up?"

Catholicism's primary claim to the divine institution of the office of the papacy rests in Matt. 16:18-19. Any passage of Sacred Scripture can be understood in one of three ways: (1) in a *literal* sense, according to the obvious denotation of the words used; (2) in a *figurative, symbolical, metaphorical* sense, such as the "keys" representing power and authority; and (3) in an *accommodated* sense, such as "*ite ad Joseph* (go to Joseph)," stated in Genesis but applied to St. Joseph, the foster father of Jesus. How any given passage in the Bible should be understood — in a literal, figurative, or accommodated sense — can be a complex problem, requiring proficiency in exegesis and the science of hermeneutics. Ultimately, the Bible must have an authoritative interpreter, which is but another reason why Christ established His Church on earth.

Protestantism, which places much faith in the written word of God as contained in the Bible, treats Matt. 16:18-19 in various ways. Some maintain that the passage was not written by Matthew but was interpolated by a later commentator who wished to buttress Church authority. The passage occurs in none of the other Gospels. Others understand the passage in a figurative sense, applying equally to all Christians and based on the Christian's faith. Others imply that Our Lord was guilty of faulty syntax when they submit that "rock" refers to Christ alone. Still others hold that the Greek word for rock, referring to Peter, is better rendered in English as *pebble*, and a different word was used for Christ as the rock. Catholicism simply takes the obvious, literal meaning of the passage and points to other passages, which we cited above, that corroborate this literal interpretation. There is no reason to doubt the authenticity or diminish the weight of a particular passage in Sacred Scripture simply because it occurs only once.

Papal Infallibility. Vatican Council I declared:

. . . we teach and define it to be a divinely revealed truth that the Roman pontiff, when, speaking *ex cathedra*, that is, when discharging

the office of pastor and teacher of all Christians, in virtue of his supreme apostolic power, he defines a doctrine regarding faith or morals,
to be held by the whole Church, through the divine assistance promised
him in the person of St. Peter, possesses that infallibility with which
our divine Redeemer wished His Church to be endowed in defining
doctrines of faith or morals; and, therefore, that such definitions of the
Roman pontiff are of themselves, not in virtue of the consent of the
Church, unalterable. Should any one, which God forbid, presume to
contradict this our definition, let him be anathema.[3]

The decree *Pastor Aeternus*, promulgated by the First Vatican Council in 1870, stated the conditions that must be present
simultaneously for an infallible papal declaration:

(1) The pope must act as supreme teacher of the Universal
Church, not as a private theologian or pastor of the diocese of
Rome.

(2) He must clearly intend to define a doctrine, settling an
issue definitively; simple exhortations and temporary decisions
on discipline are not matter for infallibility.

(3) What the pope defines must relate to faith or morals,
with the revealed message of Christianity.

(4) The pope must clearly intend to oblige the entire Church
to believe the defined doctrine, to demand an irrevocable assent.
This does not mean that the pope has given a total explanation of
the doctrine; much may have been left unsaid. But what has
been said has been said correctly.[4]

Papal authority and infallibility are assuredly stumbling
blocks for many Christians today. Hans Kung, as we have mentioned, prefers "indefectibility" to "infallibility." The Church
moves steadfastly in the path of Christ's truth, maintains Kung;
from this path the Church cannot defect. But indefectibility from
Christ's truth is not the same as ascribing infallibility to a given
statement by the Church in a given point of history.

Robert McAfee Brown has written:

Catholicism appears to commit this sin: it equates the treasure
with the earthen vessels . . . with the Catholic assertion that a human
being can ever speak in the untainted accents of the Holy Ghost. . . . To
affirm that a human being can be endowed with infallibility seems to
be claiming for that human being something that can only be claimed
for God Himself.[5]

We can only answer that papal infallibility is not of human
origin; it comes from God Himself, as indicated in Matt. 16:18-19
and in other texts of Scripture cited above. Surely no man and no
human institution would dare to arrogate to themselves and of

themselves the quality of infallibility. The frail "earthen vessel" is not to be confused with the divine "treasure": popes can sin; popes can act unwisely. But in defining an article of Christian Faith or a law of Christian morality, the Vicar of Christ will not teach error. Such is Christ's promise. Simon could and did fail; but Peter, never!

If Protestantism is appalled at the apparent arrogance of Catholicism, which claims the quality of infallibility in its teaching office, Catholicism is equally bewildered at the disunity, confusion, and contradictions that have characterized Protestantism in the last four centuries. If Catholicism has sinned by excess in terms of authority and structure, Protestantism has surely sinned by defect in these areas. Authority can be exercised democratically, as we have pointed out in Chapter VII. Catholicism sees the mind of Christ wisely providing for unity by naming one visible head of the Church, in the person of Peter and his successors. A body without a head, biologically speaking, would be a monstrosity. So too, a Church without a visible head is bound to degenerate into anarchy and error. Unity is from God; but disunity is from man.

Infallibility, like other doctrines, was a concept to be developed over the centuries, a quality to be more fully recognized by the Church in the course of time. Even before the death of St. John, the evangelist, Pope Clement of Rome (90-99) wrote to the Christians of Corinth, urging concord and submission to their ecclesiastical superiors; the Corinthians accepted Rome's message and legates gladly. The Pope's letter was placed almost on a level with the Sacred Scriptures. St. Ignatius of Antioch, in the year 117, acknowledged in a letter the supremacy of the Bishop of Rome. Pope Victor (188-198) summoned the bishops of the time to convene for the purpose of determining the date of Easter. St. Irenaeus, Bishop of Lyons, wrote a well-known letter in 180 which acknowledged the supremacy of the Church of Rome. St. Augustine acknowledged the supremacy of the Bishop of Rome in settling a dispute, with the words, "Rome has spoken; the case is closed."

The pope and the college of bishops in union with the pope are infallible because the Church is infallible; the Church is infallible because Christ (Who taught infallibly through His human nature) is infallible; and Christ is infallible because He is God. Christ instituted His Church on earth to guide mankind to its heavenly goal. A Church that could teach religious error is manifestly incompetent to lead souls to Heaven; such a Church could not be Christ's Church. Infallibility is that necessary quality that safeguards the Christian Revelation as the Church makes its pilgrim journey in time and space.

To accept the doctrine of papal infallibility requires a good deal of humility and an extra measure of the virtue of obedience, virtues which Catholics find as difficult to foster as anyone else. The primacy and infallibility of the pope constitute the primary obstacle to Christian reunion. "I am increasingly sure," writes Robert McAfee Brown, "that the fundamental cleavage between Protestantism and Catholicism comes at the point of their different understandings of *authority*."[6] Men of good will on both sides need to pray for divine guidance and understanding, that this seemingly insuperable obstacle will be resolved in God's own good time. Christian unity is a goal incumbent upon every Christian to strive to achieve.

Papal Administration. The papacy continues. "The papacy," states the *Encyclopaedia Britannica*,

is the only institution that has existed continuously from the early Roman Empire. Its activities, its influence and its claims have varied and developed and have been challenged and combated; its fortunes and prestige have waxed and waned many times. Local yet worldwide, it has always based its pronouncements upon tradition while it has taken its colour from the present; flexible in choice of means, in all the changes of social and political sentiment it has remained uncompromisingly monarchical. There have been many great and saintly popes, many nonentities and not a few worthless or bad; but the office has always been greater than the man, and it survives.[7]

The reigning pope, Paul VI, is the 261st in a continuous line dating back to St. Peter.[8] The Church honors 83 popes as saints. Of the first 31 popes, 30 were martyrs; St. Dionysius, the 25th, escaped this fate. In all, 33 popes were martyred. There have been 105 Roman popes; 107 were natives of other parts of Italy. France provided 15 popes; Greece, 9; Germany, 7; Asia, 5; Africa, 3; Spain, 3; Dalmatia, 2; Palestine, Thrace, Holland, Portugal, and England, each 1. There were 9 pontiffs who reigned less than one month. The longest reign — except for St. Peter, who reigned over 32 years — was the reign of Pius IX, who was pope for 31 years, 7 months, and 21 days. Theoretically, any baptized male having reached the age of seven could be elected pope; in practice, the College of Cardinals has never gone outside of its own ranks in selecting a pope. The last non-Italian pope was Adrian VI of Utrecht (1522-1523). For the last thousand years, with few exceptions, the popes have been Italian. This fact is not surprising, since, after all, the pope is the Bishop of Rome; furthermore, the Avignon papacy which precipitated the Western Schism was an experience that the Church does not want to repeat.

Vatican I declared that the pope has "supreme and full power of jurisdiction over the Universal Church both in matters of faith and morals and in matters of discipline and government." In practice, pontifical government is exercised by the pope through the Roman Curia, consisting of congregations, courts, and offices. The Curia has no power to legislate; it functions only in an executive and judicial capacity. In the reform of Paul VI, a new constitution was issued on August 15, 1967. The pope is no longer prefect of any Congregation. The Constitution of 1967 provides for the following Congregations:[9]

(1) The Congregation for the Doctrine of the Faith, formerly called the Holy Office — and before that, the Inquisition — is the agency through which the pope exercises his teaching office.

(2) The Congregation for Bishops, formerly known as the Consistory, supervises dioceses and appoints bishops.

(3) The Congregation for the Clergy, formerly the Congregation of the Council, handles affairs of the clergy; this Congregation is presently headed by John Cardinal Wright of the United States.

(4) The Congregation for Eastern Churches handles all matters concerning the Eastern Rite of the Catholic Church.

(5) The Congregation for the Evangelization of the World (or Propagation of the Faith) supervises the missionary activity of the Church.

(6) The Congregation for Catholic Education (formerly the Congregation for Seminaries and Universities) supervises the discipline, curriculum, and administration of Catholic schools, seminaries, and pontifical universities.

(7) The Congregation for the Discipline of the Sacraments supervises the administration of the Seven Sacraments.

(8) The Congregation of Sacred Rites supervises the liturgy, rites, and ceremonies of the Western Church. Processes of beatification and canonization of saints come under this Congregation's jurisdiction.

(9) The Congregation of Religious and Secular Institutes supervises religious communities and secular institutes.

In addition to the Congregations, the papacy governs the Universal Church through courts and offices. The pontifical courts include the Sacred Penitentiary, which handles cases arising from the Sacrament of Penance; the Rota, which is the ultimate court of appeal in matrimonial cases; and the Signatura Apostolica, a kind of pontifical supreme court. The papal offices include the Secretariate of State, concerned with foreign affairs; representatives of the Holy See abroad, known as legates; the Apostolic Chancery, which prepares pontifical documents; the Apostolic Datary, which handles appointments to certain benefices; and the Apostolic Camera, which administers the temporal affairs of the Church following the death of a pope. The prefects of all Congregations lose all powers at the death of a pope. A final office includes the Secretariate for Latin, which is entrusted with the composition of pontifical documents in the official language of the Church. Since Vatican II Secretariates for Promoting Christian Unity and for Non-Christians have been instituted.

A legate is called a *nuncio* when sent to a country having diplomatic relations with the Holy See; countries having no ambassador at the papal court (e.g., the United States) receive an Apostolic Delegate. Legates may not interfere with any bishop's right of jurisdiction.

From the foregoing sketch, one can see that the government of the Church Universal, which includes more than a half billion souls, is complex and far reaching; no other governmental structure in the world today is comparable to this vast system of ecclesiastical administration.

III. THE EPISCOPACY

The English word *bishop* comes from a Greek word, *episkopos*, meaning *overseer*. (A bishop is one who "oversees," but does not "overlook.") The monarchical bishop as known in Catholicism today does not appear in the New Testament, according to John L. McKenzie. The episcopacy appeared to be originally exercised in a collegial manner. Before the end of the apostolic period, however, the bishop emerged as the chief officer of the local Church. The monarchical bishop is clearly evidenced in the epistles of Ignatius of Antioch, written at the beginning of the second century. Structure existed in the apostolic Church; but the structure was not yet fixed and was open to development.[10]

The Church teaches that the bishops are true successors of the apostles. The Council of Trent taught that "the bishops have succeeded in the place of the apostles, and have been placed to govern the Church of God." Vatican Council II, in its *Dogmatic Constitution on the Church* (n. 22), declared:

The order of bishops is the successor to the college of the apostles in teaching authority and pastoral rule; or, rather, in the episcopal order the apostolic body continues without a break. Together with its head, the Roman pontiff, and never without this head, the episcopal order is the subject of supreme and full power over the Universal Church. But this power can be exercised only with the consent of the Roman pontiff.

Each apostle was called personally by Christ. The original collegial body of the apostles was commissioned by Christ to teach and baptize all nations. Involved in this commission was the twofold power of orders and jurisdiction: (1) orders *(potestas ordinis)*, which empowered the apostles to ordain other bishops and priests and to administer the Sacraments; (2) jurisdiction *(potestas jurisdictionis)*, which empowered the apostles to teach and govern the Church. Orders constitutes the sacerdotal office of the episcopacy; jurisdiction constitutes the magisterial office of the episcopacy. Each member of the original body of apostles received the extraordinary commission of jurisdiction over all members of the Church; only the pope now retains this universal jurisdiction. Individual bishops do not succeed from an individual apostle, but from the collegial body of apostles. Individual bishops have ecclesiastical authority only in their respective dioceses.

One can get involved in some fine distinctions as to the manner in which the power of orders and the power of jurisdiction are communicated by Christ through the pope to the bishops. For a bishop to *licitly* rule his diocese and teach in the name of the Church, he must receive the power of jurisdiction from the pope. The power to *validly* administer the Sacraments, ordain other bishops and priests, and exercise the sacerdotal office of the episcopacy appears to be received directly from Christ in the rite of ordination to the episcopacy. Thus, the Church has recognized the validity of the episcopacy and priesthood of the Eastern Orthodox Churches. John L. McKenzie states: "The bishop has his authority by his office and not by the delegation of the pope."[11] The Council of Trent taught that jurisdiction is required for the valid administration of the Sacrament of Penance. In short, the right to teach and govern is given to a

bishop by Christ mediately through the pope; the power to sanctify and to ordain is given to a bishop immediately by Christ
through the ordaining bishop.

There are presently more than two thousand Roman
Catholic bishops dispersed throughout the world. Together with
the pope they rule the Universal Church and teach infallibly in
the name of Christ. Individual bishops are not infallible; only as a
member of the collegial body of bishops teaching in unison with
the Bishop of Rome does an individual bishop teach infallibly.
Bishops pre-eminently exercise their infallible teaching authority in an ecumenical council (cf. *Lumen Gentium*, n. 25).

Catholicism has been accused of overemphasizing the importance of apostolic succession. The essential constitution of the
Church was established by Christ Himself. The apostles were
called personally by Christ. Peter was named personally by
Christ to govern the entire flock. The Church has no right to alter
or vitiate these truths of Christianity. There can be reform *in* the
Church, but not *of* the Church. The Church insists upon the
necessity of the papacy and the episcopacy as reflecting the mind
of Christ. Christ did not spell out precisely *how* structure and
authority would develop in the Church; but it stands to reason
that authority, as invested in the pope and bishops, would have a
visible continuity. Authority and structure in the Church are
real and have been transmitted visibly through time and space.
There is such a thing as credentials in terms of true authority
and true structure in Christianity.

Finally, in this description of the episcopacy in Catholicism
today, we note that the ordinary of a *metropolitan see* is called an
archbishop; he has no jurisdiction over the bishops of *suffragan
sees* of the *province,* but can conduct official inspections and
visitations, preside over provincial councils, and report to the
Holy See concerning abuses within the province. *Auxiliary
bishops* may be appointed to assist ordinaries; a *coadjutor bishop*
has the right of succession to the see of whose bishop he assists.
The diocesan office is usually called the *chancery,* resembling the
Roman Curia in structure. The *vicar general* can act for the
ordinary in ways not reserved exclusively to the bishop. The
chancellor is in charge of diocesan records and documents. The
officialis is in charge of diocesan courts. Other offices, such as
rural deans, the secretary to the bishop, superintendent of
schools, director of Catholic charities, superintendent of
cemeteries, etc., round out a full complement of ecclesiastical
government on the diocesan level.

IV. THE PRIESTHOOD, RELIGIOUS, AND LAITY

The Priesthood. Just as a human body is governed by a brain and nervous system, so is the Mystical Body governed by the pope and bishops; they alone were given the authority to rule the Church. However, just as one would inadequately define a human organism by naming only its brain and nervous system, so too, the Mystical Body cannot be adequately understood only in terms of the pope and bishops. The boundaries of Christ's Body extend beyond the government of the Church; priests, religious, and laity are very much a part of the Church's structure. Every cell in the Mystical Body, each with its particular function, is an integral and important part of the entire structure. St. Paul spoke of many gifts but one Spirit.

The fullness of the priesthood resides in the episcopacy. The bishop alone, under the pope, has full spiritual authority in his diocese. But it would be physically impossible for one man to minister to the spiritual needs of thousands of people. Thus, from the earliest times, bishops ordained priests, who share in the bishop's power to teach, govern, and sanctify the faithful. The apostles ordained deacons (*diakonos*, cf. Acts 6:6); Paul and Barnabas ordained priests (*presbyteros*, cf. Acts 14:22). The seventy-two disciples most probably possessed the character of the priesthood, as distinct from the episcopal office held by the apostles.

The Council of Trent taught that Christ ordained the apostles priests when He commissioned them at the Last Supper to change bread and wine into His own body and blood and thus to offer the Sacrifice of the New Law. On another occasion the apostles were empowered to forgive sins. The apostles were, therefore, ordained true priests, mediators between God and man. The constant tradition of the Church has been that a true priesthood exists in the Church, established by Christ, consisting of a hierarchy of orders: from bishops (who alone can ordain other bishops and priests), to priests, to ministers (lectors, acolytes, and deacons). The character of the priesthood, once received, cannot be effaced. Thus stated the Council of Trent: "If anyone assert that he who was once a priest can again become a layman, let him be anathema." A priest, strictly speaking, cannot be "laicized." He has always the power to offer Holy Mass, though he would do so illicitly without having *faculties* (the permission of his ordinary).

We have already considered the question of clerical celibacy in the previous chapter. There is no doubt that celibacy has been a problem for some priests; but the problem lies much deeper and broader. Celibacy, optional or mandatory, is but one aspect of the crisis of authority in the Church today. Many priests have found loneliness, isolation, and oppressive authority to be unbearable and unacceptable *before* they realized that compulsory celibacy is unacceptable to them. To say this is not to imply that marriage came as an afterthought to more fundamental considerations; celibacy and marriage must simply be viewed in the total context of a priest's life-style.

Commentators on the subject of the priesthood in Catholicism today are asking these questions: Is the priestly ministry necessarily fulltime, lifetime, celibate, and restricted to men? St. Paul worked at a trade. What about support systems for the clergy? What about the so-called "hyphenated priest" — the priest-teacher, the priest-scientist, the priest-politician, the priest-physician, the priest-administrator? Vatican II acknowledged the propriety and long-standing tradition of priest specialists. St. Jerome was a secretary to Pope Damasus. Robert Drinan, S.J., currently serves in the House of Representatives of the U.S. Congress, representing a district in Massachusetts. The Church officially discourages, but does not absolutely forbid, such political participation by the clergy. Canon law requires the special permission of one's ordinary to hold a civil office. The Church has known the perils of an identification of Church and state, especially in a pluralistic society.

And so the priesthood continues, as it will continue till the end of the world, as Christ promised. The priesthood has always responded to the needs of the age, producing such great men as Ignatius of Antioch, Ambrose, Jerome, Augustine, Francis of Assisi (who remained a deacon), Dominic, Aquinas, Ignatius Loyola, Alphonsus Liguori, the Curé of Ars (the patron saint of parish priests; he nearly missed ordination because of failure in seminary studies), and many great popes. Compulsory celibacy for the clergy was itself a response of the Church in terms of the needs of the times. In the present period of Church history, we may rightly ask: does celibacy make a priest more capable or less capable of loving and serving God and the People of God?

The priesthood will emerge from the present crisis of transition purified, strengthened, and fully committed to the Great High Priest, Jesus Christ. The priesthood is today what Fulton J. Sheen described in 1963:

Every priest knows himself, by divine election, to be a mediator between God and man, bringing God to man and man to God. As such the priest continues the Incarnation of Jesus Christ Who was both God and Man. . . . Inasmuch as every priest is an *alter Christus*, each of us is another Jacob's ladder — having vertical relations to Christ in Heaven and horizontal relations to men on earth.[12]

Religious. Religious communities have held a long-standing and venerable place in the life of the Church. Monasticism in the Eastern Church is based primarily on the rule of St. Basil. Western monasticism became, and has remained, Benedictine, after the order established by St. Benedict of Nursia in Italy in the fifth century.

In 1965 there were 330,107 men and 1,209,159 women living throughout the world in 201 and 1,116 religious communities, respectively.[13] Most Catholics, and many non-Catholics, are familiar with such religious orders as the Society of Jesus, the "Jesuits," the largest order in the Church, with a membership in 1963 of 35,788; the Order of Friars Minor, the "Franciscans," existing in three separate orders (O.F.M., O.F.M. Conventuals, and O.F.M. Capuchins), with a combined membership of 47,635 in 1963; the Order of Preachers, the "Dominicans"; the Order of St. Benedict, the "Benedictines"; Cistercians; Carthusians; Carmelites; Redemptorists; Crosiers; etc. Each order — a kind of spiritual family within the Church — has its own unique historical origin, tradition, and quality of spirituality. Canon law requires that the supreme heads of religious communities of *men* (unwarranted discrimination against women again appears in the Church) be allowed to attend an ecumenical council with the power to vote.

Religious orders of women are far too numerous for us to attempt even a partial listing. Nuns take *solemn* vows (which are perpetual, invalidate acts contrary to those vows, and can only be released by the pope); whereas sisters take *simple* vows (which may or may not be perpetual, make acts contrary to those vows illicit but not invalid, and are more easily released by the pope than are solemn vows). In popular parlance the terms *nun* and *sister* are used interchangeably.

Many teaching orders of sisters find themselves without jobs, with the decline in Catholic school enrollment. Which came first: the decline in vocations to the sisterhood or a decline in Catholic school enrollment? This writer recalls teaching a class of forty-six third graders in a Catholic school in the late 1950s; the enrollment was there, but the staff was half lay because of a lack of available sisters. With Catholic education taking a different form in Catholicism today, the sisters will find new ways to offer their services to the Church.

Religious take vows (either solemn or simple) of poverty, chastity, and obedience, which are known as the evangelical counsels. They are called *evangelical* because they are found in the Gospels; *counsels*, because they are recommended, but not commanded or required for all. They are recommended as counsels to achieve Christian perfection. According to Aquinas, it is the religious state that constitutes the "state of perfection," in the objective sense.

Modern civilization owes much to the monasteries. Almost all of the surviving literature of the ancients was preserved and transmitted by the monks. Monasteries gave the Church many popes and bishops, as well as such illustrious scholars as Alexander of Hales, Bonaventure, Roger Bacon, John Duns Scotus, Albert the Great, and the brightest light of them all, Thomas Aquinas.

Like all phases of Catholicism today, the religious life has been subjected to critical scrutiny. What place does monasticism and the religious life hold in the world today? One's answer, of course, will depend largely upon one's philosophy of life and religion. Prayer does count. The *contemplative orders*, whose members are strictly cloistered and spend most of their time in prayer, are few today. We submit that God will always call special souls for this unique service, to pray for mankind and quite possibly be the deciding factor in holding back the wrath of God upon a rebellious and sinful planet. Most of the religious orders have an *active* ministry. Most of the Church's missionary activity is conducted by religious orders. Francis of Assisi was especially insistent that his "little brothers," or friars, not remain in a monastery, but mingle with the people and carry the message of Christ to all. Likewise, the Dominican friars were to engage primarily in preaching.

There has been a decline in the numbers of religious. We do not pretend to have the solution to the crisis of identity that has befallen the religious life. We are confident that the place of the religious life in the life of the Church is secure and will endure. This life is obviously a special calling and not for all; even a man like Cardinal Newman, who once felt inclined to enter a religious order, declined to do so because he felt he could not accomplish within the confines of that order what God wanted him to do.

Let us further recognize that one can take a vow of poverty and yet enjoy a kind of corporate wealth and security unknown to most of the laity who take no such vow. One order erected a building whose cost averaged out to more than $16,000 per occupant. Likewise, the vow of obedience — which most religious will say is the most difficult to keep — has been somewhat mitigated in modern times to exclude what has been called "blind obedience." Concerning the vow of chastity, some have suggested the possibility of a religious community composed of families, where only the vows of poverty and obedience would obtain.

Our religious orders are here to stay. The Church needs them; and God needs them to do His special work.

The Laity. And finally, we come to the last, but by no means the least, sector of the Church's structure: the laity. Our division of the Church's structure into clergy, religious, and laity is not completely accurate, since there can be some overlapping. The official language of the Church recognizes only two major categories of the faithful: clerical and lay; each of these in turn may be either religious (or "regular") or secular.. Thus, such combinations as clerical-secular, lay-religious, and clerical-religious are possible.

St. Peter called the laity "a chosen race, a royal priesthood, a holy nation, a purchased people" (1 Pet. 2:9). The laity have been coming into their own in Catholicism today. Vatican II paid the laity their highest compliment when it stated: "The body of the faithful as a whole, anointed as they are by the Holy One, cannot err in matters of belief" (*Lumen Gentium*, n. 12). Thus, an "infallibility of believing" exists in the Church as well as an "infallibility of teaching." We already mentioned in Chapter VI Cardinal Newman's essay *On Consulting the Laity in Matters of Doctrine*. Karl Rahner's *Free Speech in the Church* must also be rementioned as a landmark in the development of the laity's role in the Church.

The laity always have been, are, and will be a vital and necessary element in the structure of the Church. The laity, as such, have no power to govern, to legislate, to define doctrine, or to administer the Sacraments (except Baptism, in an emergency); the constitution of the Church, we repeat, is essentially monarchical, with full authority and jurisdiction residing in the pope. The Church is secondarily oligarchical, inasmuch as the bishops teach, govern, and sanctify with and under the pope. Such is the mind of Christ as taught in Scripture and tradition.

Who, precisely, are the laity? We are face-to-face here with a deeper theological problem, to which we briefly alluded in Chapter II. Is the Church coterminous with all "men of good will"? Are the boundaries of the Church visible or invisible? In this last quarter of the twentieth century, is it still realistic to speak of "the one, true Church"?

The Church treads carefully in the area of ecumenism. The Church earnestly strives for Christian unity in accord with Christ's prayer that all may be one. But the Church has not and will not abandon the fundamental truths declaring that Christ's Church has a visible structure and government, a true and apostolic priesthood, Grace-giving Sacraments, a true and perfect Sacrifice, and an infallible teaching authority. In short, Christ's Church is *recognizable* today, as always. This being true, the Church simply is unable to say that *all* Christians, all of the baptized — whether of water, blood, or desire — belong *equally* and *fully* to Christ's Mystical Body. Pope Pius XII was careful to make this distinction in his 1943 encyclical *Mystici Corporis*. While all men of good will are in some way *"related"* (the word used by the pope) to the Mystical Body, a Christian's incorporation in that Body is not full and complete unless one accepts all of the elements — magisterial and sacramental — of that Body.

Thus, Vatican II taught:

They are fully incorporated in the society of the Church who, possessing the Spirit of Christ, accept her entire system and all of the means of salvation given to her, and through union with her visible structure are joined to Christ, Who rules her through the Supreme Pontiff and the bishops. . . .

The Church recognizes that in many ways she is linked with those who, being baptized, are honored with the name of Christian, though they do not possess the Faith in its entirety or do not preserve unity of communion with the successor of Peter. . . . Likewise, we can say in some real way they are joined with us in the Holy Spirit, for to them also He gives His gifts and graces and is thereby operative among them with His sanctifying power (*Lumen Gentium*, nn. 14 f.).

The Council taught that many of the elements that make up the life of the Church can exist outside of its visible boundaries: e.g., the written word of God; the life of Grace; faith, hope, and charity (cf. *Unitatis Redintegratio*, n. 3). Yet there still remains one, true Church of Christ, teaching by direct authority in His name unto the consummation of the world. Such is the mystery of the Church, the Sacrament of Christ, on its pilgrim mission among men.

The 1973 issue of the *Annuario Pontificio* puts the world Catholic population at more than 600 million souls, the largest single religious body in the world.

V. AUTHORITY IN THE CHURCH

The Meaning of Authority. Authority can be viewed in the abstract or in the concrete. Abstractly, *authority* can be defined as "the right to lead the members of a society toward the attainment of the common end to be realized by their association."[14] Viewed concretely, authority denotes the *bearer* of the right or power to govern a given society. Authority is essential to any society, since the proper end of that society cannot be achieved without order, cohesion, direction, and legislation. Authority is never purely abstract; authority functions through a visible structure, will be manifested in the form of government, and will reside in a person or persons. Rule by one is called an *autocracy* (or *monarchy*, which is generally hereditary); rule by a few is called an *oligarchy* (whether an *aristocracy*, or rule by a privileged class; *plutocracy*, or rule by the wealthy; etc.); rule by the people is called a *democracy*. Since not all the people can rule at a given time, democracy takes the form of *representative* or *republican democracy*, in which chosen representatives of the people form the government.

St. Thomas Aquinas advocated a mixed form of government — partly autocratic, partly oligarchic, partly democratic — as being the best:

> The best form of government is in a state or kingdom, wherein one is given the power to preside over all; and yet a government of this kind is shared by all, both because all are eligible to govern, and because the rulers are chosen by all.[15]

One can see that Aquinas' view is substantially the system of government that prevails in modern republican states, a system of representative democracy. Nietzsche denounced democracy as "this mania for counting noses." The Church has never endorsed a particular form of government as being absolutely the best. Government must be just and equitable and seek the common good, regardless of the form taken. The Church, like Christ before Pilate, insists that all true authority comes from God; human governments represent a share in the divine governance of the cosmos.

Authoritarianism and Authority Today. Authority has always been a problem for mankind, beginning in the Garden of Eden. Man is free, yet he must live under authority — the authority of the natural law, both physical and moral; the authority of the family, the state, and international society; the authority of God's revealed word; and the authority of Christ's Church. Hence, there exists a natural tension between authority and freedom.

There is a crisis of authority in Catholicism today, precipitated not only by those who deny the supremacy of the pope, but from those who question the quality and competency of ecclesiastical leadership on all sides. Andrew M. Greeley writes:

The most serious problem facing the Catholic priesthood today, beyond all question, is the problem of authority. . . . The real authority problem is not so much one of oppression as it is one of the collapse of confidence, credibility, and consensus. . . . Many priests under 40 no longer believe a thing that the collective hierarchy says. . . . I am not asserting that priests deny the need for authority, nor am I arguing that they will engage in a revolution to overthrow authority. . . . The problem is not a theoretical rejection of authority but rather the absence, at least in many dioceses and certainly in the collective hierarchy, of the capacity to lead.[16]

We believe the Church today is moving away from what can be called ultramonarchicalism, in which the government of the Church too closely patterns itself after a monarchical state. We see a return to the New Testament teaching of authority as *diakonia*, or service. Authority is meant to *serve*. John L. McKenzie writes:

If one wished to be captious, one could maintain that the [New Testament] texts which give *diakonia* as the function of authority and which liken persons in authority to lackeys and children not only do not recommend command and control, but positively forbid it. . . . It is plain that a simple adoption of the thesis would produce instant chaos in the Church which we know. What is to be sought is not administrative chaos, but a transformation of the idea and the use of authority. . . . Things can be guided, controlled, coerced; persons can be led.[17]

Critics of the Catholic Church find a favorite theme in alleging that the Church is guilty of authoritarianism — religious coercion and a straitjacketing of the human mind. The allegation is partly true but mostly false. Authoritarianism in the sense of religious coercion was manifested in the tactics of the Inquisition, already described and evaluated in the previous chapter.

Hopefully, what traces of the Inquisition remain in Catholicism today will eventually disappear altogether.

Authoritarianism in the sense of stifling human freedom and straitjacketing the human mind needs some elucidation. First, the Church does not fundamentally ask blind obedience to an institution, a structure, or even to a human being; the Church asks its members to fully commit themselves to Jesus Christ and *all* that He taught — which, of course, includes the institution of the Church. Secondly, the relationship between the Church and its members is essentially a relationship of *love* and *unity;* where empathy exists, obedience follows more easily and naturally. Lastly, it is simply false to say that the Church stifles reason and intellectual inquiry.

On the contrary, Catholicism places much more emphasis upon reason and philosophical inquiry than does Protestantism and most other religions. The *Summa Theologica* of St. Thomas Aquinas treats all sides of a question; this monumental work is in reality a comprehensive survey of *heresy* and *error* as well as being an outstanding statement of orthodoxy and the *philosophia perennis.* The best arguments for atheism ever written are in the *Summa;* Voltaire knew this, and spent six months studying them to gain ammunition for his attack upon Christianity. A noted Communist once said that the best and fairest exposition of Communism that he ever read was in the papal encyclical *Divini Redemptoris.*

Instruction in all of the important philosophical systems known to man forms a part of every Catholic seminarian's course of study — from the ancient Greeks and Romans to the Church Fathers to the medieval Scholastics to Descartes, Bacon, Locke, Hume, Spinoza, Hegel, Kant, Schopenhauer, Nietzsche, Spencer, Kierkegaard, and the Existentialists of our own day. This writer can say from personal experience that philosophy classes in a Catholic seminary are generally ebullient and open sessions, with plenty of give-and-take between professor and students. The truth was allowed to speak for itself; we experienced no brainwashing or intellectual intimidation.

The Church believes in *truth,* which is basically its own defense. The Catholic Church straitjackets the human mind only to the extent that truth itself restricts the human mind. A triangle is free to be a triangle only by keeping its three sides; should it decide — in a great burst of freedom — to add one side, the triangle ceases to be a triangle, but becomes a quadrilateral.

The Church is fully committed to the truth, which may at times seem to eclipse human freedom and creativity; but real freedom lies in the truth, not in error. One is free to say that 2 times 2 equals 5; but this kind of freedom will not produce accurate results and maintain contact with reality. A train remains free to function by staying on its tracks. There is freedom in the truth, but only slavery and calamity in error. Thus, Our Lord said, "You shall know the truth, and the truth shall make you free" (John 8:32).

Commitment to the truth and obedience to lawful authority are not the same thing as slavery. It is interesting to note that some of the saints exhibited a remarkable spirit of freedom and independence in the face of authority. St. Catherine of Siena — declared a Doctor of the Church by Pope Paul in 1970 — probably did not slap the face of Pope Gregory XI, but he must have often felt as though she had. Pope Innocent III, the most powerful of popes, told Francis of Assisi that Peter can no longer say, "Silver and gold I have none"; the saint replied that neither can Peter now say, "Arise and walk" (cf. Acts 3:6). No one but professional historians will recognize the name of Etienne Tempier, the Archbishop of Paris who condemned the writings of Thomas Aquinas in 1277; the Angelic Doctor lives on in Catholicism today, but the authority who suppressed him is forgotten. We mentioned St. Joan of Arc and Jerome Savonarola in the previous chapter as being victims of the Inquisition. Savonarola was never canonized, probably because he seemed to lack the necessary amount of humility and docility that one would expect to find in a saint. The great St. Teresa of Avila (1515-1582), who was declared a Doctor of the Church by Pope Paul in 1970, was not always on the best of terms with the Holy Inquisition. St. Ignatius Loyola, founder of the Jesuits, spent a short time in a prison of the Inquisition. St. Thomas More had almost no episcopal support. St. John Fisher said in a public sermon: "If the pope does not reform the Curia, God will." Catholicism is not the monolith that many Protestants portray. There is a real role for the prophet in the Church today, even though a prophet may be without honor in his own country. Catholicism today needs its Catherine of Siena, its Jerome Savonarola.

The Church will never abandon the authority it has received from Christ; but there is a positive and, we believe, a salutary trend away from overcentralization in the Church. "So many centuries of edifying popes," writes F. J. Sheed, "have affected our perspective — it seems to have affected the perspective of Pius IX, if he really said, 'I am tradition.' Public questioning of papal action by Catholics almost vanished. Now it is back."[18] Finer distinctions have been made concerning the extent of infallible papal authority. The values of democratic procedures are being increasingly recognized in the Church today. Perhaps such a Church will be more readily acceptable to Protestant Christians. Authority will thus become true *diakonia*, service to God and to the People of God.

Criticism of authority ought to be of a positive and constructive nature. Mere negative carping profits nothing, and can do much harm. "Bishop-baiting" has become a favorite indoor and outdoor sport for a certain element in the Church. Father Peter J. Riga writes:

All — including bishops — must listen to and learn from the only true teacher in the Church, the Holy Spirit. This does not mean that bishops should abdicate their essential role as teachers; but only that they, like all good teachers, can and must learn from their students. Bishops learn with all the rest of us on matters of busing, civil rights, poverty, war and peace, Vietnam, the economy, welfare, etc. Only through this listening can their moral leadership be credible in the Catholic community. We must help them in this function — not knock them.[19]

Authority is inherently in the Church of Christ. Christ's Mystical Body has its human element as well as its divine element. Just as Christ walked the dusty roads of ancient Palestine, so does the Church today tread the dusty and oftentimes perilous roads of this world. Just as Christ sometimes grew tired and hungry and thirsty, so does His Church at times grow tired and hungry and thirsty. Just as Christ could cry from the Cross, what are probably the most terrifying words in all Scripture, "My God, My God, why have You forsaken Me?" (Mark 15:34), there are times when the divine element in the Church seems to have been eclipsed by the human.

One might be tempted at times, as Christ in the fullness of His humanity seemed to have been tempted in the agony of His Crucifixion, to feel that God has forsaken His Church, that the human and divine elements have become permanently separated. Here is the great mystery of the Church: how it can continue on its pilgrim way in the world, teaching, governing, sanctifying in Christ's name, all the while being administered by weak and fallible flesh and blood. Authority in the Church has not always been all that it should be; it would be all too easy for the People of God to become disenchanted and impatient with Church authority. One of the fundamental errors of the Reformation was the failure to distinguish between what is human in the Church and what is divine.

Simon can fail; but Peter, never! The laity today must see this twofold aspect of authority in the Church. Every pope was partly Simon and partly Peter. It is right and proper to criticize where criticism is warranted; and the Church has always been subject to an internal reformation. There can be reform *in* the Church but never *of* the Church and its essential constitution as established by Christ.

Authority must ever strive to be true *diakonia*, to walk in the footsteps of the Divine Master, Who said:

Whoever wishes to become great among you shall be your servant; and whoever wishes to be first among you shall be your slave; even as the Son of Man has not come to be served but to serve, and to give His life as a ransom for many (Matt. 20:26-28).

Written in letters of gold across the dome of St. Peter's in Rome are these words, possibly the most powerful and prophetic words in all Scripture: *"Tu es Petrus, et supra hanc petram aedificabo Ecclesiam Meam"* (Matt. 16:18). Shortly after Christ made Peter the Rock and Foundation of the Church and had given him the keys of authority, with the power to bind and loose, Our Lord would need to call Peter "Satan"! Peter tried to persuade Jesus not to go to Jerusalem to suffer and be put to death (though He said He would rise on the third day). "Get behind Me, Satan, you are a scandal to Me; for you do not mind the things of God, but those of men" (Matt. 16:23). These startling words of Our Lord make clear the twofold aspect of ecclesiastical authority: every pope and every bishop are partly Simon and partly Peter. Not every utterance of ecclesiastical authority will necessarily "mind the things of God." Every pontiff needs to recall the sobering and humbling words of Matthew 16:23, which counterbalance the powerful commission of Matthew 16:18-19.

EPILOGUE

THE FUTURE OF CATHOLICISM

Behold, I am with you all days, even
unto the consummation of the world.
                          — Matt. 28:20

THE FUTURE OF CATHOLICISM

[*The Catholic Church*] *may still exist in undiminished vigour when some traveller from New Zealand shall, in the midst of a vast solitude, take his stand on a broken arch of London Bridge to sketch the ruins of St. Paul's.*

— Lord Macaulay

Something is afoot in the universe, something that looks like gestation.

— Pierre Teilhard de Chardin

Some men see things as they are and say, Why? I dream things that never were and say, Why not?
— Robert F. Kennedy, quoting George Bernard Shaw

To marry the Spirit of the Age is to be a widow in the next.
— Fulton J. Sheen

The lights begin to twinkle from the rocks:
The long day wanes: the slow moon climbs: the deep
Moans round with many voices. Come, my friends,
'Tis not too late to seek a newer world.

— Alfred, Lord Tennyson, "Ulysses"

It is our future that lays down the law of our today.
— Friedrich Wilhelm Nietzsche

Those who cannot remember the past are condemned to repeat it.
— George Santayana

And I saw a new Heaven and a new earth. . . . 'And God will wipe away every tear from their eyes. And death shall be no more; . . . for the former things have passed away. . . . Behold, I make all things new!'
— Apoc. 21:1 ff.

T O conclude this study of Catholicism today, we present some thoughts concerning the future of Catholicism. It is not our purpose to indulge in chiliastic speculation; it is part of the Christian Faith that the present order will end, that Christ will come again to rule the new Heaven and the new earth.

Christ assured us that no man knows the time or the hour when this great eschatological event will occur. Meanwhile, we face the problems of the present order in terms of the future.

(1) There is such a thing as a *Zeitgeist*, or a Spirit of the Age.[1] There are fads in philosophy and theology, just as there are fads in style and dress. Materialism, idealism, scepticism, rationalism, romanticism, positivism, pantheism, empiricism, pragmatism — one could go on *ad nauseam* — each has had its day. Existentialism is currently in vogue.

Besides the *Zeitgeist* there is the *philosophia perennis*, the perennial philosophy, which can be defined as "the continuously existent and consistent system of philosophic thought that man may find in all the records of his race."[2] The *philosophia perennis* represents the best expression of the consensus of mankind throughout the ages concerning the ultimate realities of life.

The Church has refused to marry the Spirit of the Age, for to do so would make her a widow in the next. The sixteenth century demanded a new Church (e.g., Luther, Calvin, Zwingli, Henry VIII); the eighteenth century demanded a new religion (e.g., Voltaire, Diderot, Hume, Kant); the twentieth century has demanded a new God (e.g., Nietzsche, Alexander, Whitehead, Russell). Nietzsche announced that God is dead: "If there were gods, how could I bear to be no god?"[3] For Professor Samuel Alexander, in his *Space, Time and Deity*, God's body consists of space and His soul consists of time. Alfred North Whitehead, like many writers of today, buries God in a grave of semantics: God is "the harmony of epochal occasions," "the principle of concretion," "the principle of limitation." Bertrand Russell states: "Brief and powerless is Man's life; on him and all his race the slow, sure doom falls pitiless and dark."[4]

Lyricism in philosophy and theology goes on; but the Church refuses to be wedded to any particular philosophy other than the *philosophia perennis*, inasmuch as it is identified with truth itself. The Church is wedded to no particular theology other than the revealed word of God as known through Scripture and tradition. The Church is wedded to no particular personality other than the Person of Christ. The Church is wedded to no particular culture other than the Kingdom of God. The Church is wedded to no particular age other than the Age of Christian Redemption. The Church is wedded to no particular people other than the People of God. The Church is not behind the times but beyond the times.

(2) Although the Church is not inseparably bound to any particular philosophical system other than the *philosophia perennis*, the place of Thomism in Catholicism, we believe, is secure. In this study we have had to differ from time to time with a view held by the Angelic Doctor; but no one in the history of Catholicism has succeeded so well in harmonizing philosophy and theology as did Thomas Aquinas.

There are those today who would favor a de-emphasis of the Greco-Scholastic, Aristotelian-Thomistic influence in Catholicism. Leslie Dewart favors a de-Hellenization of Catholic theology.[5] We personally do not find the existentialization of theology to be a suitable substitute. In *The Future of Belief*, Dewart defines God as "that which we experience as the open background of consciousness and being"; and Dewart proposes that "God cannot be said to exist." These statements do not strike a responsive intellectual chord with us. To say that it is more correct to say that God does *not* exist than to say He exists, and still not claim to be atheistic, is simply incomprehensible to this writer. Being and existence are, of course, basically undefinable because they have no genus; we cannot see, however, that being limits and defines the divine nature. The only alternative to being is nonbeing, which is nothing.

There is one aspect of Thomism that is frequently overlooked. Here was a man who spent a lifetime harmonizing philosophy and theology. Toward the end of his life he received special revelations which, he said, made his previous writings seem to him nothing but "straw." Josef Pieper makes a good case to show that Aquinas could have finished his masterpiece, the *Summa Theologica*, so far as time is concerned; but he purposefully *chose* not to finish it. Here was a man supremely dedicated to reason and the human intellect; but in the face of an intuitive revelation, the greatest teacher in Christendom — the "dumb ox" of Sicily whose bellowing, as Albert predicted, was heard throughout the world — had to remain silent. Thomism ends in eloquent silence.[6]

Could it be that the future of Catholicism lies not so much in philosophy, theology, or structure, as in direct mystical experience? If an ounce of Revelation is worth a ton of philosophy, is not an ounce of intuitive mystical experience worth a ton of Revelation? It is rarely noted that Aquinas began his treatise on the existence of God by saying, "We are not capable of knowing what God is, but we can know what He is not."[7] From the *Quaes-*

tiones Disputatae we find Aquinas saying, "This is what is ultimate in the human knowledge of God: to know that we do not know God."[8] One might detect a hint of agnosticism here; but we believe the Angelic Doctor was simply indicating that there is a level of knowledge above reason and the Christian Faith as expressed in theology. We do not know the essence of a fly, much less the essence of God.

(3) Vatican II described the Church as the salvation of the world. The Church is in the world to transform the world, something like a catalyst in chemistry. Catholicism of the future will become more and more an influential force in world affairs. The older emphasis of "despising the world," of an unnatural dualism between body and soul as characterized in Platonic, Augustinian, and Cartesian philosophy, will be replaced with the organic unity of all creation — creation which Genesis calls "good." Catholicism and theology will enter the market place.

The influence of the papacy will increase. One finds a non-Catholic historian, Will Durant, stating:

The greatest rulers in Europe have been popes, and the greatest ruling body has been the Church. But in the Church heredity had no place, and any man might work his way from the plough to the Vatican. The strongest government in history was an aristocratic democracy. Perhaps some day that is the sort of government which we shall be wise enough to have.[9]

Catholic theology must come down from its ivory tower and into the dust, toil, sweat, and tears of human existence. Moral theology in particular has too long been dominated by a celibate-monk mentality.[10] Georges Clemenceau ("The Tiger") said that war is too important to be left only to the generals; perhaps theology is too important to be left only to the theologians. Addressing an assembly of theologians in London, Cardinal John Wright said:

All I am asking you to do is not replace the Faith with your theology.... The Faith was revealed by Jesus Christ. Theology was dreamed up by you. Faith is a total personal response to the word of God Who speaks through Jesus Christ. Theology is some smart guy's scientific systematization of his opinion about the matter and how he explains it to himself — if he does.[11]

Theology and Faith are not identical. The Christian Faith will of necessity be expressed in the form of theology; but theology, like philosophy, is a human enterprise, an attempt to express in human terms the realities of Divine Revelation. Theology is fraught with danger; heresy is always lurking around the corner. Christ Himself warned against being too clever and wise in worldly wisdom, when He said: "I praise Thee, Father, Lord of Heaven and earth, that You hid these things from the wise and prudent and revealed them to little ones" (Matt. 11:25). The author of *The Imitation of Christ* said he would rather feel compunction than be able to define it.

Theology has its rightful and necessary place in the future of Catholicism. We do not favor an anti-intellectual approach; there is a need for expertise in theology as in other sciences. We simply say that theology must above all be humble and docile and in touch with the realities of the world. The Church of the future, being the salvation of the world, will be what it has to be to do what it has to do.

(4) There exists in Catholic theology what can be called "the Jansenist-laxist polarity," each pulling in its own direction. Jansenism — named after Bishop Jansenius of Ypres and based on his posthumous work *Augustinus* – originated in the seventeenth century as a reaction against the Jesuits. Pope Urban VIII condemned Jansenism in 1642. Jansenism espoused a one-sided view of the Church and morality. There is no Grace and salvation outside of the visible Church; only a few are predestined by irresistible Grace. One ought to rarely receive Holy Communion, and then only after the severest self-probing. Austere penances are recommended. A rigorist view of sexual ethics is maintained.[12]

The Church has steadfastly condemned both Jansenism as well as laxist positions in theology. St. Pius X, as we have noted, especially opposed the Jansenist position advocating infrequent reception of Holy Communion. Traces of Jansenism remain in Catholicism today, especially in the area of sexual ethics. Catholicism of the future must continue to resist the Jansenist-laxist polarity: Christianity is not the religion of a spiritual elite, as the heresy of gnosticism maintained; nor is Christianity so strict that it is beyond the reach of most of mankind. Christianity is for all; Christ died for all; and the Church of the future must continually reach out to all.

(5) The early 1970s saw the phenomenal success of a rock opera entitled *Jesus Christ Superstar*, written by two young

Englishmen. "Jesus Christ Superstar, do you think you're what they say you are?"

Could it be that Judaism and ultraliberal forms of Protestantism are progressively discovering the divinity of Christ? There is a movement within Judaism today that is re-examining the claims of Christ. Could it be that Judaism today is being led to Christ, twenty centuries after His birth, just as the Three Wise Men of old were led by a "superstar" from the Gentile world to Christ? Vatican II declared the innocence of the Jewish people as a whole of the crime of Christ's death.[13]

(6) Ecumenism must continue in the Church of the future. The approach of "triumphalism" — attributed by some to Pope Pius XII — which sees Christian unity being achieved only in terms of the separated, errant brethren returning to the one true fold of the Church of Rome, will not be sufficient. It was Cardinal Newman who said: "Win an argument and lose a soul." Vatican II acknowledged that the blame for Christian disunity rests partly on both sides. Sources of division must continue to be analyzed and explored, and sincere attempts made to eradicate that which divides Christendom, without doing violence to one's own sincere convictions.

The spirit of ecumenism has stimulated new theological approaches. At this writing joint studies have been undertaken by Catholic and Lutheran theologians on such topics as the place of Peter in the New Testament. Catholic-Anglican dialogue has focused on the Mass and the Eucharist. Broad areas of agreement have been reached. Pope Leo XIII's ruling concerning the invalidity of Anglican orders is being re-examined. There seems to be a genuine concern on both sides to get at the gut issues which divide Christians.

Mahatma Gandhi (1869-1948) believed that "there is no such thing as conversion from one faith to another." He believed that Jesus "came as near to perfection as possible." All religions are "equally true." Gandhi felt that people should not "even secretly pray that anyone should be converted, but our innermost prayer should be that a Hindu should be a better Hindu, a Moslem a better Moslem, and a Christian a better Christian."

One can find some Catholic theologians today saying that Protestants who are at peace in their own faith should not be urged to convert to Catholicism. We hear that membership in the Roman Catholic Church is not central to Christianity; rather the salvation of one's soul is paramount. And some might better save their souls outside of the Catholic Church. Some feel that the phrase "the one true Church" as applied to Roman Catholicism ought to be dropped.

Vatican II recognized that the Holy Spirit operates in and through non-Catholic religions. But the Council Fathers refused to dilute one iota the unique character of the Roman Catholic Church. The Council documents continue to speak of "the one true Church" which is recognizable today as always. The Council took into account the subjective and existential realities of Christian salvation and human freedom; but the Council was equally insistent upon the objective content of Divine Revelation and one's duty to seek out the truth of that Revelation.

Catholic ecumenism of the future, therefore, simply cannot subscribe to the doctrines that Christ's Church on earth is totally human; that the "one true Church" is an ecumenical goal toward which all Christians strive but nowhere exists today; that all world religions are equally true and complete so far as the human condition will allow. The worthy and necessary cause of ecumenism is not well served by dodging the truth as one believes it to be. Nevertheless, there is real hope for the future.

"Every truth without exception," taught Thomas Aquinas, "— whoever may utter it — is from the Holy Spirit." Non-Catholic Christians possess a segment of the circle of Christian truth; and the Holy Spirit can build upon that segment of truth to bring about Christian unity in a way that would be humanly impossible. Possibly a sharper and more developed definition of what constitutes membership in Christ's Mystical Body will be forthcoming in Catholic theology. Of this we are certain: "They [non-Catholic Christians] bear the name of Christ on their forehead" (Pope John XXIII).

(7) We believe the permanent diaconate will find a secure place in the future of Catholicism. The diaconate as a terminal office in the Church flourished in the pre-Nicene period; from the fourth century on, with the rise of sacerdotalism, there was a gradual decline of the permanent diaconate, the office becoming a preliminary step to the priesthood. The Council of Trent defined the powers of the diaconate; but it was not until Vatican II that the office was restored as a terminal order in the Church.

Deacons share with bishops and priests the ministries of the liturgy, the word, and charity. A deacon may administer Baptism, witness marriages, distribute Holy Communion, officiate at funerals, administer sacramentals, and preside at prayer services. A deacon cannot offer Mass, hear confessions, or administer the Sacrament of the Anointing of the Sick. As a minister of the word, a deacon may read the Gospel and preach at the liturgy. Through the ministry of charity a deacon serves the community, his chief Christian witness being person-to-person encounters.[14]

(8) Catholicism of the future ought to make public its financial condition, giving full account of all income and expenditures, assets and liabilities. A survey compiled by the Corporate Information Center of the National Council of Churches reported that 10 U.S. denominations and the National Council of Churches have nearly $203 million invested in 29 of the top 60 defense material producers. *No specific information was obtainable concerning Catholic investments.* Protestant, Catholic, and Jewish agencies have an estimated $22 billion invested in the stock market. In 1970 the 10 denominations noted above and the NCC earned slightly more than $6.2 million on almost 2 million shares in 29 corporations involved in heavy defense production.[15]

One wonders what happened to the spirit of poverty that ought to characterize the religion of Christ. Robert J. Leuver, C.M.F., writes that some priests in Chicago estimate their annual income to be equivalent to about $20,000, which includes room, board, salary, Mass stipends, stole fees, and gifts; priests of one suburban Chicago parish probably average closer to $40,000.[16] One estimate places the combined total assets of all Catholic units in the U.S. and Canada at more than $80 billion, with an annual income of nearly $12.5 billion. James Gollin, author of *Worldly Goods,* notes that the Church is real estate-rich and cash-poor.

Some religious communities have declared assets in the millions. Catholics are repeatedly asked to donate to help the starving people of the world (about two-thirds of the world population go to bed hungry every night); yet the Vatican is repeatedly accused of possessing enormous wealth and extensive financial investments, allegations that are never adequately answered. Yes, perhaps Peter need no longer say, "Silver and gold I have none"; but will Catholicism of the future be able to say to the world, "Arise and walk"?

(9) Pentecostalism is a movement within Christianity which, at this writing, is gaining considerable momentum, both within Catholicism and within Protestantism. From a handful of persons who started the Catholic Charismatic Renewal in the spring of 1967, total membership is now estimated at between 60,000 and 100,000; more than 500 Pentecostal prayer groups are now functioning in the United States. The Pentecostal movement thrives mainly on college campuses.

The Pentecostal movement seeks to foster a deeper experience of the Holy Spirit in the lives of individuals and in community, bringing a continuing and fuller conversion and commitment to Jesus Christ. "Baptism in the spirit" is followed by speaking in tongues, prophecy, exorcisms, laying-on-of-hands, which constitute the charismatic gifts which were familiar to the early Church and are being repeated today.

So far the Church has neither officially condemned nor officially approved of the Pentecostal movement. Some see it as an emotional, anti-intellectual, antistructural, antiauthoritarian form of ecumenical indifference which would reduce Christianity to a society of the spiritual elite. Others more favorable to the movement see in Pentecostalism a common meeting ground for Catholicism and evangelical Protestantism, a purified Christianity more in keeping with the practices and spirit of the pristine apostolic Church.

It is impossible to predict the future of the Pentecostal movement, what forms it will take and what success it will have. Pentecostalism seems to be gaining increasing respect and credibility within Catholicism today; some bishops have participated in Pentecostal meetings. The movement at this writing seems to be very much a part of the future of Catholicism.

(10) Pope John XXIII called for *aggiornamento*, an updating and renewal within the Catholic Church, a letting in of some "fresh air." Just as each individual cell in the Mystical Body constantly needs to renew itself in the face of the vicissitudes of this life, so does the entire Mystical Body renew itself from time to time in its pilgrim path through this world. Just as Christ retreated to the desert for forty days for prayer and fasting and renewal, so does His Mystical Body periodically undergo a period of intense prayer, fasting, and profound introspection. G. K. Chesterton, the noted English convert and master of literary paradox, said that the Church has had a thousand deaths and a

thousand resurrections. "Science," wrote Chesterton, "explained it away; and it was still there. History disinterred it in the past; and it appeared suddenly in the future. Today it stands once more in our path; and even as we watch it, it grows."[17]

Aggiornamento is an ongoing process. With a return of the deacons, a call for optional clerical celibacy and the election of bishops, one is advocating nothing new in the Church, but reverting to former practices. A universal election of the pope and the ordination of women to the priesthood would be unique innovations in Catholicism. By and large, however, one must say that there is basically little that is new in Catholicism; as Will Durant has put it, "Nothing is new except arrangement." Required reading for disturbed Catholics of today ought to be a good history of the Church, such as studies by Joseph Lortz or Philip Hughes. The problems faced by the Church today, for the most part, have been faced by the Church many times in the past. The "conciliar theory" of the Middle Ages, for example, would have put the authority of an ecumenical council above the authority of the pope. Gallicanism, Febronianism, and the Old Catholicism of Ignatius Dollinger (1799-1890) denied the supreme authority of the pope. One rarely hears those terms used today; but the papacy goes on.

One need not be unduly apprehensive about the future of Catholicism. We should note well the prophetic words of the redoubtable Archbishop John Ireland, written nearly a century ago, but equally applicable to Catholicism today:

What! The Church of the living God, the Church of ten thousand victories over pagans and barbarians, over heresies and false philosophies, over defiant kings and unruly peoples — the great, freedom-loving, truth-giving civilizing Catholic Church — this Church of the nineteenth century afraid of any century, not seeing in the ambitions of the nineteenth century the fervent ebullitions of her own noble sentiments, and in its achievements for the elevation of mankind the germinations of her own Christlike plantings, this Church not eager for the fray, not precipitating herself with love irresistible upon this modern world to claim it, to bless it, to own it for Christ.

I preach the new, the most glorious crusade, Church and age! Unite them in the name of humanity, in the name of God.[18]

Toward the end of his life, Thomas Aquinas was kneeling before a crucifix in the Friars' church in Naples. A Voice from the crucifix spoke: "You have written well of Me, Thomas. What would you have as a reward?" St. Thomas, tersely reflecting the supreme goal of all human striving, answered, "Only Thyself, Lord."

Life is a pursuit of that Perfect Life, Perfect Truth, and Perfect Love, which is God. The entire cosmos of God's manuscript, revealing the beauty, truth, and goodness of the Creator.

The profound grandeur of a Tchaikovsky symphony, orchestrating the entire gamut of human emotions; the grandiloquence of a Shakespeare, Wordsworth, Newman, or Thompson, giving verbal expression to man's deepest feelings and insights; the artistic proficiency of a Michelangelo or a Raphael, capturing in paint and marble nature's most delicate nuances of form and color; the bombastic power of a Niagara Falls; the yawning abyss of a Grand Canyon; the splendor of autumn, with its riot of color chanting a requiem over summer's effete body; the gentle kiss of emerald spring, reviving a slumbering nature; rosy-footed dawn, standing tiptoe, shooting her golden arrows to slay the night and capture the stars; the flaming sun, like a brilliant Host in a sapphire monstrance, traversing the sky; the gorgeous effulgence of an evening's sunset, announcing day's death; the moon's silver fingers sweetly cajoling the ebon stillness of the day's dead sanctities; the white chastity of new-fallen snow, adorning mortal nature with intimations of immortality; the quivering beauty of a butterfly, freshly resurrected from its metamorphic chrysalis — if these beauties of nature thrill our aesthetic sensibilities, what must Beauty Itself be like, the Beauty that is ever ancient yet ever new?

The intellectual acumen of men like Socrates, Plato, Aristotle, Augustine, Abélard, Albert, Aquinas, Bonaventure, Scotus, Descartes, Bacon, Spinoza, Kant, Newman, Spencer, Teilhard, and Rahner; the epochal accomplishments of such scientists as Newton, Copernicus, Galileo, Lamarck, van Leeuwenhoek, Redi, Harvey, Darwin, Lyell, Pasteur, Curie, Marconi, Einstein, Edison, Burbank, Oppenheimer, Goddard, Steinmetz, Farnsworth, and Salk, as they decipher nature's hieroglyphics in reading the handwriting of the Almighty and coaxing from nature her innermost secrets — if the great truths of philosophy, theology, and science stir and effervesce the waters of the human soul, what must the contemplation of Truth Itself be like, the Truth that knows all things?

The edifying sanctity of a Francis of Assisi, Joan of Arc, Catherine of Siena, Elizabeth of Hungary, Teresa of Avila, Vincent de Paul, Bernadette, Curé of Ars, Therese of Lisieux, or a

Pope Pius X, who were "fools for Christ"; the legitimate pleasures of this world, which minister unto the well-being of both
man's soul and body: a delicious meal; a refreshing sleep; an
exhilarating swim; the union of bodies in Holy Matrimony; the
subtle fragrance of a rose; the joy of companionship and good
friends; the joy of worship; a sincere faith and a good conscience,
producing peace of soul — if these finite goods bring a partial
satisfaction of human desires, what must the possession of
Goodness Itself be like, the Good that is the *Summum Bonum*
and the Love that surpasseth all understanding? "If the spark be
so bright, O, what must be the Flame!"

Life is replete with intimations of immortality. No sane
person has ever said that he was perfectly and completely happy
in this life. The romance of life is the thrill of the chase, a pursuit
of Perfect Life, Perfect Truth, and Perfect Love. Man is not
satisfied with life for a time, life adulterated with suffering,
misfortune, disappointment, disease, and finally death; man is
not satisfied with incomplete truth, adulterated with an admixture of error and doubt and cynicism, and often accompanied
with dissension, wrangling, and vituperation — so characteristic
of most human intellectual enterprises; man is not satisfied with
the fleeting and precarious goods of this earth, which "make
hungry where most they satisfy" and often betray man "in their
traitorous trueness and loyal deceit." The unanimous verdict of
history proclaims with St. Paul that this present earth is not
man's lasting city. Like a mighty space ship, planet Earth makes
its odyssey through space and time toward the new Heaven and
the new earth.

"Come to Me, all you who labor and are burdened," said the
Divine Master, "and I will give you rest" (Matt. 11:28). Knowing
that this life is not the be-all and the end-all, man can begin to
truly enjoy the things of this world and can "suffer the slings and
arrows of outrageous fortune" with a smile, knowing that all will
be made right in an afterlife. Macbeth was wrong: life is not "a
tale told by an idiot, full of sound and fury, signifying nothing."
Man's "brief candle" conquers "the way to dusty death" by a life
of faith and trust in the Almighty. As small mountain rivulets,
mighty rivers, lakes, and seas must ultimately find their way to
the expansive oceans, so must man ultimately find his total
happiness in the everlasting arms of God, Who is Alpha and
Omega, the beginning and the end, the final meaning of the
universe and human existence, the end of all human endeavor.

God is that Perfect Life, Perfect Truth, and Perfect Love for Whom all men yearn.

In closing this study of Catholicism today, we echo the poignant words of St. Augustine, which he wrote in his immortal *Confessions:* "Thou hast made us for Thyself, O Lord, and our hearts are restless until they rest in Thee!"

NOTES

INTRODUCTION

[1]A Gallup Poll taken in June, 1972, reported that a record high of 64 percent agreed with the statement, "The decision to have an abortion should be made solely by a woman and her physician"; 56 percent of Catholics polled agreed with the statement; and 68 percent of Catholics approved of making birth control information and services available to teenagers.

[2]Maritain died on April 28, 1973, at the age of ninety. A convert and probably the most capable Thomist of this century, Maritain was called "my teacher" by Pope Paul VI. *Time* magazine (May 14, 1973, p. 85) referred to Maritain as the "pilgrim of the Absolute." "No modern Roman Catholic had done more," said *Time*, "than this French layman to make the mind a subtly flashing sword in the defense of faith."

CHAPTER I

CATHOLICISM AND APOLOGETICS

[1]Cf. Will Durant, *The Story of Philosophy*, p. 104; *ibid.*, "Preface to the Second Edition," p. xi.

[2]Raymond E. Brown, S.S., "The Current Crisis in Theology As It Affects the Teaching of Catholic Doctrine," *National Catholic Reporter*, May 11, 1973, p. 10.

[3]Cited by Fulton J. Sheen, *Philosophy of Religion*, p. 336.

[4]Cited by Fulton J. Sheen, *Life Is Worth Living*, p. 31.

[5]*Ibid.*

[6]*Ibid.*, p. 32.

[7]G. K. Chesterton, *The Everlasting Man*, p. 111.

[8]Cf. Joseph V. Kopp, *Teilhard de Chardin: A New Synthesis of Evolution*, p. 57.

[9]Joseph H. Fichter, S.J., *Textbook in Apologetics*, p. 42. Cardinal Newman's refutation of David Hume's objections to the possibility of miracles makes for interesting reading.

[10]*Ibid.*, p. 45.

[11]*De Fide*, III., Can. 4.

[12]Cf. *Reality and the Mind*, by Celestine N. Bittle, O.F.M. Cap.

[13]The five arguments of Thomas Aquinas are restated in relation to modern knowledge by Fulton J. Sheen in *Philosophy of Religion;* cf. Part II.

[14]In reasoning to the existence of God, Aquinas did not include the "moral argument," which can be briefly stated as follows: Man is aware of conscience and a moral law which guide his free choices and fundamental options in terms of right and wrong. Man's sense of moral obligation cannot be wholly ascribed to either society or to human nature alone. There must be a supreme lawgiver and underwriter of the moral law who will reward the good and punish the wicked in an afterlife. Such a being men call God. The argument not only posits the existence of God but also argues for the immortality of the human soul. Man longs for perfect happiness, which is not to be found in this life; the rational, teleological organization of the universe requires that this natural and univer-

sal longing of mankind be capable of fulfillment in an afterlife. God is the *Summum Bonum* Who alone is capable of making man perfectly happy. Thus, the moral argument establishes the twin truths of God's existence and the human soul's immortality.

The metaphysical, physical (teleological), and moral arguments for the existence of God all rest ultimately on the principle of causality. Kant considered the moral argument to be the strongest proof for God's existence.

[15]Will Durant, *Caesar and Christ*, p. 557.

[16]John A. O'Brien, *Truths Men Live By*, p. 397.

[17]Percentages are taken from *Maryknoll* magazine, Feb. 1960.

[18]Cf. "Saint Peter," *Ency. Brit.* (1965 ed.), XVII, 635: "All this evidence [*supra*] taken together makes it highly probable that Peter did go to Rome and was martyred there."

[19]Cf. Fulton J. Sheen, "The History of a Word," *The Rock Plunged into Eternity*, p. 29.

[20]Cf. John A. O'Brien, *The Faith of Millions*. Part I deals with the topic, "Which Is Christ's True Church?" *The Roman Catholic Church*, by John L. McKenzie, gives an up-to-date description and appraisal of Roman Catholicism.

[21]Cf. John A. O'Brien, *The Reformation*, p. 8.

[22]Cf. Chap. VI, "Is Religion Purely Individual," *Preface to Religion*.

[23]The reader is referred to the great pioneering effort of Gustave Weigel, S.J., and Robert McAfee Brown in ecumenism, expressed in *An American Dialogue; Steps to Christian Unity*, edited by John A. O'Brien, is another outstanding contribution to the ecumenical movement.

[24]Cf. "Orthodox Eastern Church," *Ency. Brit.* (1965 ed.), XVI, 1122, 1125.

[25]We recommend John L. McKenzie's perceptive book, *Authority in the Church* (1966), especially Chaps. 11 and 12, for an honest critique of the nature and function of Church authority.

Vatican II taught that all of us share the guilt of Christian disunity. One may rightfully ask: Did Pope Nicholas I handle the case of Photius as well as it should have been? Did Pope Leo IX deal the best way with Michael Cerularius? Did Pope Leo X take Martin Luther seriously enough, as the Catholic Church has had to take him seriously ever since?

In an allocution of Sept. 29, 1963, marking the opening of the second session of Vatican II, Pope Paul VI stated in regard to Christian disunity: "If we are in any way to blame for that separation, we humbly beg God's forgiveness and ask pardon too of our brethren who feel themselves to have been injured by us. For our part, we willingly forgive the injuries which the Catholic Church has suffered, and forget the grief endured during the long series of dissensions and separations."

Similarly did Pope John XXIII speak concerning one of the primary objectives in convening the Council: "We do not intend to conduct a trial of the past; we do not want to prove who was right or who was wrong. The blame is on both sides. All we want is to say: 'Let us come together. Let us make an end of our divisions.'"

Thus far has the attitude of Catholic apologetics moved from a spirit of "triumphalism" to a spirit of Christian charity and understanding. The *Decree on Ecumenism* of Vatican II taught that "one cannot impute the sin of separation to those who at present are born into these [separated] Communities and are instilled therein with Christ's faith. The Catholic Church accepts them with respect and affection as brothers. For men who believe in Christ and have been properly baptized are brought into a certain, though imperfect, communion with the Catholic Church. . . . All those justified by faith through Baptism are incorporated into Christ. They therefore have a right to be honored by the title of Christian, and are properly regarded as brothers in the Lord by the sons of the Catholic Church" (n. 3).

[26]We are indebted to Fulton J. Sheen's excellent chapter, "Comparative Religion and Philosophy," *Philosophy of Religion*, for much of the content of this section.

[27]Will Durant, *Our Oriental Heritage*, p. 431.

[28]*Ibid.*, p. 434.

[29]*Ibid.*, p. 652.

[30]Cf. Will Durant, *The Age of Faith*, p. 186.

[31]Cf. Fulton J. Sheen, Chap. 17, "Mary and the Moslems," *The World's First Love*; the author shows that Mohammed held Mary in esteem. Mohammed stated, concerning his daughter Fatima, "Thou shalt be the most blessed of all women in Paradise, after Mary." Significantly, Our Lady appeared in 1917 at Fatima, Portugal, named after a Moslem chief's daughter. Sheen writes: "The Moslems should be prepared to acknowledge that, if Fatima must give way in honor to the Blessed Mother, it is because she is different from all the other mothers of the world and that without Christ she would be nothing" (*ibid.*, p. 175).

CHAPTER II

CATHOLICISM AND DOGMATIC THEOLOGY

[1]F. J. Sheed, *God and the Human Condition*, p. 187.

[2]Personal correspondence of the author, letter from Will Durant, March 27, 1963.

[3]Chap. III.

[4]Cf. George D. Smith (ed.), *The Teaching of the Catholic Church*, pp. 31 ff.

[5]*Contra Ep. Fundament.*, C. 5.

[6]Cf. Chaps. XI-XIV in *God and the Human Condition*, by F. J. Sheed. Mr. Sheed, whose theological prowess is considerable, at times *almost* seems to lift the veil from the profound mystery of the Trinity.

[7]Cf. Frederick Copleston, *A History of Philosophy*, II, Pt. I, 60.

[8]Cf. *Summa Theologica*, I, Q. 50.

[9]Cf. John A. O'Brien, *Evolution and Religion*. Though published in 1932, the work is still one of the best analyses of the philosophical and theological implications of evolution.

[10]Cf. Joseph V. Kopp, *Teilhard de Chardin: A New Synthesis of Evolution*, p. 44.

[11]Cited by John A. O'Brien, *op. cit.*, p. 93.

[12]Cf. Chap. VII, Sec. VI, for the author's views on Adam and Eve.

[13]According to Canon Henry de Dorlodot, who has extensively researched the thought of St. Augustine, the Bishop of Hippo subscribed to a form of complete natural evolution which posited a single, direct creative act of God, producing the potentialities *(rationes seminales)* of all forms of life. Concerning the human soul, Dorlodot concludes that Augustine believed it was created at the first instant of time, to be united to the human organism by a natural inclination when the body had become sufficiently developed through evolution to receive the rational soul (cf. John A. O'Brien, *Truths Men Live By*, pp. 328 f.).

[14]Concerning the time when the rational soul animates the unborn fetus, see Chap. IV, Sec. I.

[15]Cf. *Summa Theologica*, I, Q. 100.

[16]Cf. M. C. D'Arcy, *The Teaching of the Catholic Church*, pp. 492-93.

[17]The reader is referred to two beautiful books by Fulton J. Sheen: *The Eternal Galilean* (1934) and *Life of Christ* (1958); Frank J. Sheed's *To Know Christ Jesus* (1962) is also highly recommended.

[18]W. Wilmers, *Handbook of the Christian Religion*, p. 248.

[19]An interesting note concerns the opinion of St. Thomas Aquinas in regard

to the Immaculate Conception. The doctrine was freely discussed in the Middle Ages. Duns Scotus and the Franciscan school of theology championed the cause for the Immaculate Conception; Aquinas rejected the doctrine. "Thomas," writes Will Durant, "not foreseeing that the Church would decide in favor of the Immaculate Conception of the Virgin ... thought that Mary too had been 'conceived in sin'; he added, with tardy gallantry, that she was 'sanctified before her birth from the womb'" (*The Age of Faith*, p. 973).

Msgr. Paul J. Glenn explains the Thomistic teaching concerning Mary's sanctification in *A Tour of the Summa*, pp. 334-35; St. Thomas treats the problem in his *Summa Theologica*, III, Q. 27. He felt that Mary, like Jeremias and St. John the Baptist, was sanctified prior to her birth, but not from the first moment of conception.

[20]Cf. Fulton J. Sheen's beautiful treatise on the Blessed Mother, *The World's First Love* (1952); Richard Klaver, under whom this writer was privileged to study, treats each title of Our Lady in *The Litany of Loreto* (1954).

[21]Cf. Chap. I, Sec. IV.

[22]Contra Haer., IV 33, 7.

[23]Letter 185, Sec. 50; for the teaching of Aquinas on Christ as the Head of the Mystical Body, cf. *Summa Theologica*, III, Q. 8, and *Compendium Theologicae*, Cap. 215.

[24]Pope Pius XII, *The Mystical Body of Christ*, n. 39.

[25]F. J. Sheed, *Theology and Sanity*, pp. 272 f.

[26]Father Leonard Feeney, S.J., took an ultraconservative view of the time-honored dictum, "Outside the Church there is no salvation." He maintained that a visible, practicing membership in the Roman Catholic Church was necessary for salvation, making no allowance for invincible ignorance and an honestly formed conscience. The Church has rejected the position of Fr. Feeney.

Pope Pius XII wrote in *The Mystical Body of Christ* (1943): "For even though unsuspectingly they [non-Catholics] are related to the Mystical Body of the Redeemer in desire and resolution, they still remain deprived of so many precious gifts and helps from Heaven, which one can only enjoy in the Catholic Church" (n. 117).

[27]John A. O'Brien, *Catching Up with the Church*, p. 92.

[28]Cf. Fulton J. Sheen, *The Life of All Living*, for a deeper study and comparison of natural biology and the supernatural life of Grace; Sheen cites Bk. IV, Chap. 11, of St. Thomas' *Summa Contra Gentiles* as the inspiration for *The Life of All Living*.

[29]For the author's views on clerical celibacy, cf. Chap. VII, Sec. III.

[30]For the author's views on contraception, cf. Chap. VI, Sec. IV; regarding divorce, see Chap. VII, Sec. VII.

[31]The other two are the existence of God and the freedom of the human will.

[32]Billy Graham, *World Aflame*, Chap. 20.

[33]Cf. Celestine N. Bittle, *From Aether to Cosmos*, pp. 472 ff.

[34]The Apocalypse of St. John makes for interesting reading. For the most part, the Church has made no solemn definitions; theologians are free to explore its depths and significance. The Church does warn, however, against constructing an entire system of theology based on one or two verses of Scripture. Jehoveh Witnesses, for example, take quite literally the 144,000 who have been purchased for a heavenly Paradise. The Church rightly insists that Sacred Scripture be taken in its totality. One has no right to accept and reject what suits his fancy. Once again, one sees the supreme necessity for an authoritative interpreter of Sacred Scripture, apart from the light given each individual by the Holy Spirit.

[35]Cf. Bertrand L. Conway, *The Miniature Question Box*, p. 204.

[36]Jean-Paul Sartre, *No Exit*, cited by Will and Ariel Durant, *Interpretations of Life*, p. 181.

[37]Cf. *Summa Theologica*, III Suppl., Q. 97.

[38]Aquinas believed that more souls go to Hell than to Heaven; he cites Scripture, which says that narrow is the way that leads to eternal life, and *few* there are who find it. St. Teresa of Avila (1515-1582), the great mystic, said she saw souls descending into Hell like leaves from a tree. Will Durant cites the testimony of a twelfth-century monk, Tundale: "In the center of Hell . . . the Devil was bound to a burning gridiron by red-hot chains; his screams of agony never ended; his hands were free, and reached out and seized the damned; his teeth crushed them like grapes; his fiery breath drew them down his burning throat. Assistant demons with hooks of iron plunged the bodies of the damned alternately into fire or icy water, or hung them up by the tongue. . . . Sulphur was mixed with the fire in order that a vile stench might be added to the discomforts of the damned; but the fire gave no light, so that a horrible darkness shrouded the incalculable diversity of pains" *(The Age of Faith*, p. 733).

Excesses of imagination notwithstanding, Hell is a somber reality for the Christian to ponder.

[39]J. P. Arendzen, *The Teaching of the Catholic Church*, p. 1256. For a time Pope John XXII inclined toward the view that the blessed in Heaven will not enjoy the Beatific Vision until the consummation of the General Judgment. Even Thomas Aquinas favored this view in his earlier writings. Both gradually changed their minds: The Pope, on his deathbed in 1334, declared in a bull that the blessed "see God . . . face-to-face. . . ." Aquinas, in later writings, maintained that the Beatific Vision remains the same in *intensity* after the General Judgment, but increases in *extent* after the Resurrection of the Body. One should note that there has always been general agreement that the blessed before Christ's Ascension into Heaven enjoyed only a natural beatitude "in Abraham's bosom."

[40]Fulton J. Sheen, *Preface to Religion*, pp. 169 ff. Space has prevented us from giving adequate attention to the Protestant position concerning the various heads of Christian doctrine. Karl Barth, regarded by many as the preeminent Protestant theologian of the twentieth century, has succinctly stated that a three-letter word, *and*, separates Protestants and Catholics on matters of doctrine: Protestants say, Jesus; Catholics say, Jesus *and* Mary; Protestants say, Christ; Catholics say, Christ *and* His Vicar, the Pope; Protestants say, the merits of Jesus; Catholics say, the merits of Christ *and* good works; Protestants say, the Scriptures; Catholics say, Scripture *and* tradition; Protestants say, faith alone; Catholics say faith *and* reason (cf. *Steps to Christian Unity*, p. 90). Paul Tillich spoke of "the Protestant Principle": no human agency, or anything less than God, may be respected as though it were divine.

We feel that many of the differences are largely a matter of emphasis. The great stumbling block to doctrinal unity, of course, is papal supremacy and infallibility; but even this difficulty can be traced to a divergent view between Catholicism and Protestantism in terms of the nature of the Church on earth: Protestants prefer *church* with a lower case *c*; Catholics prefer *Church* with a capital *C*. We can only see a solution to this impasse in the doctrine of the Mystical Body of Christ, which both Protestants and Catholics need to explore more deeply.

CHAPTER III

CATHOLICISM AND MORAL THEOLOGY

[1]Will and Ariel Durant, *The Lessons of History*, p. 42.
[2]*Ibid.*, p. 96.
[3]Richard McKeon (ed.), *Introduction to Aristotle*, p. 308.
[4]"What then is time? If no one asks me, I know; if I wish to explain it to one that asks, I know not" (St. Augustine, *Confessions*, Bk. 11).

[5]Celestine N. Bittle, *Man and Morals*, p. 185.

[6]Thomas Aquinas, *Summa Theologica*, Ia IIae, Q. 90, A. 4: *"Ordinatio rationis ad bonum commune ab eo, qui communitatis curam habet, promulgata."*

[7]Bittle, *op. cit.*, p. 194.

[8]See Chap. VI, Sec. II, for a critique of natural law theory in the light of recent scholarship.

[9]Cf. Heribert Jone, *Moral Theology*, pp. 20-21.

[10]See Chap. VI, Sec. II, for a critique of the Bible as a source of moral doctrine.

[11]*Quis*, who? *Quid*, what? *Ubi*, where? *Quibus auxillis*, by what means? *Cur*, why? *Quomodo*, how? *Quando*, when?

[12]The problem of a doubtful conscience has been clearly explained by Msgr. Paul J. Glenn: "It is never lawful to act while in a state of positive practical doubt. . . . To dispel positive practical doubt, a person must use the direct method of study, inquiry. . . . If this method prove unsuccessful . . . then the indirect method (called the appeal to the reflex principle) must be applied. . . : a law that is of doubtful application cannot beget a certain obligation. In this case, certitude is attained, not of the case itself, but of the person's freedom from obligation. . ." (*An Introduction to Philosophy*, p. 375).

[13]Cf. Hugh J. O'Connell, *Keeping Your Balance in the Modern Church*, Chap. XI, "Does Love Need Laws?" The late Karl Barth (1886-1965) has said that even though adultery is objectively wrong, he could conceive of a case where it would be right to commit it (cf. F. J. Sheed, *Is It the Same Church?*, p. 29).

[14]"Under a Catholic signature I read: 'Morality is not based on immutable laws'; the question is 'What is the Christlike thing to do?' The Christian must do what love calls him to do, under no compulsion, even from God.

"In all this there is a lot of self-deception. . . . Man's power to persuade himself that the thing he is aflame with desire to do is the loving thing to do seems to be limitless. . . . Those who dismiss clearly stated moral laws — Thou shalt, thou shalt not — as legalism, and not according to the mind of Christ, can read the New Testament very strangely" (Sheed, *op. cit.*, pp. 29 ff.).

[15]The best treatment of existentialism by a Catholic writer, in our judgment, is Jacques Maritain's *Existence and the Existent*.

[16]Jone, *op. cit.*, p. 46.

[17]James Kavanaugh, *A Modern Priest Looks at His Outdated Church*, p. 96. Feeling and emotion dominate reason in many instances where the author criticizes his Church; yet, Kavanaugh makes a number of valid points concerning legalism, birth control, Catholic schools, and personalism. A recurring theme of the book is, "my arrogant Church."

[18]Aristotle, *Nichomachean Ethics*, Bk. II, Chap. 6.

[19]W. Wilmers, *Handbook of the Christian Religion*, p. 425.

[20]What about the fallen-away Catholic? God gives everyone sufficient Grace to save his soul, or at least the possibility of natural beatitude for infants and the retarded who were unable to receive either Baptism of water, blood, or desire. Insofar as faith is necessary for salvation, it follows that the gift of faith is given to all in Baptism. The "gift of faith" does not necessarily mean the gift to recognize and practice the Catholic Faith; this special gift is dependent upon human factors: childhood training; good example; intellectual factors; etc. The gift of faith must remain basically a mystery. Fulton J. Sheen has said that one never leaves the Church to become a holier person; the trouble is usually not so much with the Creed as with the Commandments. Insofar as a fallen-away maliciously — with a bad will, and with sufficient knowledge of what he or she is doing — rejects the Catholic Faith, to that extent is guilt imputable. Again, conscience is the final arbiter.

The aforementioned applies also to the infidel and the heretic. A heretic may be guilty of *material heresy* — i.e., the doctrine he holds is objectively erroneous according to the judgment of the Church; *formal heresy* implies a malicious, obstinate, culpable intention on the part of the heretic. When burning at the stake was in vogue in the Middle Ages, the distinction between material and formal heresy was nebulous indeed.

[21]Jone, *op. cit.*, pp. 73-74.

[22]Gottfried Wilhelm von Leibniz (1648-1716) especially grappled with the problem of evil. His *Theodicy* was written as a justification for the existence of God, despite the existence of evil. Leibniz concluded that this is "the best of all possible worlds." Francis Thompson spoke of evil as "the shade of His hand outstretched caressingly."

[23]Jone, *op. cit.*, p. 75.

[24]*Maryknoll* magazine (June 1973, p. 12) reports that 20 percent of the people of the world receive 80 percent of the world's income. The wealthiest nation on earth, the United States, has 6 percent of the world's population and 46 percent of the earth's wealth. Two-thirds of the earth's people are undernourished. In 1974 an estimated 10,000 human beings died daily of starvation. Six million Africans are dying of starvation. Hidden in these statistics are problems of ecology, technology, and distribution. But distributive justice requires that this *moral* problem of world poverty be solved by the affluent nations of the world.

[25]Durant, *op. cit.*, p. 40.

[26]Cf. Ex. 20:1-17; the Commandments are also given in Deut, 5:6-21. The precise division of these precepts into "ten commandments" is somewhat uncertain; we have followed the Catholic tradition.

[27]Charles E. Curran has pointed out that there is no intrinsic connection between the Sabbath observance of the Old Law and the Sunday observance of the New Law. Both the natural law and the Code of Canon Law demand divine worship. There is considerable disagreement among theologians concerning the Sunday rest and servile work. Curran believes an ultralegalism has tended to smother the true spirit of Sunday, which is to celebrate the Paschal Mystery. The purpose of the Sunday rest is to make such a celebration possible at the perfect form of divine worship, Holy Mass (cf. *Christian Morality Today*, pp. 107-19). Christ said: "The Sabbath was made for man, and not man for the Sabbath" (Mark 2:27).

[28]Papal encyclicals have dealt with marriage, contraception, celibacy, social justice, Communism, the Church, Sacred Scripture, Scholasticism, etc. When will a papal encyclical be devoted to the moral problem of alcoholism, which afflicts some 10 million Americans — not a few of which are Catholics? *Education U.S.A.* states that 60 percent of the nation's high schoolers get drunk at least once a month, and 50 percent have driven while drunk. The United States leads in the number of alcoholics proportional to the population (cf. "Alcoholism," *Ency. Brit.* [1965], I, 551). One-half of all driving fatalities are alcohol related.

[29]Thomas Aquinas gives his view on the necessary conditions for a "just war" in his *Summa Theologica*, IIa, IIae, Q. 40, A. 1.

[30]In June, 1972, by a vote of 5 to 4, the U.S. Supreme Court ruled that capital punishment is in violation of the 8th and 14th Amendments to the Constitution. The decision applied only to cases where juries hold discretionary power to choose between life and death penalties; the constitutionality of mandatory death penalties was not considered by the Court. In 1976 the Court upheld capital punishment in certain restricted cases.

[31]Aquinas, *op. cit.*, IIa, IIae, Q. 151, A. 2.

[32]Cf. Norman Vincent Peale, *Sin, Sex and Self-Control*, pp. 53 f.

[33]Cf. John F. Cronin, *Catholic Social Principles*, Chap. VI, for an excellent analysis and appraisal of communism; Fulton J. Sheen's *Light Your Lamps* is also to be highly recommended. Sheen points out that in formulating the rationale for communism, Karl Marx borrowed from the dialectical idealism of Hegel, the materialism of Feuerbach, and the sociology of Proudhon (cf. pp. 31-33).

[34]For some further precisions concerning the nature of lying, see Chap. V, Sec. III.

[35]*Op. cit.*, Bk. I, Chap. XX.

CHAPTER IV
AMERICA AND ABORTION

[1]*Op. cit.*, pp. 317 ff.

[2]*Op. cit.*, p. 372.

[3]*Summa Contra Gentiles*, III, C. 77.

[4]*Op. cit.*, p. 303.

[5]*Ibid.*, pp. 137 ff.

[6]*Ibid.*, p. 321.

[7]Cf. Bernard Haring, "The Enemies of Love," *Sign* magazine, Feb. 1971, p. 13.

[8]*Op. cit.*, IIa, IIae, Q. 120.

[9]Cf. *Theologia Moralis*, I, 201.

[10]Cf. "Jews," *Ency. Brit.* (1965 ed.), XII, 1076.

[11]Cited in *Time* magazine, Aug. 13, 1965, p. 48.

[12]*Op. cit.*, p. 72.

[13]Cf. "Arnold Joseph Toynbee," *Ency. Brit.* (1965 ed.), XXII, 337.

[14]*Op. cit.*, p. 146.

[15]Blackmun made no mention of the beginning of mitosis (cell division), nidation (implantation in the uterus), or even birth itself (separation from the mother) as possible norms for determining the beginning of a human life.

[16]In an interview with *U. S. Catholic* (March 1973), Curran inclines to believe that human life begins about the seventh or eighth day after fertilization, though "I admit to being very unsure." At this blastocyst stage of gestation, twinning can take place; also, a high incidence of spontaneous abortions occurs before the seventh or eighth day. Curran would thus approve of the "morning-after" pill and intrauterine devices which act as abortifacients.

[17]The reader is referred to an excellent article on abortion in both its philosophical and biological aspects by Dr. and Mrs. J. C. Willke, "Abortion Is Killing," *Columbia*, April 1973, pp. 11-19.

The magnitude of the problem of abortion is shown by a 1973 report by Dr. J. Corbett McDonald at a conference of the International Planned Parenthood Association. A survey that covered 209 countries revealed that (1) nearly 1 out of 3 pregnancies is deliberately terminated; (2) more than half the money spent on birth control goes for abortions; (3) less than 1 fertile couple in 3 practices any form of contraception; and (4) abortion is the world's most widespread method of birth control. The major need, according to Dr. McDonald, is to create a social and educational climate throughout the world in which contraception is acceptable.

CHAPTER V
CATHOLICISM AND CHANGE

[1]*Op. cit.*, p. 12.

[2]Cf. Dante's *Divine Comedy*.

[3]Cf. Pierre Teilhard de Chardin, "Epilogue: The Christian Phenomenon," *The Phenomenon of Man;* "The Nature of the Divine Milieu," *The Divine Milieu*. We give a brief critique of Teilhard's thought in Chap. VII, Sec. V.

[4]Cf. "John Henry Newman," *Ency. Brit.* (1965 ed.), XVI, 363 f.

[5]Fulton J. Sheen, *The Divine Romance*, pp. 139 f.

CHAPTER VI
CATHOLICISM AND HUMAN SEXUALITY

[1]We are indebted to John T. Noonan's monumental work *Contraception* for much of the content of this section.

[2]*Ibid.*, p. 53.

[3]*Ibid.*, p. 348.

[4]"The failure to incorporate love into the purposes of marital intercourse was largely a failure of theological analysis. The failure occurred in a society whose mating customs made procreation, not love, the most prominent value of marriage" (*ibid.*, p. 310).

[5]"The doctrine on contraception cannot be said to have been fully, freely, and generally known and accepted by the Catholic laity; neither can it be said to have been known only to the literate clergy.... It was a teaching destined for development — both by a more instructed and self-conscious future laity, and by medieval theologians themselves who were aware of values other than those the condemnations of contraception embodied" (*ibid.*, p. 331).

[6]*Ibid.*, p. 370.

[7]"Any use whatever of marriage, in the exercise of which the act by human effort is deprived of its natural power of procreating life, violates the law of God and nature, and those who do such a thing are stained by a grave and mortal flaw" (*Casti Connubii*).

[8]Cicero, *The Republic*, III, 22.

[9]Cf. *Contemporary Problems in Moral Theology*, pp. 97-158.

[10]Perhaps posterity has been too harsh on Epicurus, putting him down as a crass sensualist. A careful reading of Epicurus will show that he never advocated pleasure at the expense of reason. Pleasure is to be fully enjoyed, which it cannot be if reason is violated.

[11]Cited by Richard Frisbie, *The Six Paradoxes of Sex*, p. 18.

[12]Cf. C. C. Martindale, *The Vocation of Aloysius Gonzaga*, pp. 88-89, cited by John L. McKenzie, *The Roman Catholic Church*, p. 231.

[13]*Coitus interruptus* and *coitus reservatus* are also contraceptive techniques. The Billings ovulation method, published by Drs. Lyn and John Billings in 1968, determines the time of ovulation by the changes in appearance of a woman's vaginal mucus secretions. The Billings method is a variant of the rhythm method of periodic abstinence.

[14]"*Consensus omnium hominum de aliqua doctrina requiruntur ... ad ordinem socialem et moralem instituendum et conservandum ... in errorem ducere nequit*" (J. S. Hickey, *Summula Philosophiae Scholasticae*, pp. 257-58).

[15]Cf. *National Catholic Reporter*, Dec. 3, 1971, p. 16.

[16]Cited by John A. O'Brien, *Family Planning in an Exploding Population*, p. 216.

[17]"The non-Catholic is ... offended by the implication of Catholic teaching that a marital practice which is approved by most Christian churches should be described by Roman Catholics as 'intrinsically immoral and unnatural'" (Archbishop Thomas D. Roberts, S. J., *Contraception and Holiness*. p. 10).

[18]Cf. *Summa Theologica*, II, II, Q. 154, A. 11.

[19]Cf. Robert E. Rothenberg, M.D., *The Doctor's Premarital Medical Adviser;* see also, Edward Sagarin, "Autoeroticism: a Sociological Approach," *Sexual Self-Stimulation:* "Today, virtually no authority on sex would consider masturbation abnormal ... just as no authority would consider other nonprocreative acts, such as heterosexual petting to orgasm or sexual intercourse with the use of contraceptives, perverted" (p. 224).

[20]Cf. John H. Tobe, *Your Prostate: Treatment and Prevention*, pp. 132 ff.

[21]The interested reader is referred to Charles E. Curran's pioneering chapter, "Masturbation and Objectively Grave Matter," *A New Look at Christian*

Morality, pp. 201-21. The book bears a *nihil obstat* and an *imprimatur*. Curran was one of the first moral theologians of prominence in America to openly question the traditional position of the manuals declaring all directly voluntary sexual actuation outside of marriage to be *ex toto genere suo grave* (grave matter). Curran's basic arguments can be summarized as follows:

(1) Masturbation does not seem to involve mortal sin understood in light of the theory of the fundamental option, which involves the very core of one's being.

(2) The condemnation of the manuals rests on an exaggerated physicism which binds all sexual actuation to *copula* (copulation) and procreation, and downplays personal values.

(3) The condemnation of the manuals erroneously defines sexual pleasure as a "reward" reserved exclusively to the married for the burdens and responsibilities of procreation.

(4) Both the Bible and patristic literature offer no clear and conclusive condemnation.

(5) No official pronouncement of the Church can be regarded as a definitive condemnation.

(6) Modern physiology and psychology have revealed the essentially banal and benign character of autosexual behavior.

Curran is careful to point out the incomplete and less than ideal nature of autosexual behavior. Human sexuality is best expressed in an interpersonal love relationship within marriage. Autosexual behavior could be symptomatic of a neurotic inversion, narcissism, or immaturity which prevents one from entering more meaningful interpersonal relations. Any form of human behavior can become perverted and degenerate into neurosis or immorality; yet, the conclusion remains that autosexual acts, though incomplete and basically unfulfilled, are not to be considered as aberrations or gravely sinful in themselves. Studies have shown that a high percentage of healthy, well-adjusted men and women, both single and married, sometimes engage in autosexual activity. Curran states flatly that adolescents should be openly taught that masturbation should not be a reason preventing one from full participation in the Eucharist (cf. *Contemporary Problems in Moral Theology*, p. 176).

See also Herbert J. Miles, *Sexual Understanding Before Marriage*, pp. 137-62. Writing from a Christian perspective, Miles denies that all masturbation is to be equated with lust and impurity. He finds no specific Biblical prohibition (not Gen. 38:8-11 nor 1 Cor. 6:9-10) and no incompatibility with Christian moral principles. He justifies the act as a form of sexual self-control in avoiding fornication and adultery — both of which are clearly forbidden by the Bible.

Father William J. Bausch, in an excellent pamphlet entitled "Masturbation," (Chicago: Claretian Publications, 1973), maintains that while excessive masturbation could involve serious matter, ordinarily such acts would not involve serious sin for one who is of "good will" and otherwise disposed toward the love of God.

Dr. Karl Menninger, in his best-selling *Whatever Became of Sin?*, regards masturbation as a normal physiological process with no specific Biblical proscription (cf. pp. 31-37). "An incalculable amount of pain could have been spared [millions of priests and nuns since Augustine], and spared millions of young boys and girls if, in some way, it could have been made common knowledge long before 1900 that there is no harm in masturbation, no evil in it, and no sinfulness in it, the former religious stipulations notwithstanding" (p. 140).

Marc Oraison is a French priest, psychiatrist, and urologist. He writes: "Scientific understanding of [sexuality] is very recent. It is difficult for us to realize that the eminent men of the sixteenth century like Leonardo de Vinci, were totally ignorant of sexual physiology. . . . There was total ignorance of the tremendous wastage in spermatognesis, and the sperm was considered as a sacred liquor. . . . Clinical observation should have been able long ago to show that the masturbaton of adolescence was a banal matter. . . . Masturbation is a common, transitory, and not alarming sign of the crisis of psychosexual awakening in adolescence. . . . It may pose some problems for moral theory. . . . But of itself it absolutely does not hold the threat of disaster brandished by sixteenth- and seventeenth-century morality and medicine. . ." *(The Celibate Condition and Sex*, pp. 134 ff.).

CHAPTER VII

PROPOSALS FOR REFORM

[1]Cf. Fulton J. Sheen, "The Signs of the Times," *Columbia* magazine, Nov. 1970, p. 17. "It is a new world. It is a new ball game. We are playing in a new park" (*ibid.*, p. 19).

[2]"The legend that a woman [Pope Joan] reigned between Leo IV (847-855) and Benedict III (855-858) has no foundation in fact and has long been discredited" ("Papacy," *Ency. Brit.*, XVII, 205).

[3]The first pope, Peter, saw fit to move the Holy See from Jerusalem to Antioch to Rome. There is danger in making a necessary and inseparable connection between the Holy See and a particular geographical area. The Holy See belongs to the world; no article of faith states that Rome must be the headquarters of the Catholic Church. The spiritual power of the papacy is guaranteed by Christ, irregardless of the particular locale from which the Holy See functions. The pope, of course, must be able to govern with freedom and independence and without state interference in matters spiritual; the Avignon experience is not to be repeated. But such independence should be possible in many democratic states existing in the world today.

[4]A common opinion of theologians is that one receives the powers of the papacy when he is recognized, either implicitly or through the existing structure for naming the pope, to be *de facto* the pope. We favor the view that the pope does possess the right to name his successor and that the whole Church would be obliged to accept such a decision, which is guaranteed by the pope's power to bind and loose. In the text we simply recommend that the pope freely place the responsibility for naming a new pope in the hands of the entire Church.

We recommend that the Church come to grips with the somewhat unpleasant prospect of replacing a pope who has become senile, neurotic, psychotic, or otherwise chronically debilitated — conditions which manifestly render a pope incapable of discharging the duties of the papal office with competence and responsibility. It borders on the scandalous that the Church has never squarely faced this problem in nearly two thousand years. The bishops of the world in union with the pope need to establish specific procedures for coping with such an eventuality. Only a few popes have resigned or were deposed, the most famous resignation being St. Celestine V, who abdicated on Dec. 13, 1294, after reigning five months. Pope Paul VI, who reached his seventy-fifth year on Sept. 26, 1972, ended speculation that he might resign at the age he has asked bishops to resign.

[5]In canon law cardinals are the heirs of the early pastors of Rome who originally elected the pope. Each cardinal is appointed titular head of a Roman church. Technically, a cardinal may live outside of Rome only by a papal dispensation. Our position is that the *world*, not just Rome, is the pope's true "diocese"; in this context the College of Cardinals becomes an anachronism that could well be eliminated in the Church of the twentieth century.

[6]On March 25, 1972, the Holy See promulgated the decree, "Procedure for the Selection of Bishops in the Latin Church," which gave to nuncios and apostolic delegates the final judgment in choosing names to constitute *ternae* submitted to the pope. The decree allowed for bishops to consult with their

priests in submitting nominations to the episcopacy (cf. *America*, Oct. 14, 1972, p. 289).

[7]Andrew M. Greeley, "The State of the Priesthood," *National Catholic Reporter*, Feb. 18, 1972, pp. 15 f.

[8]We are aware of the perils of democracy, which tends to proliferate parties, factions, and maneuvering; but one would be naive indeed to assume that such factions do not exist in the Church today under the present system. Democratic procedures would at least give all voices a fair hearing.

The 1972 convention of the Canon Law Society of America, held in Seattle in October, has made a recommendation similar to the one we have proposed. A committee of priests, religious, and laity would submit names to be screened by the priests' senate and given to the local bishop, who can exercise a "certain discretionary power over the composition of the list"; the bishop then submits the list of three to five names to the committee of the National Conference of Catholic Bishops for approval; the president of the NCCB then submits the names to the Holy See for final appointment (cf. Ladislas Orsy, S.J., "What the Canonists Recommend," *America*, Nov. 18, 1972, p. 414).

[9]Canon 2388 states that clerics in major orders (deacons, priests, and bishops) and solemnly professed religious who presume to contract marriage, even by a mere civil ceremony, and also those who marry such persons incur excommunication *simpliciter* reserved to the Holy See (cf. Heribert Jone, *Moral Theology*, p. 302). The most famous American clerics to have received the penalty of Canon 2388, at this writing, are James Kavanaugh, James P. Shannon, and Philip Berrigan. *Why Priests Leave*, edited by John A. O'Brien, relates the personal stories of twelve priests who left the active ministry.

[10]Pope Paul VI, *The Development of People*.

[11]Bernard Haring, "The Enemies of Love," *Sign* magazine, Feb. 1971, p. 10.

[12]A married clergy, of course, presents the possibilities of family scandals, divorce, and the problem of financial support; but we know that clerical celibacy is not without its share of scandals and pragmatic difficulties. The thesis is not that marriage will solve all of the problems of the secular clergy; on the contrary, marriage will present a different set of problems. Our position is simply that marriage ought not to be categorically denied as an option for the secular clergy. The economics of celibacy is interesting. William J. Whalen has concluded that most Catholic parishes would find the cost of supporting a married priest to be about the same as supporting a celibate priest; some parishes would find the cost to be *less* for a married priest (cf. "The Economics of Celibacy," *U.S. Catholic*, Sept. 1972, pp. 42-44).

[13]John A. O'Brien, *Why Priests Leave*, p. 187.

[14]We are indebted to Mary Perkins Ryan, "Hints from History," *Are Parochial Schools the Answer?*, for much of the following historical information.

[15]*Ibid.*, p. 29.

[16]*Ibid.*, p. 33.

[17]*Time* magazine, July 12, 1971, p. 36. In 1972 Catholic schools in America were closing at the rate of one per day. A study prepared under the auspices of the U.S. Catholic Conference reported that between 1965 and 1974 enrollment in Catholic elementary schools decreased from 46.5 percent to 26 percent of the total population of that age group; Catholic high school enrollment decreased from 28.1 percent to 17.6 percent during the same period. The study further noted that 43.5 percent, or 6.6 million boys and girls, receive no formal religious instruction in either Catholic schools or Confraternity of Christian Doctrine (CCD) programs.

[18]We do not intend to minimize the values of pluralism and diversity in education. The *right* of Catholics to maintain their own schools has never been seriously questioned in America. But we also see values in uniting Catholic education with the public school system. Public education need not be monolithic

and state dominated; there is latitude for diversity within public education.

[19]Ryan, *op. cit.*, pp. 43 f.

[20]Quoted by Robert T. Francoeur, "The Cosmic Christianity of Teilhard de Chardin," *Sign* magazine, Feb. 1967, p. 8.

[21]*Ibid.*, p. 13.

[22]Cited by John Kobler, "The Priest Who Haunts the Catholic World," *Saturday Evening Post*, Oct. 12, 1963, p. 50.

[23]*Ibid.*

[24]Much of the following exposition of Teilhard's doctrines is based on Fulton J. Sheen's Chap. Six, "The Origin of Man in Society," *Footprints in a Darkened Forest.*

[25]The Thomist-Scotist debate in the Middle Ages as to whether God would have become incarnate if man hadn't committed Original Sin is resolved by Teilhardism with an unequivocal "yes."

[26]Pierre Teilhard de Chardin, *The Phenomenon of Man*, p. 270.

[27]Teilhard entrusted his manuscripts to Jeanne Mortier. Within eight months after Teilhard's death, *The Phenomenon of Man* was published; the work had been completed in 1940. Teilhard's ten published books have since sold more than a million copies.

Teilhard is published in the Soviet Union. Teilhard said that *vertical* evolution has ended for man. Human evolution is now taking place on a *horizontal* plane. Man's perfection will be achieved in association and communion with his fellow man: "No evolutionary future awaits man except in association with other men." The hyperpersonal will exist in the collectivity.

Teilhard once said that Marxists look more to the future than do Christians; but he also saw in Communism "the most ghastly fetters . . . , the anthill instead of brotherhood." Roger Garaudy, a French Communist, by twisting Teilhard's evolutionary theory, has made the Jesuit acceptable to the Soviets.

[28]Cited by Francoeur, *loc. cit.*

[29]Fulton J. Sheen, *Footprints in a Darkened Forest*, p. 73.

[30]Cf. Pierre Teilhard de Chardin, "Mass upon the Altar of the World." This philosophical and mystical poem was written in the stillness and vast solitude of the Ordos Desert, and completed on Easter Sunday.

[31]Teilhard de Chardin, *The Phenomenon of Man*, p. 185.

[32]*Ibid.*, p. 188.

[33]Cf. F. J. Sheed, *Genesis Regained*, p. 159.

[34]*Ibid.*, p. 160. Sheed still feels that the human race began with a single pair, not because monogenism is essential to the doctrine of Original Sin, but because he cannot envision creatures streaming over the borderline between the human and subhuman (cf. *ibid.*, p. 159). It is worth noting that Teilhard did not believe in intermediate stages between the human and the subhuman; "the threshold had to be crossed in one stride," between one individual and the next.

[35]Fulton J. Sheen, *Preface to Religion*, p. 72.

[36]John McNeill, S.J., speaking to a Dignity convention of Catholic homosexuals, questioned the absolute Biblical prohibition of homosexual relations. McNeill, who was an associate professor of moral theology at Woodstock College, New York, maintains that the essential sin of Sodom and Gomorrah was "inhospitality" — a fact referred to more than sixteen times throughout the Bible. He sees the Pauline condemnation of homosexuality as referring only to a freely chosen form of sexual perversion committed by heterosexuals; he notes that St. Paul was ignorant of the modern concept of homosexuality as an innate psychophysiological orientation. McNeill feels that homosexual fulfillment is compatible with Christian principles and eminently in accord with personalist ethics (cf. "The Homosexual and the Church," *National Catholic Reporter*, Oct. 5, 1973, pp. 7 ff.).

The debate continues as to whether or not homosexuality should be considered as a pathological aberration and a dysfunction of the psychosexual orientation of an individual or as a normal condition for a certain percentage of human beings. Psychiatrists seem to be pretty evenly divided on the question. The gay liberation movement would have homosexuality removed from the realm of abnormal psychology. Serious questions arise: Is homosexuality a freely chosen life-style, or is it congenital and involuntary in its etiology? Would the pair-bond of a homosexual relationship constitute a true "marriage," sacramental and indissoluble in character? Are heterosexuality and the ontological possibility of procreation essential ingredients to the institution of marriage? The questions are real, even though nearly two thousand years of Christianity has traditionally looked disfavorably upon homosexuality. The problem is nuanced and will require the best minds that Catholicism today can muster. The Church has already admitted in principle that human sexuality need not always be tied to procreation, that sex can be a legitimate expression of love between two individuals; but so far the Church has not been willing to say that sexual love may be expressed in a homosexual relationship. There is no doubt that sexual promiscuity is just as immoral for a gay as for a straight.

See also "A Christian Response to Homosexuals" by Father Henry Fehren, *U.S. Catholic*, Sept. 1972, pp. 6-11, for another liberal view.

Some pertinent Biblical texts relating to homosexuality are: Gen. 13:13; Gen. 19:1 ff.; Lev. 18:22; Judges 19:22-25; Rom. 1:26-27; 1 Cor. 6:9-10; 2 Pet. 2:6; Jude 1:7. Christ once referred to Sodom and Gomorrah, and said that these inhabitants would fare better on the day of Judgment than those who refuse to receive the Christian message (cf. Matt. 10:14-15).

Kinsey reported that about 50 percent of all males are involved in homosexual behavior at some time in their lives. Among primitive societies, 64 percent accepted homosexuality as normal, as did the ancient Greeks (cf. "Homosexuality," *Ency. Brit.* [1965 ed.], XI, 648 f.).

In December, 1973, the American Psychiatric Association trustees, by a vote of 13 to 0, decided to remove "homosexuality *per se*" from the association's official manual of mental disorders. The manual will henceforth refer only to a "sexual orientation disturbance." The association also called for a repeal of laws in 42 states which make "criminal offenses of sexual acts performed by consenting adults in private," and called for an end to public and private discrimination against homosexuals, who represent one-tenth of the U.S. population, according to the "National Gay Task Force."

[37]Cf. Heribert Jone, *Moral Theology*, pp. 495-511.

[38]*Ibid.*, pp. 514-17.

[39]Cf. *Commentary on Aristotle's Metaphysics; Summa Theologica*, I,Q.92,A.1.

[40]Cf. Will Durant, *The Age of Faith*, p. 973.

[41]Cf. *Summa Theologica*, I, Q. 92, A. 3.

[42]Fulton J. Sheen, *The World's First Love*, pp. 128 f.

[43]*National Catholic Reporter*, March 31, 1972, p. 10.

[44]John A. O'Brien, *Why Priests Leave*, p. 182.

[45]Pope Leo XIII, *Brief on Historical Studies*, Aug. 18, 1893.

[46]Cf. John A. O'Brien, *The Truth About the Inquisition*, pp. 7-8.

[47]"Inquisition," *Ency. Brit.* (1965 ed.), XII, 271b, 273bc.

[48]Will Durant, *The Reformation*, p. viii.

[49]John A. O'Brien, *Why Priests Leave*, p. 184.

[50]Charles E. Curran, *A New Look at Christian Morality*, p. 131.

[51]A report published by William C. McCready and Andrew M. Greeley revealed that in 1972 only 55 percent of American Catholics attended Mass at least once a week; in 1963, 71 percent attended weekly Mass (cf. *idem*, "The End of American Catholicism?", *America*, Oct. 28, 1972, p. 334). The percentage of Europeans attending weekly Mass is considerably below the American figure.

CHAPTER VIII

STRUCTURE AND AUTHORITY IN THE CATHOLIC CHURCH

[1]Cf. John Lewis, *The Religions of the World Made Simple*, p. 132.
[2]Cf. Fulton J. Sheen, *The Rock Plunged into Eternity*, p. 30.
[3]Vatican Council I, I., *De Eccl.*, C. 14.
[4]Cf. "Infallibility," *Ency. Brit.* (1965 ed.), XII, 216d.
[5]Robert McAfee Brown, *An American Dialogue*, pp. 93, 96.
[6]*Ibid.*, p. 92.
[7]"Papacy," *Ency. Brit.* (1965 ed.), XVII, 195a.
[8]There have been 263 pontificates recognized as canonical; Benedict IX ascended the papal throne on three separate occasions: in 1032, 1045, and 1047 (cf. *ibid.*, 207).
[9]Cf. "Roman Catholic Church," *Ency. Brit.* (1972 ed.), XIX, 468a.
[10]Cf. John L. McKenzie, *Authority in the Church*, pp. 71-72.
[11]*Idem, The Roman Catholic Church*, p. 59.
[12]Fulton J. Sheen, *The Priest Is Not His Own*, pp. 23, 25.
[13]Compiled from *Annuario Pontificio* 1965, cited by McKenzie, *The Roman Catholic Church*, p. 102.
[14]Celestine N. Bittle, *Man and Morals*, p. 655.
[15]*Summa Theologica*, I, II, Q. 105, A. 1.
[16]Andrew M. Greeley, "The State of the Priesthood," *National Catholic Reporter*, Feb. 18, 1972, p. 10.
[17]McKenzie, *Authority in the Church*, pp. 93, 96.
[18]F. J. Sheed, *Is It the Same Church?*, p. 5.
[19]Peter J. Riga, "Let's Stop Knocking Bishops," *U.S. Catholic*, July 1972, p. 14.

EPILOGUE

THE FUTURE OF CATHOLICISM

[1]Cf. Fulton J. Sheen, *Philosophy of Religion*, p. 3.
[2]Paul J. Glenn, *An Introduction to Philosophy*, p. 21.
[3]Friedrich Nietzsche, *Thus Spake Zarathustra*, cited by Will Durant, *The Story of Philosophy*, p. 416. At the age of twelve, Nietzsche wrote: "I saw God in His splendor in a vision." As a young man he wrote: "I want to know You, Unknown One, You Who are reaching deep into my soul and ravaging my life, a savage gale. You Inconceivable yet Related One! I want to know You — even serve." In Latin Nietzsche wrote in his notebook: "Life, thou art my cross; cross, thou art my life." He condemned the "slave morality" of Christianity, extolling "power" and the advent of "superman." He died an insane man.
[4]Bertrand Russell, *Mysticism and Logic*.
[5]According to Dewart, the "employment" by the Catholic Church of Scholasticism gradually became its "adoption" in the sixteenth century, then its "establishment" in the early nineteenth century, its "beatification" in 1879 by Leo XIII, and finally its "canonization" in 1917 by Benedict XV (cf. *The Future of Belief*, p. 164). Charles E. Curran has reminded us that Christianity managed to get along without Scholasticism for nearly a thousand years. Dewart does not deny the real contributions made by Scholasticism to theology; but he believes that theology "in a world come of age" is now ready to advance beyond some of the naive concepts of Scholasticism.
[6]Cf. Josef Pieper, *The Silence of Saint Thomas*, pp. 38-41.
[7]*Summa Theologica*, I, Prologue.
[8]*Op. cit.*, 7, 5 ad 14.
[9]Will Durant, *The Pleasures of Philosophy*, p. 315.

[10]For some reason Catholic moral theology has been slow to adopt scientific terminology, especially in the area of sexual morality. Aquinas, for example, never used the word *vagina*, though the term was known in his day; he spoke only of "the fit vessel" in relation to coitus. Textbooks in moral theology speak of orgasm as "pollution"; autosexual behavior is called "mollities" (softness), or simply self-abuse. The word *masturbation* is derived from two Latin words, *manus* (hand) and *stuprare* (to defile); obviously, whoever coined the word had already made up his mind concerning the moral quality of the act.

We submit that neither euphemisms nor pejoratives have a legitimate place in moral theology, which ought to pre-eminently seek accuracy and objectivity. Loaded words — words with unscientific connotations and words which are prejudgmental in character — ought to be purged from moral theology. This will be no small task for the future of Catholicism.

[11]Cited by James Conroy, *Our Sunday Visitor* (Ft. Wayne-South Bend ed.), June 9, 1972, p. 3.

[12]Cf. Joseph Lortz, *History of the Church*, p. 432.

[13]The word *deicide* was dropped from the final draft, which reads: ". . . what happened in His passion cannot be blamed upon all the Jews then living, without distinction, nor upon the Jews of today" *Nostra Aetate*, n. 4).

Concerning non-Christian religions in general, the Council taught: "The Catholic Church rejects nothing which is true and holy in these religions. She looks with sincere respect upon those ways of conduct and life, those rules and teachings which, though differing in many particulars from what she holds and sets forth, nevertheless often reflect a ray of that Truth which enlightens all men" *(ibid.,* n. 2).

[14]Cf. Carl Balcerak, "The Return of the Deacons," *Columbia*, July 1972, pp. 6-14.

[15]Cf. *National Catholic Reporter*, Jan. 14, 1972, p. 1.

[16]Cf. *U.S. Catholic*, Sept. 1972, p. 44.

[17]G. K. Chesterton, *The Everlasting Man*, p. 260.

[18]Cited by Andrew M. Greeley, "The State of the Priesthood," *National Catholic Reporter*, Feb. 18, 1972, p. 17.

The words of Archbishop Ireland take on added significance when one realizes that he wrote them at a time when official Church policy continued to look askance, if not with downright hostility, toward "modern culture." The *Syllabus of Errors*, issued by Pius IX in 1864, ended with this unprophetic proposition, calling it an error to say that "the Roman Pontiff may and ought to reconcile and adapt himself to progress, liberalism, and modern civilization." Pius X condemned modernism in his encyclical *Pascendi*, issued in 1907. The Church no longer requires its priests at ordination to take an oath against modernism.

We doubt that the Council Fathers of Vatican II would have approved of the two documents in totality, if they had been submitted; the Council, in fact, made declarations directly opposed to statements of the popes in the above-mentioned documents. In fairness to Pius IX and Pius X, their views must be seen in the context of their times, when pantheism, deism, rationalism, and naturalism threatened the purity and supernatural character of Christian doctrine. The Church has since learned that it can and should unite with the age in all that is good and truly progressive and truly beneficial for mankind; this is not the same as uniting with the transient *spirit* of the age, which is ephemeral and not always grounded in unchanging truth.

BIBLIOGRAPHY

A. REFERENCES FOR FURTHER READING

The Holy Bible. Confraternity edition. New York: Catholic Book Publishing Co., 1953.

ABBOTT, WALTER M. (ed.). *The Documents of Vatican II.* New York: Guild Press, America Press, Association Press, 1966.

Annuario Pontificio. 1964, 1965, 1973.

AQUINAS, THOMAS. *On the Truth of the Catholic Faith (Summa Contra Gentiles).* 4 bks. Garden City, N. Y.: Image Books, 1955-57.

———. *Summa Theologica.* 3 vols. New York: Benziger Bros., 1947; 22 vols. London: Burns, Oates, 1912-36.

AUGUSTINE, SAINT. *The City of God.* Garden City, N.Y.: Image Books, 1958.

———. *The Confessions of St. Augustine.* New York: Washington Square Press, Inc., 1951.

BARTLETT, JOHN. *The Shorter Bartlett's Familiar Quotations.* New York: Pocket Books, Inc., 1953.

BIRMINGHAM, WILLIAM (ed.). *What Modern Catholics Think About Birth Control.* New York: The New American Library, 1964.

BITTLE, CELESTINE N. *The Science of Correct Thinking* (Logic). Revised edition. Milwaukee: The Bruce Publishing Co., 1950.

———. *Reality and the Mind* (Epistemology). Milwaukee: The Bruce Publishing Co., 1936.

———. *The Domain of Being* (Ontology). Milwaukee: The Bruce Publishing Co., 1939.

———. *From Aether to Cosmos* (Cosmology). Milwaukee: The Bruce Publishing Co., 1941.

———. *The Whole Man* (Psychology). Milwaukee: The Bruce Publishing Co., 1945.

———. *Man and Morals* (Ethics). Milwaukee: The Bruce Publishing Co., 1950.

———. *God and His Creatures* (Theodicy). Milwaukee: The Bruce Publishing Co., 1953.

BRENNAN, ROBERT EDWARD. *Thomistic Psychology.* New York: The Macmillan Co., 1941.

BROWN, ROBERT MCAFEE, AND GUSTAVE WEIGEL. *An American Dialogue.* Garden City, N.Y.: Anchor Books, 1960.

CALLAHAN, DANIEL. *Abortion: Law, Choice, and Morality.* New York: The Macmillan Co., 1970.

———. *The Mind of the Catholic Layman.* New York: Charles Scribner's Sons, 1963.

CHESTERTON, G. K. *The Everlasting Man.* Garden City, N.Y.: Image Books, 1925.
——. *Orthodoxy.* Garden City, N.Y.: Image Books, 1936.
——. *St. Francis of Assisi.* Garden City, N.Y.: Image Books, 1924.
——. *St. Thomas Aquinas.* Garden City, N.Y.: Image Books, 1933.
CONNOLLY, DONALD L. (ed.). *The Protestants Among Us.* Huntington, Ind.: Our Sunday Visitor Press, 1958.
CONWAY, BERTRAND L. *The Miniature Question Box.* New York: The Paulist Press, 1950.
COPLESTON, FREDERICK C. *Aquinas.* Baltimore: Penguin Books, 1955.
——. *A History of Philosophy.* 8 vols. Garden City, N.Y.: Image Books, 1946-66.
COX, HARVEY. *The Seduction of the Spirit.* New York: Simon and Schuster, 1973.
CRONIN, JOHN F. *Catholic Social Principles.* Milwaukee: The Bruce Publishing Co., 1955.
CURRAN, CHARLES E. *Christian Morality Today.* Notre Dame, Ind.: Fides Publishers, Inc., 1966.
——. *Contemporary Problems in Moral Theology.* Notre Dame, Ind.: Fides Publishers, Inc., 1970.
——. *A New Look at Christian Morality.* Notre Dame, Ind.: Fides Publishers, Inc., 1968.

DEWART, LESLIE. *The Future of Belief.* New York: Herder and Herder, 1966.
DULLES, AVERY. *Models of the Church.* Garden City, N.Y.: Doubleday and Co., Inc., 1974.
DUPRÉ, LOUIS. *Contraception and Catholics: A New Appraisal.* Baltimore: Helicon Press, 1964.
DURANT, WILL. *The Pleasures of Philosophy.* New York: Simon and Schuster, 1953.
——. *The Story of Philosophy.* New York: The Pocket Library, 1933.
——. *Transition.* New York: Simon and Schuster, 1927.
——. *The Story of Civilization.* 11 vols. New York: Simon and Schuster, 1935-75:
    Pt. I: *Our Oriental Heritage.* 1935.
    Pt. II: *The Life of Greece.* 1939.
    Pt. III: *Caesar and Christ.* 1944.
    Pt. IV: *The Age of Faith.* 1950.
    Pt. V: *The Renaissance.* 1953.
    Pt. VI: *The Reformation.* 1957.
——, AND ARIEL. Pt. VII: *The Age of Reason Begins.* 1961.
    Pt. VIII: *The Age of Louis XIV.* 1963.
    Pt. IX: *The Age of Voltaire.* 1965.
    Pt. X: *Rousseau and Revolution.* 1967.
    Pt. XI: *The Age of Napoleon.* 1975.
——————. *The Lessons of History.* New York: Simon and Schuster, 1968.
——————. *Interpretations of Life.* New York: Simon and Schuster, 1970.

Encyclopaedia Britannica. 1965, 1972 editions. 24 vols. Chicago: Encyclopaedia Britannica, Inc.

ETEROVICH, FRANCIS H. *Approaches to Natural Law*. New York: Exposition Press, 1972.

FICHTER, JOSEPH H. *Textbook in Apologetics*. Milwaukee: The Bruce Publishing Co., 1947.

FLETCHER, JOSEPH. *Situation Ethics*. Philadelphia: Westminster Press, 1966.

FRISBIE, RICHARD. *The Six Paradoxes of Sex*. Chicago: Claretian Publications, n. d.

FUCHS, JOSEF. *Natural Law*. New York: Sheed and Ward, 1965.

GALLAGHER, DONALD AND IDELLA (eds.). *A Maritain Reader*. Garden City, N.Y.: Image Books, 1966.

GILSON, ETIENNE. *The Elements of Christian Philosophy*. New York: The New American Library, 1960.

GLENN, PAUL J. *The History of Philosophy*. St. Louis: B. Herder Book Co., 1929.

———. *An Introduction to Philosophy*. St. Louis: B. Herder Book Co., 1944.

———. *A Tour of the Summa*. St. Louis: B. Herder Book Co., 1960.

GOLLIN, JAMES. *Worldly Goods*. New York: Random House, 1971.

GRAHAM, BILLY. *World Aflame*. Minneapolis: Billy Graham Evangelistic Association, 1965.

GREELEY, ANDREW M. *The New Agenda*. Garden City, N.Y.: Doubleday and Co., Inc., 1973.

———. *Priests in the United States*. Garden City, N.Y.: Doubleday and Co., Inc., 1972.

GRISEZ, GERMAIN G. *Abortion: The Myths, the Realities, and the Arguments*. New York: Corpus Books, 1970.

———. *Contraception and the Natural Law*. Milwaukee: The Bruce Publishing Co., 1964.

GUTTMACHER, ALAN F. *Understanding Sex: A Young Person's Guide*. New York: The New American Library, Inc., 1970.

HARDON, JOHN A. *The Catholic Catechism*. Garden City, N.Y.: Doubleday and Co., Inc., 1975.

———. *Christianity in the Twentieth Century*. Garden City, N.Y.: Image Books, 1972.

———. *Religions of the World*. 2 vols. Garden City, N.Y.: Image Books, 1963.

HARING, BERNARD. *Morality Is for Persons*. New York: Farrar, Straus, and Giroux, 1971.

HICKEY, J. S. *Summula Philosophiae Scholasticae*. 3 vols. New York: Benziger Bros., 1919.

HUGHES, PHILIP. *A Popular History of the Catholic Church*. New York: The Macmillan Co., 1962.

JONE, HERIBERT. *Moral Theology*. Sixteenth edition. Trans. Urban Adelman. Westminster, Md.: The Newman Press, 1951.

KAVANAUGH, JAMES. *A Modern Priest Looks at His Outdated Church.* New York: Pocket Books, Inc., 1967.

KEEN, SAM. *Gabriel Marcel.* Richmond, Va.: John Knox Press, 1967.

KELLEHER, STEPHEN J. *Divorce and Remarriage for Catholics?* Garden City, N.Y.: Doubleday and Co., Inc., 1973.

KELLY, GEORGE A. *The Catholic Family Handbook.* New York: Random House, 1959.

———. *The Catholic Marriage Manual.* New York: Random House, 1958.

———. *The Catholic Youth's Guide to Life and Love.* New York: Random House, 1960.

KELLY, GERALD. *Modern Youth and Chastity.* St. Louis: The Queen's Work, 1941.

KENNEDY, EUGENE C. *The New Sexuality: Myths, Fables and Hang-ups.* Garden City, N.Y.: Doubleday and Co., Inc., 1972.

KENNEDY, ROBERT F. *To Seek a Newer World.* New York: Bantam Books, Inc., 1968.

KINSEY, ALFRED C., W. B. POMEROY, AND C. E. MARTIN. *Sexual Behavior in the Human Male.* Philadelphia: W. B. Saunders Co., 1948.

KINSEY, ALFRED C., W. B. POMEROY, C. E. MARTIN, AND P. H. GEBHARD. *Sexual Behavior in the Human Female.* Philadelphia: W. B. Saunders Co., 1953.

KLAVER, RICHARD. *The Litany of Loreto.* St. Louis: B. Herder Book Co., 1954.

KOPP, JOSEPH V. *Teilhard de Chardin: A New Synthesis of Evolution.* Glen Rock, N.J.: Deus Books, 1964.

KUNG, HANS. *Infallible? An Inquiry.* Garden City, N.Y.: Doubleday and Co., Inc., 1971.

———. *Why Priests?* Garden City, N.Y.: Doubleday and Co., Inc., 1972.

LAWLER, RONALD, DONALD W. WUERL, AND THOMAS COMERFORD LAWLER (eds.). *The Teaching of Christ.* Huntington, Ind.: Our Sunday Visitor, Inc., 1976.

LEWIS, JOHN. *The Religions of the World Made Simple.* New York: Made Simple Books, Inc., 1958.

LORTZ, JOSEPH. *History of the Church.* Trans. Edwin G. Kaiser. Milwaukee: The Bruce Publishing Co., 1939.

MACQUARRIE, JOHN. *Martin Heidegger.* Richmond, Va.: John Knox Press, 1968.

MARITAIN, JACQUES. *Existence and the Existent.* Garden City, N.Y.: Image Books, 1948.

———. *Three Reformers: Luther, Descartes, Rousseau.* New York: Charles Scribner's Sons, 1929.

MASTERS, R. E. L. (ed.). *Sexual Self-Stimulation.* Los Angeles: Sherbourne Press, Inc., 1967.

MASTERS, WILLIAM H., AND VIRGINIA E. JOHNSON. *Human Sexual Response.* Boston: Little, Brown, and Co., 1966.

MAURIAC, FRANCOIS. *Life of Jesus.* New York: Avon Book Division, the Hearst Corp., 1937.

MAY, ROLLO. *Love and Will.* New York: W. W. Norton and Co., Inc., 1969.
———. *Man's Search for Himself.* New York: The New American Library, 1953.
MAYNARD, THEODORE. *Saints for Our Times.* Garden City, N.Y.: Image Books, 1952.
MCBRIEN, RICHARD P. *The Remaking of the Church.* New York: Harper and Row, 1973.
———. *Who Is a Catholic?* Denville, N.J.: Dimension Books, 1971.
MCKENZIE, JOHN L. *Authority in the Church.* New York: Sheed and Ward, 1966.
———. *Did I Say That?* Chicago: The Thomas More Press, 1973.
———. *The Roman Catholic Church.* New York: Holt, Rinehart and Winston, Inc., 1969.
———. *A Theology of the Old Testament.* Garden City, N.Y.: Doubleday and Co., Inc., 1974.
MCKEON, RICHARD (ed.). *Introduction to Aristotle.* New York: The Modern Library, 1947.
MENNINGER, KARL. *Whatever Became of Sin?* New York: Hawthorn Books, Inc., 1973.
MERTON, THOMAS. *No Man Is an Island.* New York: Dell Publishing Co., Inc., 1955.
MILES, HERBERT J. *Sexual Understanding Before Marriage.* Grand Rapids, Mich.: Zondervan Publishing House, 1971.

NOONAN, JOHN T., JR. *Contraception.* New York: The New American Library, 1965.
——— (ed.). *The Morality of Abortion: Legal and Historical Perspectives.* Cambridge, Mass.: Harvard University Press, 1970.
———. *Power to Dissolve.* Cambridge, Mass.: Harvard University Press, 1972.
NOVAK, MICHAEL (ed.). *The Experience of Marriage.* New York: The Macmillan Co., 1964.

O'BRIEN, DAVID J. *The Renewal of American Catholicism.* New York: Oxford University Press, 1972.
O'BRIEN, JOHN A. *Catching Up with the Church.* New York: Herder and Herder, 1967.
———. *Evolution and Religion.* New York: The Century Co., 1932.
———. *The Faith of Millions.* Huntington, Ind.: Our Sunday Visitor Press, 1938.
——— (ed.). *Family Planning in an Exploding Population.* New York: Hawthorn Books, Inc., 1968.
———. *Giants of the Faith.* Garden City, N.Y.: Image Books, 1957.
———. *Happy Marriage.* Huntington, Ind.: Our Sunday Visitor Press, 1956.
———. *Pathways to Happiness.* Huntington, Ind.: Our Sunday Visitor Press, 1940.
———. *The Reformation.* New York: The Paulist Press, 1943.
———. *Religion in a Changing World.* Huntington, Ind.: Our Sunday Visitor Press, 1938.
——— (ed.). *Roads to Rome.* New York: All Saints Press, Inc., 1954.

——, *et al. Sex-Character Education.* Huntington, Ind.: Our Sunday Visitor Press, 1952.

—— (ed.). *Steps to Christian Unity.* Garden City, N.Y.: Doubleday and Co., Inc., 1954.

——. *The Truth About the Inquisition.* New York: The Paulist Press, 1950.

——. *Truths Men Live By.* Huntington, Ind.: Our Sunday Visitor Press, 1946.

—— (ed.). *Why Priests Leave.* New York: Hawthorn Books, Inc., 1969.

O'CONNELL, HUGH J. *Keeping Your Balance in the Modern Church.* Liguori, Mo.: Liguorian Pamphlets, 1968.

O'CONNOR, EDWARD D. *The Pentecostal Movement in the Catholic Church.* Notre Dame, Ind.: Ave Maria Press, 1971.

O'DEA, THOMAS F. *American Catholic Dilemma.* New York: Sheed and Ward, 1958.

Official Catholic Directory. New York: P. J. Kenedy and Sons, 1972.

ORAISON, MARC. *The Celibate Condition and Sex.* New York: Sheed and Ward, 1967.

——. *The Human Mystery of Sexuality.* New York: Sheed and Ward, 1967.

OURSLER, FULTON. *The Greatest Book Ever Written.* New York: Pocket Books, Inc., 1951.

——. *The Greatest Story Ever Told.* New York: Pocket Books, Inc., 1949.

PEALE, NORMAN VINCENT. *Sin, Sex and Self-Control.* Garden City, N.Y.: Doubleday and Co., Inc., 1965.

PIEPER, JOSEF. *The Silence of Saint Thomas.* Chicago: Henry Regnery Co., 1957.

RAHNER, KARL. *The Christian of the Future.* New York: Herder and Herder, 1967.

——. *Free Speech in the Church.* New York: Sheed and Ward, 1953.

ROBERTS, THOMAS D., *et al. Contraception and Holiness.* New York: Herder and Herder, 1964.

ROCK, JOHN. *The Time Has Come.* New York: Alfred A. Knopf, Inc., 1963.

ROTHENBERG, ROBERT E. *The Doctor's Premarital Medical Adviser.* New York: Grosset and Dunlap, Inc., 1971.

RYAN, MARY PERKINS. *Are Parochial Schools the Answer?* New York: Holt, Rinehart and Winston, Inc., 1964.

SHEED, F. J. *The Church and I.* Garden City, N.Y.: Doubleday and Co., Inc., 1974.

——. *Genesis Regained.* New York: Sheed and Ward, 1969.

——. *God and the Human Condition.* Vol. I: *God and the Human Mind.* New York: Sheed and Ward, 1966.

——. *Is It the Same Church?* Dayton, Ohio: Pflaum Press, 1968.

——. *Society and Sanity.* Garden City, N.Y.: Image Books, 1953.

——. *Theology and Sanity.* New York: Sheed and Ward, 1946.

——. *To Know Christ Jesus.* New York: Sheed and Ward, 1962.

——. *What Difference Does Jesus Make?* New York: Sheed and Ward, 1972.

SHEEN, FULTON J. *The Divine Romance*. Garden City, N.Y.: Garden City Books. 1930.
———. *The Eternal Galilean*. New York: D. Appleton-Century Co., Inc., 1934.
———. *Footprints in a Darkened Forest*. New York: Meredith Press, 1967.
———. *God and Intelligence in Modern Philosophy*. Garden City, N.Y.: Image Books, 1925.
———. *Life Is Worth Living*. New York: McGraw-Hill Book Co., Inc., 1953.
———. *The Life of All Living*. New York: The Century Co., 1929.
———. *Life of Christ*. New York: McGraw-Hill Book Co., Inc., 1958.
———. *Lift Up Your Hearts*. Garden City. N.Y.: Garden City Books, 1950.
———. *Light Your Lamps*. Huntington Ind.: Our Sunday Visitor Press, 1947.
———. *Moods and Truths*. New York: Popular Library, 1932.
———. *The Moral Universe*. Freeport, N.Y.: Books for Libraries Press, Inc., 1936.
———. *Peace of Soul*. Garden City, N.Y.: Image Books, 1949.
———. *Philosophy of Religion*. New York: Appleton-Century-Crofts. Inc., 1948.
———. *Preface to Religion*. New York: P. J. Kenedy and Sons, 1946.
———. *The Priest Is Not His Own*. New York: McGraw-Hill Book Co., Inc., 1963.
———. *The Rock Plunged into Eternity*. Huntington, Ind.: Our Sunday Visitor Press, 1950.
———. *Those Mysterious Priests*. Garden City, N.Y.: Doubleday and Co., Inc., 1974.
———. *Three to Get Married*. New York: Appleton-Century-Crofts. Inc., 1951.
———. *The World's First Love*. Garden City, N.Y.: Image Books, 1952.
SMITH, GEORGE D. (ed.). *The Teaching of the Catholic Church*. 2 vols. New York: The Macmillan Co., 1948.

TAYLOR, MICHAEL J. (ed.). *Sex: Thoughts for Contemporary Christians*. Garden City, N.Y.: Doubleday and Co., Inc., 1972.
TEILHARD DE CHARDIN, PIERRE. *The Divine Milieu*. New York: Harper and Row, 1960.
———. *The Phenomenon of Man*. New York: Harper and Row, 1959.
THOMAS, DONALD F. *The Deacon in a Changing Church*. Valley Forge, Pa.: Judson Press, 1969.
THORMAN, DONALD J. *The Emerging Layman*. Garden City, N.Y.: Doubleday and Co., Inc., 1965.
TITUS, HAROLD H. *Living Issues in Philosophy*. Second edition. New York: American Book Co., 1953.
TOBE, JOHN H. *Your Prostate: Treatment and Prevention*. New York: Pyramid House. 1967.
TODD, J. M. (ed.). *Problems of Authority*. Baltimore: Helicon Press, 1962.
TOYNBEE, ARNOLD J. *A Study of History*. 12 vols. New York: Oxford University Press, 1934-61.

Webster's Third New International Dictionary. Springfield, Mass.: G. and C. Merriam Co., 1965.
WILLKE, DR. AND MRS. J. C. *Handbook on Abortion.* Cincinnati: Hiltz Publishing Co., 1973.
WILLS, GARRY, *Bare Ruined Choirs: Doubt, Prophecy and Radical Religion.* Garden City, N.Y.: Doubleday and Co., Inc., 1972.
WILMERS, W. *Handbook of the Christian Religion.* New York: Benziger Bros., Inc., 1891.
World Almanac. Newspaper Enterprise Association, Inc., 1972.

B. DOCUMENTARY AND SUPPLEMENTARY REFERENCES

ABÉLARD, PETER. *Problems of Heloise.*
AESCHYLUS. *Prometheus Bound.*
ALBERT THE GREAT. *On the Sentences.*
———. *Summa Theologica.*
ALEXANDER, SAMUEL. *Space, Time and Diety.* 2 vols.
Apostles' Creed.
AQUINAS, THOMAS. *Commentary on Aristotle's Metaphysics.*
———. *Compendium Theologicae.*
———. *On the Sentences.*
———. *Questiones Disputatae.*
ARISTOTLE. *Metaphysics.*
———. *Nicomachean Ethics.*
Athanasian Creed.
AUGUSTINE, SAINT. *De Trinitate.*

BARTH, KARL. *Church Dogmatics.* 14 vols.
BLAKE, WILLIAM. "Auguries of Innocence."
BONHOEFFER, DIETRICH. *Ethics.*
BONIFACE VIII, POPE. *Unam Sanctam.*
BRIDGET, SAINT. *Revelations.*
BUBER, MARTIN. *I and Thou.*
BULTMANN, RUDOLF. *Jesus Christ and Mythology.*

CHRYSOSTOM, JOHN. *Virginity.*
CICERO. *The Republic.*
Codex Juris Canonici. 1917-18.
CONFUCIUS. *Morals.*
Constitution of the United States of America.
Creed of Constantinople.
Creed of the Fourth Latern Council.

DANTE. *The Divine Comedy.*
Doe v. Bolton.
DOMS, HERBERT. *The Meaning and End of Marriage.*
Dred Scott v. Sanford.

FOURTH LATERAN COUNCIL. *Omnis Utriusque Sexus.*
FRANCIS OF ASSISI, SAINT. "Peace Prayer."
FRAZER, JAMES. *The Golden Bough.*

GURY, JOHN. *Compendium of Moral Theology.*

HARING, BERNARD. *The Law of Christ.* 3 vols.
HEIDEGGER, MARTIN. *Being and Time.*
HILDEBRAND, DIETRICH VON. *In Defense of Purity.*
Hippocratic Oath.
HUGUCCIO, BISHOP. *Summa Theologica.*

INNOCENT IV, POPE. *Ad Extirpanda.*
IVO, BISHOP. *Decretum.*

JANSENIUS, CORNELIUS. *Augustinus.*
JOHN XXIII, POPE. *Mater et Magistra.* May 15, 1961.
———. *Pacem in Terris.* April 11, 1963.

KANT, IMMANUEL. *Critique of Practical Reason.*
———. *Critique of Pure Reason.*
KEMPIS, THOMAS À. *The Imitation of Christ.*
KIERKEGAARD, SOREN. *Philosophical Fragments.*
The Koran.

LEIBNIZ, GOTTFRIED WILHELM VON. *Theodicy.*
LE MAISTRE, MARTIN. *Moral Questions.*
Lemon v. Kurtzman.
LEO XIII, POPE. *Arcanum Divinae Sapientiae.* Feb. 10, 1880.
———. *Brief on Historical Studies.*
LIGUORI, ALPHONSUS. *Theologia Moralis.*
LINDNER, DOMINIKUS, *Der Usus Matrimonii.*
LOMBARD, PETER. *Sentences.*

MALTHUS, THOMAS. *An Essay on the Principle of Population.*
MARCEL, GABRIEL. *Metaphysical Journal.*
MARTINDALE, C. C. *The Vocation of Aloysius Gonzaga.*
MIDDLETON, RICHARD. *On the Sentences.*

NEWMAN, JOHN HENRY. *Essay on the Development of Christian Doctrine.*
———. *On Consulting the Laity in Matters of Doctrine.*
———. "The Pillar of the Cloud."
Nicene Creed.
NIETZSCHE, FRIEDRICH WILHELM. *Beyond Good and Evil.*
———. *Thus Spake Zarathustra.*

PAUL VI, POPE. *Ecclesiam Suam.* Aug. 6, 1964.
———. *Humanae Vitae.* July 29, 1968.
———. *Populorum Progressio.* March 26, 1967.
———. *Professio Fidei.* June 30, 1968.
———. *Sacerdotalis Caelibatus.* June 24, 1967.
PIUS IX, POPE. *Syllabus of Errors.* Dec. 8, 1864.
PIUS X, POPE. *Lamentabili.* July 3, 1907.
———. *Pascendi.* Sept. 8, 1907.
PIUS XI, POPE. *Casti Connubii.* Dec. 31, 1930.
———. *Divini Redemptoris.* March 19, 1937.

278 CATHOLICISM TODAY

PIUS XII, POPE. *Allocution to the Italian Catholic Society of Midwives.* Oct. 29, 1951.
———. *Humani Generis.* Aug. 12, 1950.
———. *Mystici Corporis.* June 29, 1943.
Profession of Faith of the Council of Trent.

RAHNER, KARL. *Theological Investigations.* 8 vols.
RICE, TIM, AND ANDREW LLOYD WEBBER. *Jesus Christ Superstar.*
Roe v. Wade.
ROUSSEAU, JEAN JACQUES. *Émile.*
RUSSELL, BERTRAND. *Mysticism and Logic.*

SACRED CONGREGATION FOR THE CLERGY. *General Catechetical Directory.* Apr. 11, 1971.
SACRED CONGREGATION FOR THE DOCTRINE OF THE FAITH. *Declaration in Defence of the Catholic Doctrine on the Church Against Certain Errors of the Present Day.* June 24, 1973.
———. *Declaration on Certain Questions Concerning Sexual Ethics.* Jan. 15, 1976.
SANCHEZ, THOMAS. *The Holy Sacrament of Matrimony.*
SARTRE, JEAN-PAUL. *No Exit.*
SCHOPENHAUER, ARTHUR. *Essay on Women.*
SHAKESPEARE, WILLIAM. *Hamlet.*
———. *Macbeth.*
———. *Measure for Measure.*
SIXTUS V, POPE. *Effraenatam.* Oct. 29, 1588.

TEILHARD DE CHARDIN, PIERRE. "Mass upon the Altar of the World."
Ten Commandments.
TENNYSON, ALFRED, LORD. "Ulysses."
THOMPSON, FRANCIS. "The Hound of Heaven."
TILLICH, PAUL. *Systematic Theology.* 3 vols.
TISSOT, SIMON ANDRÉ. *Onanism.*
TOCQUEVILLE, ALEXIS CHARLES DE. *De la Démocratie en Amérique.*

U. S. BISHOPS. *Basic Teachings for Catholic Religious Education.* Jan. 11, 1973.
———. *Theological Reflections on the Ordination of Women.* Dec. 1972.
Upanishads.

VATICAN COUNCIL I. *Pastor Aeternus.*
VATICAN COUNCIL II. *Declaration on Christian Education (Gravissimum Educationis).*
———. *Declaration on Religious Freedom (Dignitatis Humanae).*
———. *Declaration on the Relationship of the Church to Non-Christian Religions (Nostra Aetate).*
———. *Decree on Ecumenism (Unitatis Redintegratio).*
———. *Dogmatic Constitution on the Church (Lumen Gentium).*
———. *Pastoral Constitution on the Church in the Modern World (Gaudium et Spes).*

WASHINGTON, GEORGE. *Farewell Address.*
WHITEHEAD, ALFRED NORTH. *Adventures of Ideas.*
———. *Religion in the Making.*
———. *Science and the Modern World.*